LANGUAGE IN SIGN:
AN INTERNATIONAL PERSPECTIVE ON SIGN
LANGUAGE

LANGUAGE IN SIGN: AN INTERNATIONAL PERSPECTIVE ON SIGN LANGUAGE

Edited by
J.G. KYLE and B. WOLL

CROOM HELM
London • Sydney • Dover, New Hampshire

©1983 Jim Kyle and Bencie Woll
Croom Helm Ltd, Provident House, Burrell Row,
Beckenham, Kent BR3 1AT

Croom Helm Australia Pty Ltd, Suite 4, 6th Floor,
64-76 Kippax Street, Surry Hills, NSW 2010, Australia

Croom Helm, 51 Washington Street,
Dover, New Hampshire 03820, USA

Reprinted 1985

British Library Cataloguing in Publication Data

Language in sign.
    1. Deaf – Means of communication – Congresses
    2. Sign language – Congresses
    I. Kyle, J. II. Woll, B.
    419   HV2474

    ISBN 0-7099-1528-4

Printed and bound in Great Britain by
Biddles Ltd, Guildford and King's Lynn

CONTENTS

FOREWORD

The greater status now accorded to the languages of deaf people throughout the world has provided the basis for cooperation between deaf and hearing researchers. The study of sign language has implications not only for deaf people and the community, their education and development, but also for the understanding of the spoken languages of the world. Many of our psychological, educational and linguistic theories have rested on an assumption of the primacy of spoken language and as a result our ideas on language use and thought are derived from the study of speech and its functions. The test of many of these theories comes in situations where spoken language is not the primary language.

Our knowledge of sign language therefore comes not from a study *of* deaf people but from study *with* deaf people. It was in this spirit of cooperation and interchange of ideas, that the Second International Symposium of Sign Language Research took place in Bristol, U.K. in July 1981. What follows is a selection of papers from those presented. They indicate the development of sign language research in eight different countries of the world and the conference was a meeting place for deaf and hearing researchers from 17 different countries. The simultaneous interpretation of each talk into eight sign languages provided a uniquely international context for all of the papers.

In editing the contributions, we have tried to alter the content as little as possible and have included as many of the papers given at the conference as were compatible with the style and length of this volume. There is a wide range of topics and these have been grouped in rather traditional lines. However, linguists, psychologists and educators will find much of relevance in all sections of the book.

Bernard Tervoort in a special study prepared for the conference highlights the current range of attitudes and practices in the education of deaf children throughout Europe. His conclusion that despite the differing provisions of education in Europe, there is a general trend towards the use of sign language is an important one, not only in the sense of progress in education, but also because it is a development which brings deaf and hearing communities closer in mutual understanding.

William Stokoe, in a paper which provides an overview of the state of sign language research, highlights the shift in attention away from the manual aspects of sign language to a greater understanding of other features such as facial expression and lip-patterns as carriers of significant information for sign language communication. The shift is a significant one and almost certainly will lead to a much deeper analysis of the grammatical features in sign language.

It is precisely these sorts of grammatical features that Brita Bergman discusses in her paper, and it is particularly appropriate that her contribution should be first in this volume. Her work has provided a stimulus for workers not only in Sweden but throughout Europe, and without the *first* sign language conference in Stockholm in 1979, this gathering in Bristol and this volume, may never have been possible.

Acknowledgements in such a cooperative venture are inevitably due to a host of people who made this volume possible. Particular thanks are due to the Department of Health and Social Security, who provided the resources for the large international group of interpreters who took part and without whose work the symposium could not have functioned. In this respect, the work of Peter Llewellyn-Jones as co-ordinator of interpreters should be mentioned. Thanks are also due to the British Council for their financial support in conference expenses. Numerous people contributed to the running and organisation of the symposium but there should be special mention for Gloria Pullen, Lorna Allsop, Maggie Carter and Peter Wood. Eileen Nash, Maureen Devoy and Josephine O'Looney helped with the organisation and the typing. Jenny Mills-Roberts, Liz Young and Karen Threlfall typed these manuscripts and worked on the conference organisation over a period of almost two years and it was latterly Liz who administered and controlled the working of each different aspect of the symposium provision. Without this work we could not have achieved our aim in this international meeting. Finally, special acknowledgement is due to UNESCO who have provided the financial support necessary to produce these proceedings and whose grant has allowed us to undertake a small international examination of sign languages in preparation for the third international symposium in 1983.

We are deeply indebted to all these sources of help.

J. G. Kyle and B. Woll

PART ONE: LANGUAGE

INTRODUCTION

The expansion of linguistic research on sign language has taken place not only numerically, in that greater numbers of linguists are concerning themselves with the description of greater numbers of sign languages, but also in the expansion of topics considered important in sign language linguistics. The papers in this section indicate both these sorts of expansion, and include discussions of American, British, Swedish, Norwegian and Russian sign languages on a range of topics including semantics, syntax and morphology of both manual and non-manual components of sign language.

Bergman's paper examines modulation in Swedish Sign Language and relates descriptive and semantic typologies. She focusses particularly on aspectual processes as encoded both manually and non-manually, and indicates the wealth of information which can be compressed in a single sign and the richness of information which results.

Brennan also looks at modulation and sign complexity, but with the emphasis on how time is encoded in British Sign Language. She identifies a number of 'time lines' and describes the function of these lines in a number of signs with temporal features.

McDonald picks up the theme of sign complexity, but while Bergman is mostly concerned with movement types, and Brennan with location types, she focusses on the information found in sign hand shape through a description of the classifier system of American Sign Language. Her comparison of ASL classifiers with Navaho provides insights into the underlying similarities between signed and spoken languages. She also indicates the relevance of historical work on sign languages, a theme taken up in the following two papers.

Woll, like McDonald, examines handshape from a semantic viewpoint, and the role of handshape in creating meaning is explained in classifiers, temporal and quantifying signs, and loan signs. She also suggests that handshape may relate to evaluative as well as physical properties.

Wallin's paper looks at compounds in Swedish Sign Language, and changes in their forms between 1916 and the present. He describes changes such as loss of compound elements and the distinction between foreign (i.e. Swedish) type compounds and native (i.e. Swedish Sign Language) type compounds. He also suggests some constraints on compound form which may well be universal.

Deuchar confronts an important issue for sign language linguistics: what is the basic sentence structure of a sign language? Using spontaneous sign data she shows that a sign order approach is of less relevance than a functional analysis. The criteria she uses to provide this answer are drawn from spoken language linguistics, and again, show the relation of features of sign language forms to those of spoken language. She concludes that the situational context in which a language is found may be the most important variable in defining its form.

Zaitseva's paper, which is concerned with Russian Sign Language, reaches many similar conclusions to those of Deuchar, by comparing the structures found in colloquial speech with those found in sign language. She describes a number of syntactical structures and suggests functional explanations for their occurrence.

Many of the earlier papers in the section discuss the importance of non-manual elements in sign languages. Both Vogt-Svendsen and Lawson make this topic the core of their papers. Vogt-Svendsen focusses on this topic entirely, through a discussion of lip movements in Norwegian Sign Language. She presents a descriptive scheme for sign-associated lip movements and discusses a topic of great educational importance: if signs have both manual and oral components, how can sign and speech be used simultaneously in the classroom? She concludes that there remains a great deal of work to be done on the oral component of sign languages.

Lawson's paper rounds off this section with a discussion of multi-channel signs in British Sign Language. She particularly explores the relationship between hand movement, mouth movement and meaning, and suggests that very close links between mouth and hand may exist.

The papers of this section combine to extend our understanding of the linguistic structure found in sign languages. Sign language linguistics is still the core discipline in the study of sign language and this section thus forms a fitting opening to this volume as a whole.

VERBS AND ADJECTIVES: SOME MORPHOLOGICAL PROCESSES IN SWEDISH LANGUAGE

Brita Bergman

In one of the major works on American Sign Language it is characterised as an inflecting language, comparable to languages like Latin, Russian and Navajo (Klima & Bellugi, 1979). The possibility of other natural sign languages displaying different typologies is mentioned as well as a suggestion that 'the modality in which the language develops constrains its natural patterning in one direction rather than another'. (Klima & Bellugi, p. 314.) The data we are beginning to obtain from Swedish Sign Language support the latter suggestion, since many morphological processes described by Klima and Bellugi seem to be present in Swedish Sign Language. The striking similarities between the two languages are particularly interesting since, contrary to what has been claimed (Stokoe, 1974), the American and the Swedish sign languages are not genetically related (Bergman, 1979). However, other data from our study of sign language grammar (the use of classifiers and incorporation) suggest that the morphological structure can also be characterised as polysynthetic or simultaneous-polysynthetic (Ahlgren & Ozolins, 1981), which becomes especially clear when we analyse texts rather than isolated signs or sentences.

By 'morphological processes' we mean changes in forms of signs resulting in systematic changes in their meaning. Therefore, when studying these processes the following three issues must be dealt with: the form of the change; the meaning associated with that change; and the class of signs on which the process operates.

Matthews (1974) distinguishes three major categories of morphological process: affixation, reduplication and modification. In the spoken languages which are most familiar to many of the participants in this symposium, such as English, French and the Scandinavian languages, morphological changes are typically made by adding one or more sound segments to a stem: affixation. This type of process can be found in Signed Swedish (Bergman, 1979) but is not utilised at all in Swedish Sign Language, which has several kinds of reduplication and modification. These changes in sign form are not restricted to the manual component of a sign and as we shall see later they may involve the use of additional articulators such as the mouth or the head.

In this study, I have analysed 32 video-recorded stories told by 14 deaf signers. These recordings were originally made for a test of the receptive skills of hearing persons applying to train as sign language interpreters. I am grateful to the Swedish National Association of the Deaf for letting me use this material.

I have focussed on five morphological processes: fast reduplication, slow reduplication, initial stop, doubling, and initial hold. Among these, reduplication is perhaps the most familiar. When used in spoken languages, reduplication means that a part of a word or the whole word is repeated two or more times. Thus the process of reduplication differs from affixation since the reduplicated form will vary from word to word, whereas the same affix

3

can be attached to a whole class of words.

In Swedish Sign Language there are two different types of reduplication, fast and slow (cf. Susan Fischer's article on reduplication in American Sign Language, 1973). The difference between fast and slow reduplication is not just speed as implied by the terms used. Slow reduplication is certainly perceived as being slower than fast, but equally important is the uneven movement, which is not continuous but rather has pauses between each repetition (for a description of features of aspectual modulations, see Klima & Bellugi, 1979). Examples of signs reduplicated in this way in the material I have analysed are CALL, DRINK, LAUGH, LOOK-AT, SPIT, SUFFER, WAIT, and WALK. (English words in capitals are here used as names of Swedish signs.) Slow reduplication is often accompanied by simultaneous rocking movements of the body (Fischer, 1973), one of many examples of how an additional articulator is used when a morphological process is operating on a sign.

Fast reduplication gives an impression of higher speed, but is also characterised by an even, continuous movement. In my material it has been observed in signs such as DRINK, EAT-WITH-KNIFE-AND-FORK, GET-EMBARRASSED, SPIT, TAKE-MEDICINE, WAIT, and WALK.

Reduplication can also operate on signs having some kind of repetition in the citation form. One such example is WAIT, where the flat hand (palm down and fingers pointing left) twice brushes down the left side of the trunk (i.e. with thumb side of the hand in contact with the place of articulation). In such a sign only a single sequence of the citation form is reduplicated, rather than the whole citation form with its repeated movement. Another very frequent sign in the data is WALK, which also has a repeated movement in its citation form (V-hand makes two forward movements in palm of flat hand). If the sign as represented by its citation form was reduplicated, there would be an even number of forward movements. This is not the case and the number of movements most frequently observed in WALK is three. 'Modulations are applied to a basic movement unit (the sign unit) rather than to the base form.' (Supalla & Newport, 1978.)

The modification called 'doubling' simply means that signs having a single articulator add a second hand and are performed with a double manual articulator. In signs where the manual component has been doubled, the hands may move either simultaneously or alternately. Simultaneous movement has been observed in signs such as ANGRY, BE-USED-TO, FUNNY, LOOK-AT. In doubled signs with alternative movements reduplication has also taken place: GO-HOME, GET-OUT, LOOK-AT, TRAVEL, ZOOM-OFF.

The second modification found is the 'initial stop': the articulator (single or double) assumes the initial position as if starting to perform the movement, but remains in that position without completing the movement. It looks as if a whole aspect of articulation (the movement parameter) has been deleted, and therefore it appears as if the sign is not performed at all. Some of the signs when modified in this way also have an open mouth, and eye-gaze and head may be directed sideways or down. This modification has been observed in HIT, THROW, TEACH, SHOOT-WITH-RIFLE, SIGN, UNDRESS.

The third modification to be accounted for is the 'initial hold'. Here the articulation begins with a short hold before it is completed relatively quickly: COLD, DEAF, ANGRY, BE-USED-TO, IMPUDENT. A characteristic feature of this modification is the movement of the head, which turns away from the position in which the articulator is held during the initial phase of the articulation. Signs starting their movement at the ipsilateral side (same side as that of the articulator) will have the head turned towards the contralateral side. The visual impression is that the sign is enlarged – the distance between the manual articulator and the head being greater than that in the unmodified form. One can also observe a change in the orientation of the hand during an initial hold – the orientation of the palm tends to be opposite to its direction in the final phase of the sign.

Having identified some morphological processes we may now attempt to find the changes in meaning associated with them. In order to be able to describe the changes in meaning and the classes of signs on which these processes operate it is necessary first to take a brief look at the meaning of predicates.

From the English glosses used here as arbitrary names of Swedish signs, but with some of the meaning in common we can see that most denote actions while a few denote states or qualities. Following Lyons' description (1977) of the denotata of predicates we can refer to two main types of situations as static and dynamic situations. According to their duration in time, dynamic situations are further divided into processes, which are extended in time; and events, which are momentary situations. A dynamic situation under the control of an agent is referred to as an action: the agent-controlled processes and events are called activities and acts, respectively (Lyons, 1977, p. 483).

Now, with respect to the different types of situations they refer to, verbs can be classified as follows:

Situation:	*Verb:*
static	stative
process	durative
event	punctual

Standard examples of static situations are those referred to by English verbs such as 'know', 'possess' and 'weigh'. Some of my SSL examples are ANGRY, BE-USED-TO, COLD, DEAF. (They will be discussed in more detail later.)

Other examples of signs, LAUGH, SUFFER, WAIT, WALK, refer to processes, and are durative verbs. Such verbs may be used with durational adverbs having meanings like 'for hours' and 'the whole day'. In contrast punctual verbs, such as CALL, SPIT and TAKE-MEDICINE refer to acts, and may occur with adverbials having meanings like 'at one o'clock' and 'suddenly'.

Let us now return to the signs mentioned earlier which take slow reduplication. They all refer to actions and there are both durative and punctual verbs. Both types can be rendered into English by phrases like 'walk and walk and walk' and 'spit and spit and spit'. There is, however, a difference in meaning in the reduplicated forms which is due to the lexical meaning – or 'aspectual character' (Lyons, 1977) – of the signs. A durative verb like WALK with slow reduplication adds the meaning that the process was prolonged, something like 'walk for a long time'. A punctual verb with slow reduplication, though it also expresses some kind of continuation, has the meaning of an event occurring 'over and over again'.

The above mentioned changes in the meaning of verbs seem to be regular productive processes in Swedish Sign Language. They are examples of a kind of grammatical process that we do not encounter in Swedish: *aspectual* modulations, 'expressing different ways of viewing the internal temporal constituency of a situation' (Comrie, 1976). Other languages with grammaticalised temporal aspect are Slavonic languages, Turkish and of course English, which has the aspecutal opposition of the progressive (I am eating) and the non-progressive (I eat). More typical of English (and Swedish) verb morphology is inflexion for the grammatical category of tense, which locates a situation in time (past, present or future) in relation to the time of the utterance.

It is tempting to refer to these processes as aspectual *inflexions,* as in the description of American Sign Language (in Klima & Bellugi, 1979). Considering the still very limited data from Swedish Sign Language we avoid the choice between inflexion and derivation for the time being, and adopt the more neutral term *modulation* (as used by Pedersen, 1977).

For the aspectual modulations associated with slow reduplication, we will use the terms *continuative* and *iterative.* A durative verb with slow reduplication is modulated for continuative aspect, with the approximate meaning 'for a long time'. A punctual verb with slow reduplication is modulated for iterative aspect, meaning 'over and over again'. These modulations seem to be the same as those in American Sign Language described by Fischer (1973). This also applies to the rocking body movement that can sometimes be seen to accompany slow reduplication, which in Swedish Sign Language also means 'too much'.

The change of meaning rendered by fast reduplication when operating on punctual verbs is somewhat easier to capture than when it operates on durative verbs. With punctual verbs it can be described as 'often' or 'regularly' and this modulation will be referred to as *habitual* aspect. This corresponds well with the use of this modulation in a context like 'used to go there very often' where the sign ZOOM-OFF is performed as fast reduplication.

Fast reduplication with durative verbs merely emphasises the aspectual character of the sign, so the term *durational* seems to capture the meaning of this aspectual modulation (Klima & Bellugi, 1979).

To sum up this preliminary analysis of fast and slow reduplication we can set up the following table:

Morphological process	Durative verb	Punctual verb
Fast reduplication	durational aspect	habitual aspect
Slow reduplication	continuative aspect	iterative aspect

One final comment on the form of these aspectual modulations: A few signs have been observed to have a rocking movement performed by the body but with no manual reduplication: LAUGH, THINK, WAIT-WITH-FOLDED-ARMS. These signs share two formational features: continuous contact throughout the articulation of the sign and lack of movement. These features mean that in the citation form the hands do not move but remain in contact with the place of articulation. If, for example, THINK, when modulated for continuative aspect, was to be reduplicated manually, the contact of the index finger on the forehead would have to be established several times. This is not done; instead the contact is prolonged while the body makes the movements. This observation supports the claim that morphological processes do not operate on the surface form of a sign as represented by the citation form, but on some underlying form (Supalla & Newport, 1978).

Reduplicated verbs are often, though not always, accompanied by different positions of the mouth. These orally produced elements are not part of the aspectual modulations but add some more information to the modulated sign: a description of the manner in which the action is performed. They are examples of non-manual lexical items and since their function is to determine verbs we can call them oral adverbs. Once again, they are unique to Swedish Sign Language; oral verbs also exist in American Sign Language (Baker, 1976; Baker & Cokely, 1980).

In the video-recorded stories that I analysed there are two such oral adverbs frequently used. One of these is a closed mouth with somewhat protruding lips ('mm' in Baker & Cokely, 1980) and means 'normally' or 'with ease' when accompanying action verbs. It is usually found with durative verbs modulated for durational aspect. The other oral adverb is made with tense, spread, 'smiling' lips ('intense' in Baker & Cokely, 1980) and means 'intensively' or 'with effort'. It also seams to be used to express the notion of fast motion when found with signs like CYCLE and RUN modulated for durational aspect. This may, however, be another modulation, because the movement is considerably faster than in the even, continuous reduplication which here is called fast reduplication.

In connection with oral adverbs I would also like to draw attention to another use of mouth movements in combination with reduplicated verbs: the simultaneous use of Swedish words. In some cases the mouth can be seen to pronounce a Swedish word with approximately the same meaning as the sign, with the word performed as many times as the manual reduplications. The examples I have found occur both with fast and slow reduplication: CALL (fast), SUFFER (slow), WALK and WAIT (fast). In no case has the spoken word been inflected (for tense) but looks like the infinitive form. These words do not affect the meaning of the manual sign – as do oral adverbs – but seem to be completely redundant.

Let us now proceed to the modification called initial stop which is another modulation of durative and punctual verbs. It has been observed in HIT, THROW, TEACH, SHOOT-WITH-RIFLE, SIGN, UNDRESS and indicates that the action was not performed. It is used in contexts such as 'was just going to start the lesson (TEACH), but . . .' or 'I was about to hit him, when . . .'. I do now know of any language where this meaning is morphologically expressed so in want of an established term I will call this modulation 'inhibitional'.

The next modification to be accounted for is doubling. When the hands are simultaneously used in a doubled verb of action the meaning added by the modulation is 'each other', i.e. reciprocity. Many signs with a lexical reciprocal meaning use a double articulator in the citation form (CHANGE, DISCUSS, MEET), but signs like LOOK-AT and SCOLD are modulated to express the meaning that two or more agents perform the same action to each other. Doubling easily combines with reduplication, resulting in forms with meanings like 'look at each other over and over again, and 'scold each other for a long time'.

Doubled signs with alternating movements are combined with reduplication in all the examples I have found and function as inflected for the category of number (and/or distributional aspect, Klima & Bellugi, 1979). Thus the fingerspelled sign OUT (a punctual verb meaning 'leave' or 'get out') when modulated in this way has the meaning 'many (people) leave at different times'. If, instead, the same sign is doubled and performed with one simultaneously diverging movement it means 'all leave at the same time' and with still another modification it may mean 'get out, all of you!'

The last modification, initial hold, is simply a modulation for degree and means 'very'. As already mentioned, signs like COLD, DEAF, ANGRY and FUNNY take this modulation. These signs have been glossed with English adjectives which indicate their stative meaning. Signs with a single articulator tend to combine initial hold with doubling but this is not obligatory. Doubling does not take place in signs located at head level if the place of articulation is one of a pair of locations (e.g. left or right cheek) but may do so at the chin.

In the previous paragraphs I have given just a few examples of morphological processes in Swedish Sign Language. I have also tried to outline the signs on which they operate and how the meaning of the signs is changed. Though I have mentioned only some possible combinations of these processes, it should be obvious that they constitute a very complex system, both formationally and semantically, which deserves further investigation.

Before concluding I would like to make a comment on the title, which may be somewhat misleading. It states that there are both verbs and adjectives in Swedish Sign Language and that was my hypothesis when this study was begun. A more cautious, and as it seems, more appropriate title would be: 'Some morphological processes on predicates in Swedish Sign Language'. Let me explain this very briefly.

Traditional definitions of the parts of speech use semantic, syntactic and morphological criteria. As an example of the first type, verbs are said to refer to processes, events or states, whereas adjectives refer to qualities. It is, however, very difficult to argue for the difference between a state and a quality and only by using semantic criteria is it barely possible to maintain that a distinction should be made between adjective and verb.

In languages that do have a distinction between adjectives and verbs they function differently grammatically, either syntactically or morphologically. In English, as in Swedish, one such morphological difference is that verbs, but not adjectives, are inflected for tense when used predicatively. Thus 'he is nice', but not 'he nices' is grammatical in English, where the semantically empty copula is inflected for tense.

As we have seen there are some morphological processes in Swedish Sign Language operating on some predicates but not on others. The modulation for degree meaning 'very' was described as taken by stative predicates (glossed by English adjectives). It is tempting to regard this modulation as characteristic of adjectives rather than of verbs, but the distinction between stative and non-stative (i.e. durative and punctual) verbs is sufficient to capture the difference in this case. There are, however, stative verbs that do not take this modulation, like KNOW and POSSESS, but this can be explained with reference to the number of arguments associated with these predicates. KNOW and POSSESS are transitive (two arguments) and those that take the initial hold modulation for degree – COLD, DEAF, etc. – are intransitive (one argument).

The data so far available do not give any support to the assumption that there are adjectives in Swedish Sign Language. However, more knowledge about the syntactic structure of the language is needed before it is possible to draw any definite conclusions. For pedagogical reasons it may still be justified to talk about both verbs and adjectives, if we only bear in mind that 'adjectives' probably are nothing but intransitive, stative verbs.

Acknowledgement

The research project on Swedish Sign Language in which this study is being carried out is financed by the Bank of Sweden Tercentary Foundation (RJF 19/206).

MARKING TIME IN BRITISH SIGN LANGUAGE

Mary Brennan

Introduction

The aim of this paper is to provide an account of some of the ways in which time can be expressed in British Sign Language (BSL). In fact, information about time can be encoded in so many different ways that at least part of the exercise here will be to separate out the individual time-systems and then to see how systems can be overlaid upon one another to build up highly complex temporal information.

Temporal Marking

There are two initial problems facing the researcher interested in temporal marking: the first is the concept of time itself and the second is the manner of encoding within the grammar. As space and time have taxed the minds of our greatest philosophers, it is not my intention to enter such a problematic area. However, one aspect of time may be useful as a guide: this is the notion of change. One dictionary definition describes time as 'the continuous passage of existence in which events pass from a state of potentiality in the future, through the present to a state of finality in the past' (*Collins English Dictionary*), while David Hume argued that it is 'because there is a continual succession of perceptions in our minds that the idea of time is for ever present with us.' (Hume, 1896.)

The dictionary definition is partly surprising in that it tackles our expectations by beginning with the future and moving through to the past. What is important is that it is language itself which has forced philosophers to extend and expand upon their accounts of time. We are forced to turn again and again to what language can do with time in order to ensure that our philosophical or non-linguistic account encompasses the full range of possibilities. While the notion of change can actually guide us in our understanding of time, the problem is that most actions are divisible and therefore we can talk of a succession of changes within a given activity as well as, for example, a succession of activities. We will see that this is directly relevant to the linguistic category of aspect.

Our second difficulty relates to manner of encoding within the grammar. Recent work in linguistics has attempted to demonstrate that all natural languages have the same temporal expressive power no matter what their grammatical tense system. Thus, although there are tense-less languages, such as the West African Languages Yoruba and Igbo, these are without tense in the sense that the verb forms carry no specific marking to indicate the particular point of time (in relation to some other point) at which an event occurs, has occurred or will occur. However, these verbs do have aspectual marking and the languages do have other ways of marking time reference – e.g. temporal adverbials. In these languages, in the absence of temporal adverbials, the aspectual markers can also be interpreted in deictic terms, so that perfective forms are interpreted as referring to the past while imperfective forms are taken as referring to the present (Comrie, 1976, p. 82). This itself is interesting in relation to BSL in that it may well be that the marker which is typically glossed as FINISH (Figure 1), while having a primarily aspectual function as marker of the perfective, also functions, in the absence of other information, to indicate past.

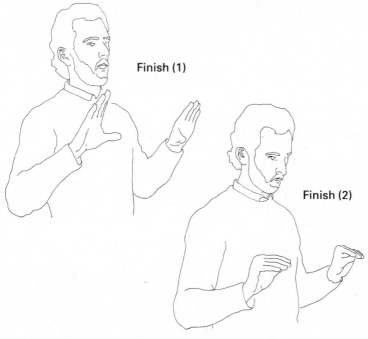

Finish (1)

Finish (2)

Figure 1

British Sign Language

The main argument presented here is that the temporal expressive power of BSL is comparable to that of other more extensively studied languages, but that one kind of temporal marking, namely aspectual marking, is more fully grammaticalised, in the narrow sense, than deictic time reference. By grammaticalised I here mean expressed by regular morphological processes: there is no suggestion that such processes are linguistically superior to other means used to express time within the language.

At this point it may be useful to mention aspect. The most helpful definition of aspect is that it is concerned with the internal temporal constituency of the situation; aspect can thus be seen as situation-internal time and tense as situation-external time (Comrie, 1976, p. 5). It should be noted, however, that perfective is normally treated as an aspect, although the function of perfective aspect is to treat the situation as 'an unanalysed whole': this might account for the fact that the perfective does seem to straddle the tense/aspect boundary. Furthermore, both aspect and tense can be grammaticalised or not, in the sense referred to above. Thus, although English does have a way of encoding certain aspectual contrasts within the verb phrase, this encoding is very limited compared with grammaticalised aspect in both American Sign Language (ASL) and BSL. It might be helpful to see the possibilities as follows:

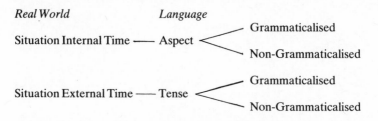

Real World   *Language*

Situation Internal Time —— Aspect Grammaticalised / Non-Grammaticalised

Situation External Time —— Tense Grammaticalised / Non-Grammaticalised

In this account of BSL, the concern is with all types of time marking and not only with grammaticalised areas. This may mean that a relatively superficial account is given of some areas, but it seems important to establish initially the wealth of interacting systems.

BSL: Tense
Accounts of temporal marking in ASL have drawn attention to the 'time-line' stretching from behind the signer's right shoulder to a foot or more in front of the signer's shoulder. This account of BSL temporal marking suggests that we are in effect dealing with several time-lines, expressed diagramatically in Figure 2.

Time-line A is almost identical to that specified for ASL. BSL seems to use the right side of the face as mid-point with the signs DAY, YESTERDAY, and TOMORROW involving initial contact on the right side of the chin. The cheek is the tab for the future marker WILL which involves a forward twisting action. A series of signs indicating past time reference are articulated above the right shoulder. Several signs are frequently given the English gloss BEFORE, but these signs can probably best be separated out into a neutral PAST marker, and a series of more specific time adverbials such as A LONG TIME AGO, LONG AGO, and RECENTLY. NEUTRAL PAST seems to occur regularly in pre-subject position but it can occur several times throughout a text, not only in initial position. A manual sign can itself be modified by a non-manual adverbial. Thus manual A LONG TIME AGO can be accompanied by a non-manual intensifier, with cheeks puffed out, emphasising the length of time. RECENTLY can be accompanied by a non-manual modifier to indicate 'just recently'.

TIME LINES

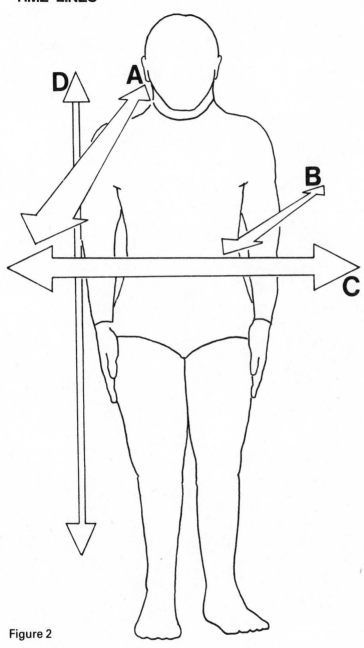

Figure 2

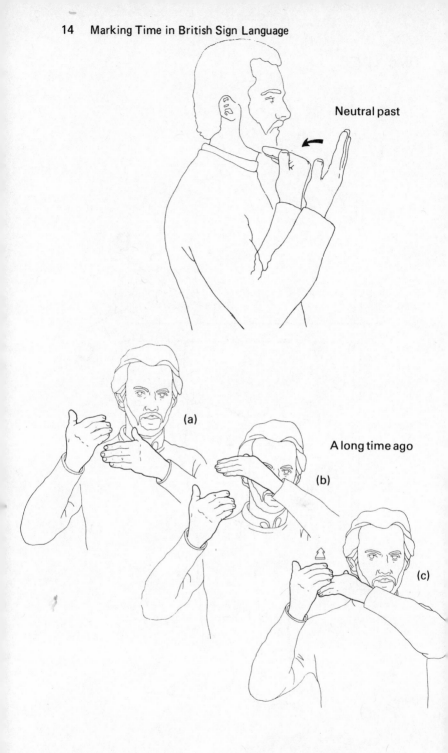

Neutral past

(a)

A long time ago

(b)

(c)

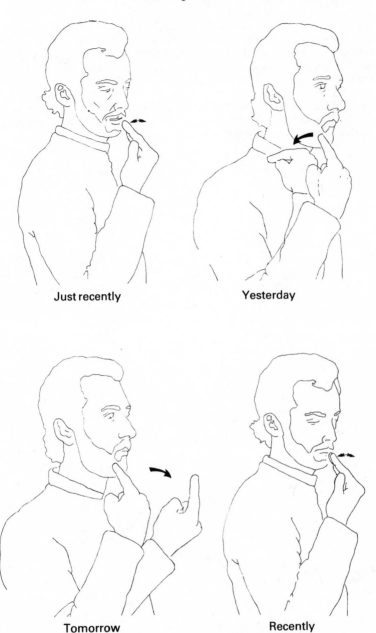

Just recently   Yesterday

Tomorrow   Recently

In some geographical areas calendric units such as week, month and year are integrated within time-line A. The most common forms are connected with day or week: hence LAST WEEK, NEXT WEEK, EVERY WEEK, and WEEK AFTER WEEK. It is important to note that when such forms are transferred to other tab areas, particularly within time-line B, then they can still be modulated for aspect. Thus we can compare NEXT WEEK, LAST WEEK, EVERY WEEK, and WEEK AFTER WEEK (Figure 4) at different time-lines. Wherever they are placed the same underlying modulations can be expressed.

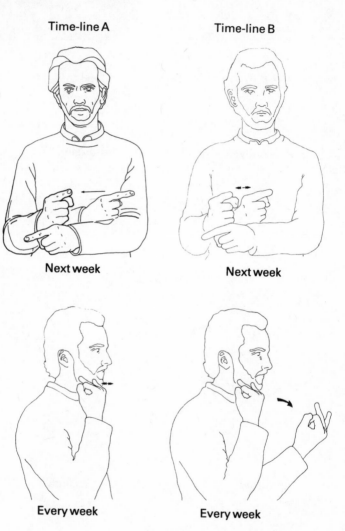

Time-line A

Time-line B

Next week

Next week

Every week

Every week

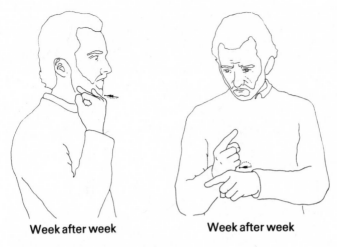

Week after week   **Week after week**

Figure 4

Time-line **B** allows for the expression of calendric units, succession (BEFORE, AFTER) and also indication of duration: A LONG TIME. The hand itself when held as a flat B in neutral position with fingers pointing up and palm right, can be used to indicate increasing or decreasing periods of time. The palm is used as Tab for forms such as HOUR, EARLY, LATE and their modulations, e.g. HOUR AFTER HOUR (Figure 5).

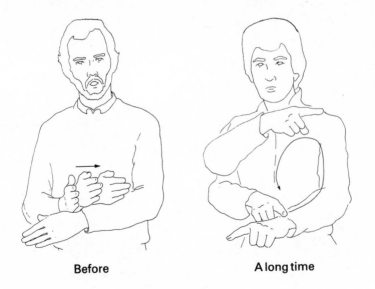

Before   **A long time**

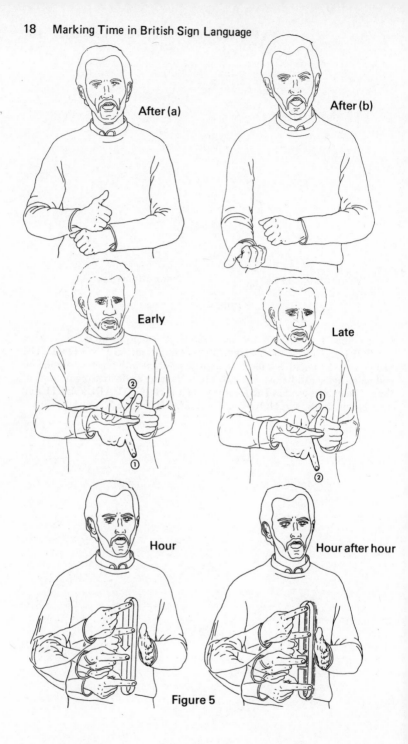

Figure 5

Line C is rather different from the first two in that this area in front of the signer's body is used primarily to indicate continousness and/or duration. It can be used to indicate that an event or state has persisted over a long period – and in many cases continues to persist. Such usage involves movement from left to right and is in a sense lexicalised in a verb such as CONTINUE (Figure 6).

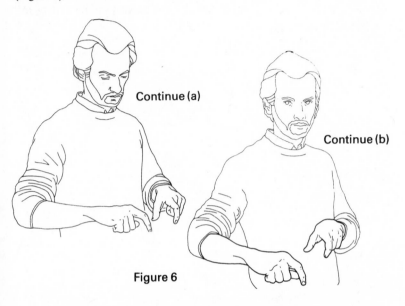

Continue (a)

Continue (b)

Figure 6

The same movement and position can be seen in a number of adverbials, but there are problems in deciding whether items such as:

7.1.   IT WILL ALWAYS REMAIN IN MY MIND
7.2.   I HAVEN'T SEEN HIM FOR A LONG TIME

should be viewed as modulated verb forms or as adverbial forms.

Figure 7.1 is made with the right index finger touching the forehead then moving downwards, changing to a bent index finger and interlocking with the bent index finger of the left hand. Both hands retain this position and move rightwards alone time-line C. We have noted a number of different versions of this sign: one involves both hands making a definite move to the left before moving firmly rightwards, apparently indicating past, present and future, i.e. 'it has remained in my mind, does remain and will remain'. Another variant of this sign simply involves the right index finger moving down from the forehead, interlocking with the left hand and then both hands moving downwards. The translation would be 'It is firmly fixed in my mind', hence this variant does not include any marking for duration (Figure 7).

Figure 7.2 begins with the index finger below the eye then moving downwards changing to an O hand: both hands in O configuration then move rightwards, and the whole manual sign is typically accompanied by the puffing out of the cheeks. A variant which can be translated as 'I saw you for a shorter time than expected', involves a shorter, faster hand movement to the right and the non-manual feature of sucked-in cheeks (Figure 8). (See Lilian Lawson's paper, this volume.)

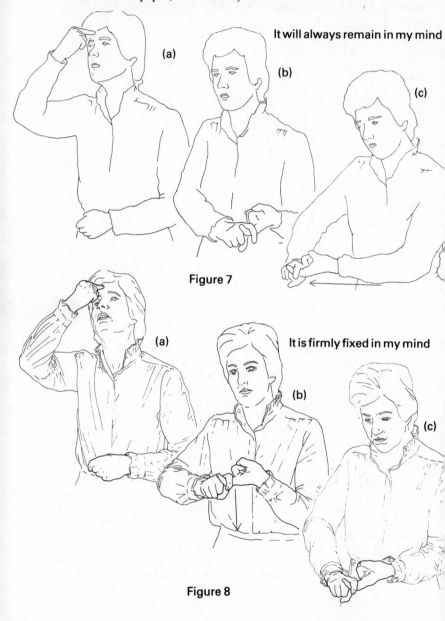

It will always remain in my mind

Figure 7

It is firmly fixed in my mind

Figure 8

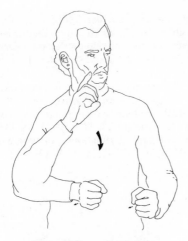

I saw X for a shorter time
than expected

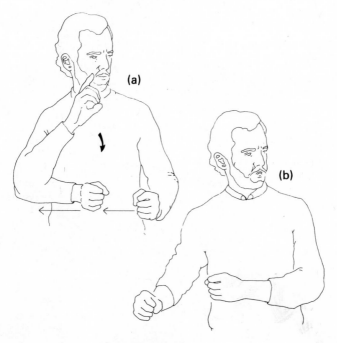

I haven't seen X
for a long time

In both sets of signs we can see that information about time (here specifically duration) can be incorporated into a single sign although the signer may prefer in other circumstances to use separate verb and adverbial forms. The argument here is that the above signs derive from an underlying Verb + Adverbial form.

The form YEAR is also articulated in neutral space and forms such as FOR EVER AND EVER can be seen as derived from YEAR. It is also worth noting that as with other calendric units, numbers can be incorporated into the signs so that we have TWO YEARS AGO, IN THREE YEARS TIME, and that again aspectual modulations can be applied to express meanings such as YEARLY, and YEAR AFTER YEAR (Figure 9).

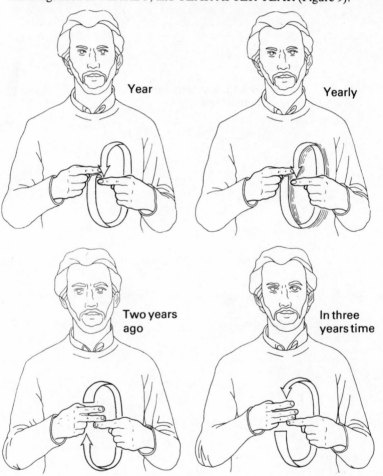

Figure 9

Age is normally expressed in BSL by using a front face tab, typically the nose: hence HOW OLD and FIVE YEARS OLD. We have noted an interesting tendency for signers to modify signs indicating age so that the sign begins at the nose but is then moved to time-line D, e.g. WHEN I WAS THREE, so that there is reference to what one might think of as ontological time, i.e. an individual's life-time. This use of time-line is more frequent than might be expected, although it is linked to a rather narrower set of meanings. Signers often use time-line D in conjunction with an aspectual modulation expressing the notion of 'gradually over time'. Thus in the statement 'As he grew older he gradually acquired sign language', three main signs are involved: /GROW OLDER/ ACQUIRE /SIGN LANGUAGE/. (Figure 10.) The first, made with palm facing down, involves a slow movement upwards: the second continues this slow movement upwards but involves a change to an Ô hand at the forehead. The slow deliberate movement expresses the meaning of 'gradually'.

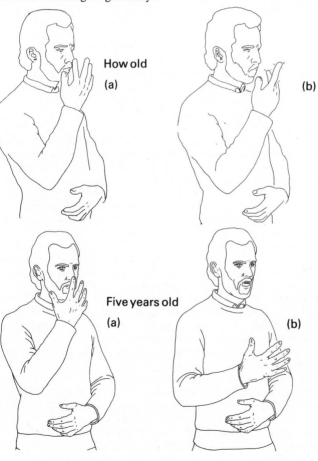

How old
(a)

(b)

Five years old
(a)

(b)

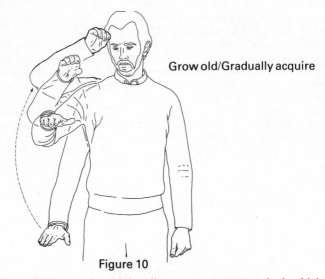

Grow old/Gradually acquire

Figure 10

BSL thus exploits a number of time-lines to create temporal adverbials. Sometimes the adverbial element appears to be incorporated into the verb itself so that the temporal information is presented within a single unit. The frequency and placement of these adverbials is at present under investigation but some initial observations may be worth noting. Firstly, we have been surprised at the frequency of marking for deictic time. The video tapes of our primary data contain a number of accounts of war-time events. These accounts were stimulated by a piece of film which formed part of a structured elicitation task. In these accounts, the signer frequently gives highly specific temporal information such as 'in 1940' or 'at the end of the war', but then goes on to include numerous markers of past time. At this stage we are unsure whether story-telling itself encourages such multiple marking, but in every case the observer is left in little doubt as to the time in which the event took place.

One further type of marking for time has been noted in a number of signers. This is the tendency to localise particular time reference in space. In the sign sequence: AROUND e-a-s-t-e-r HOLIDAY AROUND THEN, THEN is simply the deictic marker G (i.e. hand held closed with index finger extended). The signer points to a particular position in space and sets this up as a time-point. This allows the signer the opportunity to refer back to that same position in space again and again throughout the text. Such spatial markings of temporal reference are quite arbitrary and thus independent of time-lines.

Finally in this section, we turn to what is for most English speakers the most obvious realisation of tense, namely the use of inflections. Of course, in English, inflections are only used to mark past tense: present and future are expressed by a variety of other means. In BSL we have noted a very small number of verbs which appear to have clearly distinct past tense forms. In some cases they may be regarded as 'blends' which have incorporated into one sign the lexical verb and the completion sign glossed as FINISH. The 'past tense' of SEE may be viewed in this way. WON also involves the closing action found in FINISH but the past form bears no phonetic relation to the present form. The question of whether these forms should be described as past tense or perfective forms is discussed further below. We have also noted a number of forms which do not exploit the FINISH element at all. Examples include LEFT and SAID, both used in Scotland, but not as far as we know, in England. These examples are closer to such English irregular forms as go/went; leave/left. The two frequently used 'existence' markers, which make use of either a flat 5 hand with fingers flickering, or an Å hand with side to side movements, do not appear to be marked for tense.

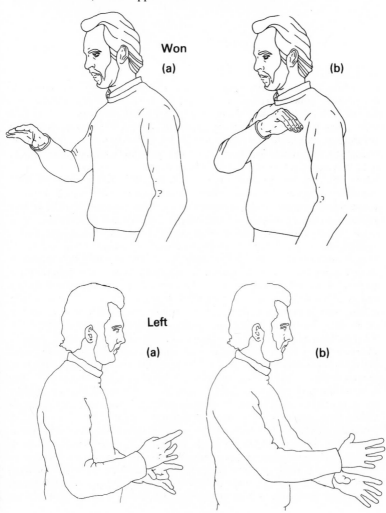

Won
(a)   (b)

Left
(a)   (b)

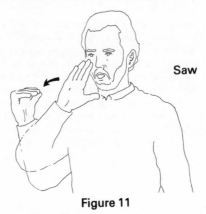

Saw

Figure 11

BSL: Aspect

The grammatical category of aspect allows us to take different temporal perspectives concerning the action, process or state described. An action may be seen as completed, continuing over a period, happening again and again, just beginning, occurring gradually, etc. This kind of temporal information can be just as important as deictic time reference and indeed cuts across such deictic marking. Thus an event can be viewed as occurring again and again, whether it is placed in past, present or future.

One immediate question in relation to aspect in BSL is whether FINISH should be seen as an aspectual marker indicating perfective. As noted above, one inherent problem is the tendency to gloss this item as FINISH. In fact what we can see, in many extracts from our data, are differing realisation of this item occurring within verbs, after verbs and in adverbial forms. This is one case where it will be interesting to discover whether the phonological form of the Scottish variety (B hands closing to O hands) links with a range of related forms which do not occur in the English varieties. The English form uses two Å hands and involves a circular rather than a closing action. At this stage I do not know the answer, but English deaf people may be able to help us out here. However, it is interesting to note that several of our Scottish informants use both forms, but with slightly differing functions, the 'English' variant often being used to mark the end of a text or even the end of a sentence: it is often translated by such English glosses as 'that's all', 'that was it' and 'there you are'. The essential phonetic feature of the Scottish version is the closing action, from fully open B to closed tapered O. This same action occurs in lexical signs such as COPY and PHOTOGRAPH which could be said to have the notion of completion built into them. (I realise that this may be pushing the connection too far – there is no suggestion that this combination of phonetic features does not occur in other signs which do not inherently imply completion, cf. repeated action in TALK.) However, more significantly it occurs in time adverbials such as BRIEFLY (Figure 12). The suggestion of an underlying pattern realised in both verb and adverbials has been discussed above in relation to duration and is discussed below in relation to iteration.

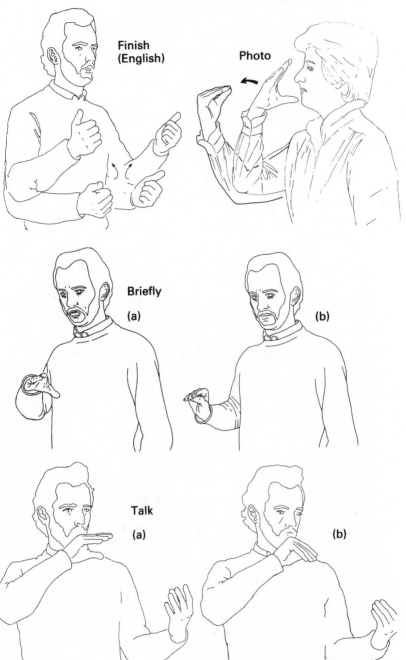

Finish
(English)

Photo

Briefly

(a)

(b)

Talk

(a)

(b)

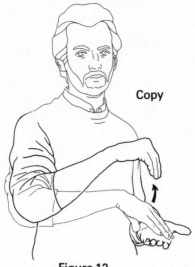

Copy

Figure 12

The main question which remains is whether this form should be seen as perfective or not. Comrie (1976) has suggested that perfective treats an event or state as an unanalysed whole – with emphasis on the *complete* rather than *completed* action. This latter gives greater emphasis to the final part of the action. On present evidence, it is doubtful whether we are here dealing with perfective in this sense. As pointed out earlier, we have also noted items which we have been tempted to treat as past tense forms (SAW, WON, LEFT), but these again appear to stress completion as opposed to simple past or perfective in Comrie's sense: it may be helpful for the moment to treat all of these under the category 'perfect' (i.e. completed), leaving perfective as the aspectual term indicating a whole action.

Other accounts of sign languages, Klima and Bellugi (1979) for ASL and Bergman (this volume) for Swedish Sign Language (SSL), have noted a considerable number of aspectual modulations operating on verbs and/or adjectives. In this presentation, I merely wish to mention several aspectual contrasts which emerge very clearly from our data. At this stage, no claims are made as to the specific categories of verbs which exploit such modulations: the ongoing work of the project involves noting and tabulating these forms. Similarly, we are at present noting only 'gross' differences, i.e. we have not used any special timing devices or artificial mechanisms to plot the formational features of modulations. However, we have tested out our own initial hypotheses by using specific elicitation tasks with informants. These include presenting informants with 'modulated' time adverbials such as WEEK AFTER WEEK or WEEKLY and asking signers to use these adverbials with different verbs. In this way we can note the obligatory contexts for specific modulations.

The major phonetic options exploited by modulated verbs include reduplication, changes in the length and quality of the movement, speed of movement and freezing or holding of the initial or final movement. Like other researchers we have noted at least two types of reduplication: the first involves long slow repetitions either with or without an end-hold, the second involves short rapid repetitions, again with or without an end-hold. The latter type is seen in the adverbial WEEKLY, while the former (with end-hold) is seen in WEEK AFTER WEEK. The verb COME used with WEEKLY would be marked aspectually for habitual aspect; the same verb used with WEEK AFTER WEEK (Figure 13) would be marked aspectually for iterative aspect. In some cases the operation of the modulation upon the verb-form produces a form which is iconically less expected. Thus, in the verb SMOKE (as in 'smoke cigarettes') we have observed the end-hold in the iterative modulation occurring at the lips, in fact touching the lips, rather than as we might expect, a few inches in front of the mouth.

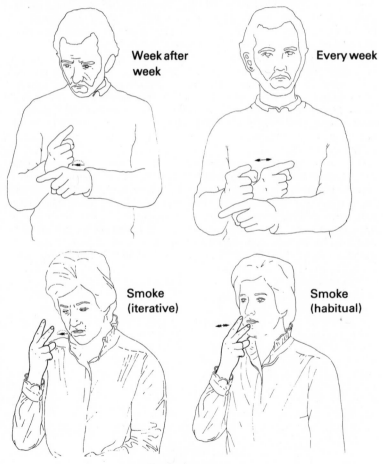

Week after week

Every week

Smoke (iterative)

Smoke (habitual)

Figure 13

Klima and Bellugi (1979) suggest that the same verb (their example is 'look at') can be seen as having a 'punctual' or 'durative' sense. According to this analysis the *punctual* verb can have the following modulations:

1. 'incessant'   realised by short iterated movements
2. 'habitual'   rapid non-tense repetitions
3. 'iterative'   tense, end-marked repetitions with a slow
                    elliptical return.

The *durative* verb is said to have the following modulations:

1. 'protractive'   realised by a long tense hold
2. 'durational'   realised by smooth circular repititions
3. 'continuative'   realised by slow elongated elliptical
                    reduplications.

While all of these distinctions have emerged from our own data, we feel less able to make definitive statements about the occurrence of 'durational' and 'continuative' than we are about the occurrence of the other aspectual modulations. This may be because the dynamic qualities of the movements involved demand rather finer measurement than we have yet used.

Our observations do suggest that the continuative modulation is typically accompanied by a non-manual feature involving the lips pushed out and a slight head-tilt. If our observations are correct, this feature is itself a marker of continuity and does not necessarily add further information. There are, of course, other non-manual adverbials which may supersede the continuity marker: several of those noted by Liddell (1980) also occur in BSL. Thus the non-manual Cs (involving shoulder raise, head turned to the side and the mouth twist), and 'th' (lips apart, tongue protruding), appear to be used in BSL in ways directly comparable to ASL. Here they clearly are supplying extra (adverbial) information, rather than acting as a direct marker of aspect. It will be interesting to see whether any other directly aspectual information is supplied non-manually either in BSL or other sign languages.

Finally, it should be noted that the phonological echoing which we have seen operating between verb modulations and adverbials in relation to, for example, the perfective, also appears to operate in relation to, for example, iterative. Both PERSISTENT and AGAIN AND AGAIN (Figure 14)

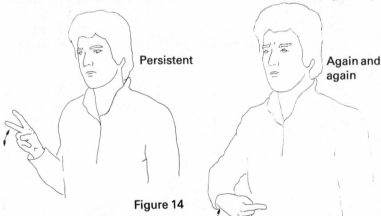

Persistent   Again and
                                    again

Figure 14

demand intensive repetition: it would be odd (i.e. ungrammatical) to use a non-modulated verb form with such an adverbial.

This short account has only hinted at the complexity of temporal marking in BSL: what is emerging is an interplay of systems, both manual and non-manual and a multiplicity of options for the fluent signer.

LEVELS OF ANALYSIS IN SIGNED LANGUAGES

Betsy McDonald

Levels of Analysis in ASL

In this paper, I would like to address considerations in sign language study which have surfaced during the course of this symposium. Ulfsparre (1981) described the rich possibilities for communicating actions in Swedish Sign Language and pointed out the necessity in sign language instruction of accurately stating the rules for these complex sign constructions.

Kyle (this volume) 'Looking for Meaning in Sign Language Sentences' made the by-now familiar observation that signers are very concerned with the 'picture' which their moving hands create and stated that we need a way to account for this. None of these concerns are new ones to sign language research in general. Specifically, research in American Sign Language (ASL) has been struggling with these issues in recent years.

Early research into the American Sign Language (ASL) disproved the idea that it was a primitive system composed of gestures with general conceptual meaning. William C. Stokoe, in his 1960 work, showed that signs could be characterised as combinations of a finite number of meaningless units. Based on the corpus of ASL available at that time, he established the analogy between the various parameters of a sign (handshape, movement, and location) and the meaningless units known as phonemes in linguistic theory. This established the sign as the smallest meaningful unit in ASL. Later work extended this analogy to other levels, without revising it. Signs were seen as unanalysable words. The characteristics of parameters (such as the bentness of fingers, or thumb position) were seen as analogous to *distinctive features* in linguistic theory. (Woodward, 1973; Lane et al, 1976.) As more ASL data accumulated, however, huge areas of the language did not seem to fit this analogical model. Increasingly, researchers reported on sign constructions which were not translatable by a single word, but which required an entire sentence to communicate the meaning accurately. This was noticed especially in the verb signs. Moreover, signs which were related in meaning were seen to be similar in production, with a vast number of meaning differences signalled by slight differences in movement, orientation, location, or handshape (DeMatteo, 1977). Because of the unstated acceptance of the analogical model described previously, the masses of data tended to be treated in one of two ways. First, they were considered to be non-ASL or mime. Alternatively, they were treated as the core of ASL, and the conclusion was drawn that ASL, and signed languages in general, were very different from all and any spoken languages. These solutions did not answer the questions: 'What are the rules of ASL? How do signers understand each other, and why do non-signers not understand ASL?' Therefore, these solutions were not satisfying. Further research seems to indicate that ASL can be characterised as a well-defined system of multi-morphemic sign constructions. I would like to summarise the research which points to this type of analogical model.

Klima and Bellugi (1979), expanding upon Fischer (1973), have given us a detailed description of the system of aspectual modulation in ASL verbs. In this system, a number of types of movements and repetition signal similar aspectual meanings regardless of the handshape or location of the sign.

These repetition patterns certainly consitute abstractable units of meaning in ASL. Type of movement has also been shown by Supalla and Newport (1980) to signal word class – that is, noun and verb distinctions in ASL. The path of movement in verbs has been shown to signal various types of adverbial (or verbal) information in the following way: in the complex sign which means 'a person came towards me' in ASL, the information contained in the movement can be labelled as either 'linear movement along a path' or as 'to or towards'; with the handshape signalling 'a human being' (Forman and McDonald, 1978, 79; Kegl, 1978, 79; Supalla, 1978). Location in signing has been shown to signal pronominal information (Fischer, 1973; Friedman, 1975; Kegl, 1978). Handshape in ASL has been shown to indicate the shape of objects across various movements and locations (Klima and Bellugi, 1979; Kegl and Wilbur, 1976; Supalla, 1978; Forman and McDonald, 1978, 79).

As these attempts show, we are still very concerned as a field with the need to discover the rules for the highly productive verbal signs which lie at the core of many sign languages. In addition, we want to know if the event-oriented, picture-oriented sign languages that we know of, with their vast amount of information packed into one unit, are unique among the world's languages.

Our study of signed languages would be greatly enhanced by the ability to draw upon a body of existing research into a similar language. Yet the study of *signed* languages is just beginning. It would help immeasurably to find a spoken language with the following characteristics:

1. The language compresses an incredible amount of information into a single unit, which is very difficult to analyse as a combination of separate units.
2. There is an incredible amount of information concerning the shape of objects in the verbal system of the language.
3. The use of these forms would be the basis for most of the words in the langage and cut across all word classes.

In fact, these statements accurately describe Navaho, an American Indian spoken language of the Athabaskan family. Navaho is a highly synthetic language. The units in its verbs bind together very tightly and the relations between the morphemes are very complex, semantically and phonetically. Nevertheless, at least some linguists (Sapir and Hoijer, 1967; Young and Morgan, 1980) have analysed Navaho verbs as consisting of a verb stem and up to ten prefixes. These prefixes signal different types of adverbial, pronominal and aspectual information. A great many verb stems for movement and location in Navaho are based on the shape of the involved object. In traditional linguistic terminology, Navaho is said to exhibit a predicate classifier system.

Consider the Navaho data below (taken from Young and Morgan, 1980).

Example 1. -*lts'id   'independent movement of a solid round object'
Example 2. -*Ødéél   'independent movement of a slender flexible
                        object'
Example 3. *Øna'   'independent movement of a flat flexible object'
                        (the stems are listed in the forms which they
                        would take for the perfective aspect)

In addition, the stems also differ as to the causation for the movement, depending on whether it is independently caused, caused by continuing manual contact, or only initiated by an agent.

Example 4. -*lts'id   'independent movement of a solid round object'
Example 5. -*á   'movement of a solid round object through
                        continuing manual contact', e.g., carrying a ball,
                        lowering a box from a wagon.
Example 6. -lne'   'movement initated by an agent involving a solid
                        round object' (e.g., a clock falls or a ball bounces).

These forms are built up to form a full verb in Navaho. The especially important information in specifying the verb is the addition of adverbial particles in the first prefix position.

Example 7. h à ǹ ' aà . h 'you take a round solid object out of an
                                enclosed space.'
            out you handle a   (from Sapir and Hoijer, 1967)
                     RSO
Example 8. ǹ   n í ' à . h 'you put a round solid object down'

            down you handle a
                     RSO

We find that over time, the verbs freeze and come to represent more specific unanalysable meanings which may be far from their original ones. The forms also cross word class boundaries and appear in the nominal system.

Example 9.   -nííh   'act with the hand and arm'

This form has come to be used in verbs which mean 'distribute', 'buy', 'sell', and 'trade'.

Example 10. -bą́ą́z   'movement by rolling'

This form yields 'nilbą́ą́z' 'I drove a wheeled conveyance' (such as a wagon).

The word for 'fence', 'ant'i', is derived from the verb for 'something extends encircling'. The word for a 'bolo tie' or 'necktie', zéédéeláhí, is derived from the verb zéédéelá, meaning 'a slender flexible object is placed around the neck'.

In light of these resemblances, let us change a few of our assumptions about ASL. Let us assume that the sign is not the smallest unit of meaning. Recent research cited above points to this conclusion as being correct. Let us suppose that a single sign is made up of many morphemes which combine in an incredibly tight fashion. Further, let us assume nothing about the meaning of a particular morpheme until we have examined a number of signs in which it occurs. Then let us assign it a meaning. If we do this with the system of shape specification in ASL verbs, a very neat system results. I would like to briefly describe some aspects of this system. Data from previous research, such as Klima and Bellugi (1979), Supalla (1978), Kegl (1978, 1979), Forman and McDonald (1978, 1979) is incorporated here, as well as new data from my own research with native signers. I will be able to describe only the underlying verb forms in ASL in this paper. I will not have time to deal with the combinatory possibilities of these morphemes with other morphemes in the ASL verb. I will claim that the handshape is the core or stem of the ASL verb and is used to signal the motion or location of a given type of object. The forms which I will present here are abstracted from other aspects of a sign, such as the location of the signing hand, the movement of the hand and the orientation of the palm of the hand: up, down, etc. The meaning of these forms was determined by examining a range of signs in which the form was used, and by finding the semantic element which was constant across all of these signs.

This system in ASL verbs distinguishes between objects perceived as an undifferentiated whole and objects perceived as a collection of more than one individual object, or as the 'sum of its parts'. This distinction is achieved by having the extended fingers touching each other for the stems signalling objects seen as undifferentiated wholes. (Example 11.) The stems which signal a collection of individuated objects have the extended fingers spread apart. (Example 12.)

Example 11. 'motion or location of a narrow object' (e.g., location of a bed, or movement of skateboard)

Example 12. 'motion or location of an object with two straight thin extensions' (such as movement of scissor blades, or a pair of legs)

Example 13. 'motion or location of a narrow curved object' (e.g. the motion of a spoon or the location of a whistle at the mouth for the sign for 'referee')

Example 14. 'motion or location of an object with two curved thin extensions' (e.g. the location of fangs for the sign for 'vampire', or bent legs in the sign for 'knee', or quotation marks in the sign for 'topic')

The system also distinguishes between flat and curved objects. The stems which signal the motion or location of flat objects keep the extended fingers straight and those which signal the motion or location of curved objects bend the extended fingers. Examples 11 vs. 13 exhibit this distinction, as do examples 12 vs. 14. An additional example of this type of distinction can be seen in Examples 15 and 16.

Example 15. 'motion or location of a flat wide object' (e.g., the location of a door or a poster, or the motion of feet).

Example 16. 'motion or location of a curved wide object' (e.g., the motion of a big spoon or a snow plow blade).

The system distinguishes between the motion and location of curved vs. circular objects. In the forms above which are labelled 'curve' (Examples 13, 14, 16), it can be seen that the fingers are bent but the thumb is not opposed. The forms for the motion or location of round objects have the thumb opposed, as can be seen in Example 17.

Example 17. 'motion or location of small round objects' (e.g., motion of raindrops, location of bullet holes or spots).

Example 18. 'motion or location of wide cylindrical object, (e.g., the location of a glass or telescope).

In addition to these distinctions, others can be seen, such as a system of singular, dual, plural. That is, the verb system makes distinctions, for example, between the motion or location of one vs. two vs. many upright straight thin objects. It also distinguishes between the location or motion of an object consisting of one vs. two vs. many thin curved extensions.

A system of thin, narrow and wide also cuts across the bent, straight and round dimensions and contributes forms, as in the forms for the motion or location of a thin vs. narrow vs. wide flat object.

We can see, however, that there are not an infinite variety of forms. We do not have infinite degrees of curvature or width. Among objects of the world which are perceived of as 'wide' we may find varying degrees of actual width, but they are nevertheless represented by the same form 'motion or location of a wide (flat or curved) object'.

At this point, I would like to mention verbal forms which are semantically different from those which I have mentioned above. The forms above dealt with and could be described in terms of the motion or location of a particular shape of object. However, when we look at a range of signs using this second type of form, we find that a notion of the object being *handled* must be included in the semantic label of the form.

Example 19. 'handle a compact or small cylindrical object (e.g., handle a dagger, paddle or lawnmower handle) (the label 'small cylindrical object' was first used in Forman & Fischer, 1979).

Example 20. 'handle a thin flattish object' (e.g., handle paper, a credit card or cloth)

Example 21. 'handle a round object' (e.g., handle a TV knob, a ball, a jar lid).

Example 22. 'handle a small object' (e.g., handle a coin, a needle , a feather).

Example 23. 'handle a light narrow object, (e.g., handle a fork, a plug, a light switch).

These forms are 'fleshed out' with the information contained in movement, location and orientation in ASL to produce a full verb.

As in Navaho, we find that the signs resulting from the combinations of these verb stems with other grammatical information tend to 'fuse', and produce more specific or more abstract 'frozen' verbs (or prepositions in some cases, like the ASL sign for 'under'). The form labelled as 'handle a compact or small cylindrical object' in example 19 above, has come to be used in frozen combinations which mean 'practice', 'make', 'work', and 'with'. In addition, the meaning of the underlying verb stem itself can change to become more general and signal the same verb, regardless of the other information with which it is combined. The form labelled 'handle a compact or small cylindrical object' in example 19 can mean 'take; grab', the form labelled 'handle a thin flattish object' in example 20 above can mean 'give', and the form for 'handle a small object' in example 22 above can mean 'choose, volunteer'. The forms also cross to the nominal system of the language, as with the ASL sign for 'fence', which can be analysed as being derived from the verb sign 'an object consisting of many straight thin objects extends'. Many so-called 'lexical' signs can easily be seen as frozen members of this productive predicate classifier system.

The analysis of ASL which I have begun to describe shows the advantages of considering a sign to be a complex word, made up of many morphemes. Using this approach, we can begin to state the rules for sign formation and we can easily trace the changes in sign formation over time. Further we can explicitly state the relationships between related signs in ASL, on a basis other than 'iconicity' or 'mime'.

It is very much an open question whether all signed languages are morphologically complex. A gesture takes twice as long as a word to produce (Bellugi and Fischer, 1972). Does this mandate morphological complexity? A second question is whether all signed languages 'pay attention' to the shape, location and handling of objects in the verb systems of their grammar. Do they all have predicate classifier systems? I do not know the answer to these questions. Perhaps we can begin to answer them together.

THE SEMANTICS OF BRITISH SIGN LANGUAGE SIGNS

B. Woll

A number of sign language linguists have explored the relationship between the constituent elements (parameters) of a sign (handshape, location, movement) and its meaning, and observed both that groups of signs with related meanings often share some constituent element, and that certain inflectional processes can be identified by the appearance of a common constituent element in sign underlying that inflection.

The existence of signs showing 'generalisation of meaningful parameter values' (Klima & Bellugi, 1979) (for example, signs with a common place of articulation all referring to 'feelings'), and signs where some regular parameter value appears as part of a grammatical process (for example, classifier insertion), have, however, been considered by sign language researchers as separate linguistic events. In this paper, I will discuss some data from BSL and suggest that these types of data are closely related, and that they should not be regarded as arising from separate processes. The signs I will discuss have in common that they share handshape and some feature of meaning. The data I would like to consider are in four groups:

1. Generalised Meaningful Parameter Values
2. Classifiers
3. Number Elements
4. Loan Signs

1. Generalised Meaningful Parameter Values

There are numerous signs in BSL which share some parameter value and some meaning. If we examine location, for example, many signs which could be labelled as 'emotional processes' are made on the chest (FEEL, LOVE), while many signs relating to cognitive processes are made at the forehead (THINK, KNOW, UNDERSTAND).

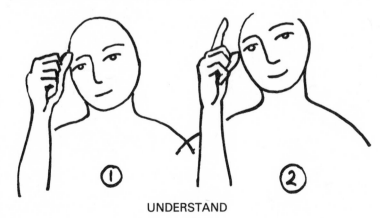

UNDERSTAND

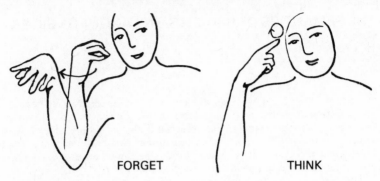

FORGET   THINK

Example 1. Signs with Shared Handshape, Location and Related Meaning.

Many signs which share a meaning connected to 'looking' share the handshape V.

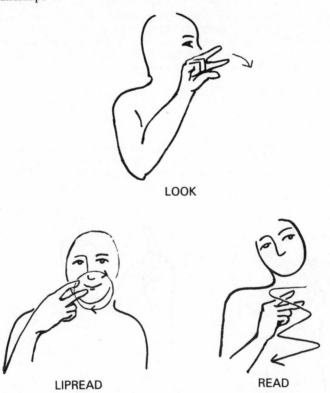

LOOK

LIPREAD   READ

Example 2a. Signs with Shared Handshape and Related Meaning.

Other signs with related meanings share both location and handshape (ANGRY, HATE, INTEREST).

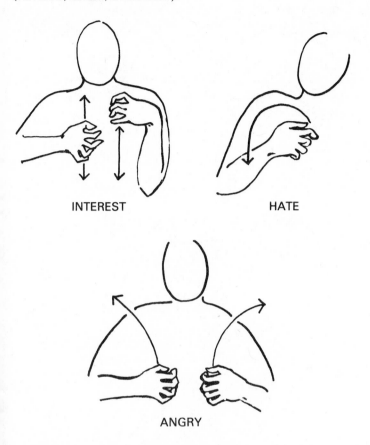

INTEREST   HATE

ANGRY

Example 2b. Signs with Shared Handshape and Location, and Related Meaning.

This feature of generalised meaningful parameter values is common in a wide variety of sign languages (Woll, in preparation); Klima and Bellugi (1979) have suggested that it resembles sound symbolism in spoken language, but that it is unrelated to the type of handshape substitution which occurs in classifier insertion.

Another very large group in BSL is formed by signs which share handshape, and which relate to 'good' or 'bad' attributes. Signs such as GOOD-BAD, SUCCEED-FAIL, etc., differ only in handshape, the 'good' signs having Å, the 'bad' signs having I.

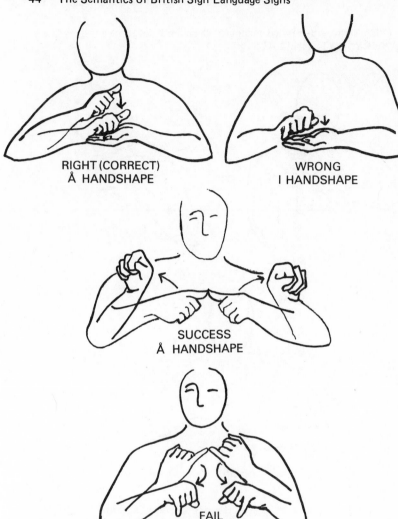

RIGHT (CORRECT)
Å HANDSHAPE

WRONG
I HANDSHAPE

SUCCESS
Å HANDSHAPE

FAIL
I HANDSHAPE

Example 3. Signs with Contrasting Handshape

The pervasiveness of these handshapes in signs with meanings relating to 'goodness' or 'badness' may be seen in a count of such signs in the BSL lexicon. In a study of 2000 signs in the lexicon the following was observed:

Handshape Å
The majority of signs with Å handshape bore a meaning connected with 'goodness'. They are grouped as in Table 1.

Table 1. Distribution of Å handshape signs by meaning

Meaning	% in Lexicon	Examples
GOODNESS	56%	CLEVER APPROVE
DEIXIS	30%	LEAGUE AFTER
OTHER	14%	WHO AMERICA

Example 4 illustrates these groups.

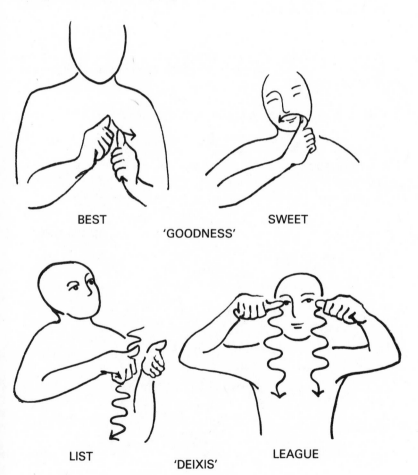

BEST   SWEET

'GOODNESS'

LIST   LEAGUE

'DEIXIS'

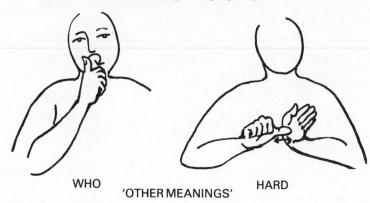

WHO   'OTHER MEANINGS'   HARD

Example 4. Å Meanings.

Handshape I
The majority of signs with I handshape bore a meaning connected with 'badness'. The distribution is shown in Table 2 and further illustrations are provided in Example 5.

Table 2. Distribution of I handshape signs by meaning

Meaning	% in Lexicon	Examples
BADNESS	83%	WICKED REJECT
ENDING	10%	LAST LATE
OTHER	7%	SATURDAY SIX

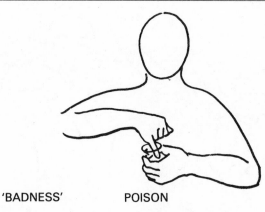

'BADNESS'   POISON

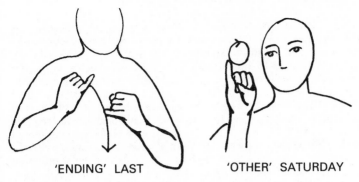

'ENDING' LAST   'OTHER' SATURDAY

Example 5. I Meanings

Apart from the sign for 6 (see Section (c) below), and three finger-spelled loan signs (see Section (d)), every occurrence of I in this lexicon relates to 'badness' or 'ending'.

For several of these signs, a variant exists with the same meaning, but with a handshape different from I or Å (see Example 6a). In other cases, a sign with a similar meaning, but without a 'good' or 'bad' connotation and identical in all respects but handshape may be found. (See Example 6b.)

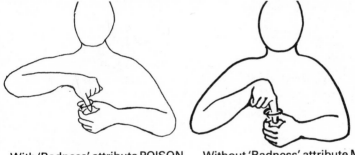

With 'Badness' attribute POISON   Without 'Badness' attribute MIX

Example 6a. Related signs.

ARGUE (I handshape)   ARGUE (G handshape)

Example 6b.

The process by which signs change handshape to match this pattern may be observed historically (Woll, 1981). Signs with connotations of goodness and badness which had distinct handshapes 100 years ago, have changed handshape to conform to this pattern. Thus we see signs such as HEALTH and SORRY, which both had B handshapes in the last century, differentiating, so that HEALTH now has the Å and SORRY, the I handshape. There is informal evidence that the association of 'badness' with I handshape is equally strong in Australian Sign Language (a language closely related to BSL). Ray Jeanes (personal communication) has told of attempts to introduce signs with American alphabet initialisations into the Australian deaf community. Signs such as I (first person singular pronoun) (with I handshape) were rejected as having some, unspecified, 'bad' connotation, and were considered unacceptable by adult deaf signers.

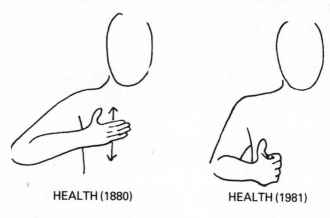

HEALTH (1880)   HEALTH (1981)

Example 7. Change of Handshape.

2. Classifiers

Classifiers in BSL are similar to those in ASL (McDonald, this volume), and may be described as functioning to pick out a set of signs which have in their semantic description shared physical characteristics. Kegl (1979) has described how classifiers substitute for handshapes in verbs of motion. In the following examples, the handshape of the verb specifies the class of items which form the subject of the verb. Classifiers are thoroughly discussed in McDonald's paper, and are therefore only mentioned briefly here.

Classifiers are, of course, handshapes with attached meanings, and for those signs which undergo classifier insertion, the handshape indicates membership of a nominal class, and therefore contributes to meaning in a systematic way. They have been considered as unrelated to the first group discussed above, but the Number Elements discussed below form an intermediate group between the classifiers and signs with Generalised Meaningful Parameters.

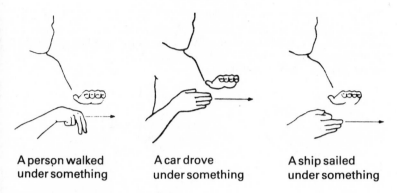

| A person walked under something | A car drove under something | A ship sailed under something |

Example 8. Classifiers in verbs.

3. Number Elements

The appearance of elements in the lexicon which reflect numerical properties is interesting for a number of reasons. To some extent, the phonology of number signs is different from the rest of the lexicon: some handshapes only appear in number signs, and handshapes found in signs other than number signs may reflect number properties. For example, the classifier 'moving on two-legs' shown above, and the signs connected with 'looking' discussed in Section 1, Example 2, both convey some meaning of the 'two-ness' of two eyes and two legs. Similarly, the classifier 'many-individuals' has the 5 handshape; the classifier 'one-person' has the 1 handshape. There are also several signs with handshapes reflecting number properties, for example, AGAIN and ANOTHER.

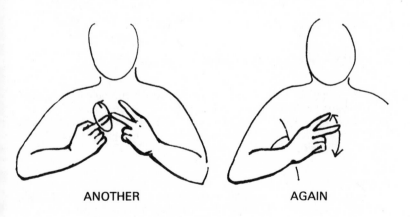

ANOTHER   AGAIN

Example 9. Number Elements in Handshape.

Numbers can also be incorporated into 'time' signs. For example, the sign TOMORROW, signed with V handshape (=2), rather than G, means THE-DAY-AFTER-TOMORROW; with W handshape (= 3), 3-DAYS-FROM-NOW. The signs, WEEK, YESTERDAY, and AGE are other signs which can incorporate number handshapes.

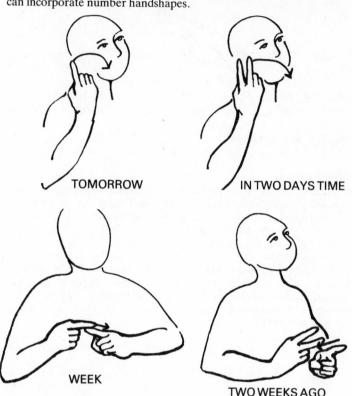

Example 10. Number incorporation in time signs.

Some signers, as well as incorporating number handshape into the time-related signs discussed above, also incorporate number handshapes into other signs. For example, one signer, when describing a photograph of three girls, signed GIRL with W (3) handshape. Another signer produced BED with 4 handshape to describe 4 bedrooms (Example 11).

4. Loan Sign

A fourth group I would like to consider are loan signs and those signs showing 'initialisation'. Despite very recent attempts to introduce American 1-handed fingerspelling into schools for the deaf, adult signers and most school-age signers use the British 2-handed alphabet. This alphabet was used

GIRL   THREE GIRLS

BED (ROOM)   FOUR BEDROOMS

Example 11. Number incorporation in other signs.

at one time as the primary means of communication in many schools for the deaf, and older signers, in particular, may use fingerspelling extensively in place of BSL signs.

Possibly because with a 2-handed alphabet opportunities for initialisation appear limited, there is no evidence that initialisation of signs has ever occurred under the influence of educators or Signed English users and, thereore, signs with handshapes resembling those of the manual alphabet must be assumed to be loan signs, reduced from fully-fingerspelled words. There are large numbers of these, undoubtedly deriving their handshapes from the initial letter of a fingerspelled English word, and they include such common signs as MOTHER, FATHER, ENGLAND, PAPER, GOLD, SATURDAY, SHOE, FEBRUARY and many others.

The loan signs described by Battison (1978) in ASL differ somewhat from these loan signs. In all the BSL signs which derive from 2-handed fingerspelling, only the initial letter appears in the handshape. Most of the ASL loan signs have movements derived from the movement required to make the transitions between 1-handed statically articulated letters. The movements of the BSL loan signs fall into three groups. The movement may be the same as that of the articulation of a single letter (all 2-handed letters involve movements such as touching, grasping, etc.). In some signs a

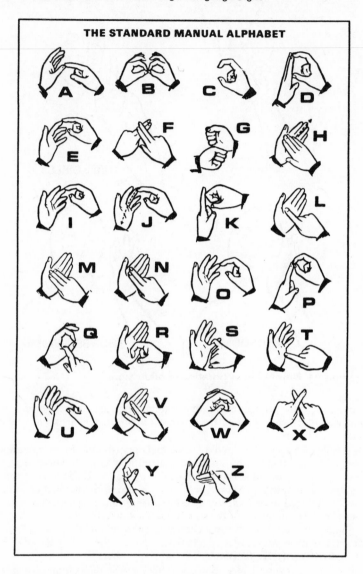

Table 3. Fingerspelling: British Sign Language.

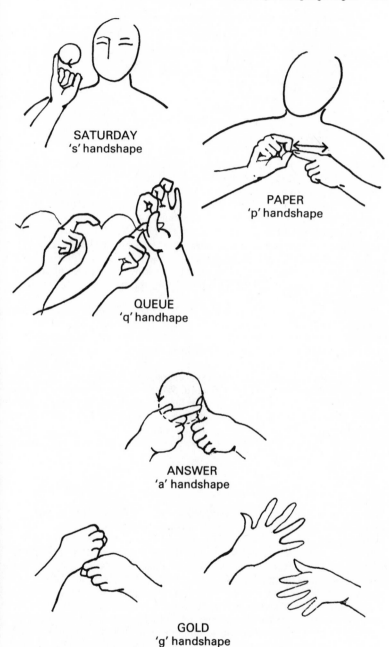

SATURDAY
's' handshape

PAPER
'p' handshape

QUEUE
'q' handhape

ANSWER
'a' handshape

GOLD
'g' handshape

Example 12. 'Initialised' loan signs.

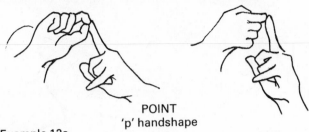

POINT
'p' handshape

Example 12a.

specialised movement may have replaced the original movement of the letter (ENGLAND, GOLD, PAPER). While most of these changes are to such movements as stroking, in some cases this specialised movement may be the same as a similar sign with a non-alphabet handshape (SATURDAY: in this sign only one hand is used, but with the handshape of 's'). In other cases the specialised movement may appear iconic (GOLD, QUEUE). In a sign such as GOLD, the movement is the same as in the signs BRIGHT, LIGHT, SUN, etc., while the handshape is the initial 'g' of 'gold'. In QUEUE, the right hand moves rightwards; with repeated flicking of the index finger, the same movement as in OBJECTS-LINED-UP; the handshape begins with the hands in 'q' configuration.

Initial letters as symbols for spelled words (and their referents) can be seen in English where abbreviations such as 'pee' for 'new penny', and 'ess-ess' for 'steam ship' or more complex derivatives such as 'beeb' representing 'Bee Bee Cee' which in turn represents 'British Broadcasting Corporation' are very common. It is reasonable to assume that the alphabet itself has some iconic or symbolic value for both English speaker and signers. The initial letter symbolises the entire spelled word. We cannot tell from signs such as GOLD and QUEUE if a movement has been added to a handshape (loan sign in Battison's terms) or if a handshape has been added to a movement (initialised sign in Battison's terms). If the second is the case, then these signs show generalisation of a meaningful parameter in the same way that the first group of signs discussed do.

Summary

Four groups of data have been discussed so far. The first and last groups can easily be treated as analogic formations, the second as a rule-governed morphological process. This analysis would be congruent both with Kegl's description of classifiers and Klima and Bellugi's discussion of generalised meaningful parameter values, and these two phenomena can be treated as wholly distinct. The third group however – number elements – do not fit neatly into this scheme. If we follow Kegl's definition of classifiers as functioning to pick out a set of nouns which have in their semantic description shared physical characteristics of shape and animacy, then we can hardly label as classifiers those number elements which represent the 'two-ness' of a class of items (eyes, two persons, etc.). That is, we presumably must describe such elements as functioning to pick out some shared characteristic of number. But even if we broaden our description of classifiers to include these, we still find that we must separate signs with a generalised meaningful handshape linked to number (LOOK, etc.). Similarly, while we may establish a rule permitting the insertion of a handshape representing a number element into 'time' signs, we cannot describe the insertion of number elements into other types of signs in the same rule-governed way. What I would like to propose, in place of these separate groupings is a continuum of structure types, from unique lexical items, through no-longer-productive analogic formations, through productive analogic formations to general grammatical processes. Handshape may be used to mark physical, quantitative and qualitative attributes. Analogic formations may be so productive that virtually all signs with a given handshape may have related meanings (e.g. I: 'bad' or V: 'two'). Rather than regarding signs with generalised meaningful parameters as a curiosity, like sound symbolism in spoken language, it should be regarded as an organising principle for the representation of meaning in sign language.

COMPOUNDS IN SWEDISH SIGN LANGUAGE IN HISTORICAL PERSPECTIVE

Lars Wallin

First of all, I would like to give some background information about how I became interested in observing compounds in Swedish Sign Language. In the beginning my intention was to look at historical change in Swedish Sign Language, that is, how the form of signs has changed. For this study I used the oldest Swedish Sign Language dictionary *Teckenspraket* (The Sign Language). It was compiled in 1916 by a deaf man, Oskar Österberg, who had gone to the school for the deaf in Stockholm – Manillaskolan. This dictionary is the only one of its kind from that time in Sweden. In the dictionary the signs are either described with photographs together with written descriptions, or in written form only. There is also a short list of Swedish words and corresponding signs described by Österberg. He compiled the dictionary not only to facilitate the learning of sign language by hearing people, but also having in mind 'that the dictionary should facilitate, for such deaf-mutes who already know sign language, a better understanding of the Swedish language'. (Österberg, 1916.)

For my study, I transcribed all the signs described by Österberg (about 1,200 signs). The sign notation used is based on the one described in *Tecknad Svenska* (Bergman 1977). This notation system was originally constructed for Signed Swedish. My intention in using transcription was to compare the sign language of 1916 with today's, and to observe how the form of the signs has changed and developed. As I transcribed these signs I observed that Österberg used more than one sign to translate or paraphrase many Swedish words which now are translated with only one sign. I also observed that signs which now are single signs, were previously rendered by sentence-like strings of signs; for example, the word 'family' was signed: MAN WOMAN MARRIED CHILDREN TOGETHER. Today, 'family' is signed with the same form as the sign TOGETHER, but the movement is repeated twice. According to Osterberg the sign 'pension' was signed: OLD REST MONEY RECEIVE; today the form approximates the last sign RECEIVE. 'Pension' is signed close to the signer's face – thumb and index receive money from the air.

I have also observed that signs which now can be regarded as simple were described as compound signs by Österberg. Thus, 'hotel' was signed with the compound LIVE/SIGN, though today it is a simple sign, similar to SIGN. However not all compounds in Österberg's dictionary have become single signs.

My study in the end has focussed on compounds, both on what distinguishes *form* and to some extent on *historical change*.

What is a Compound?
A compound is a word composed of two or more separate words, such as the Swedish word 'grasten' (granite), composed of 'gr)' (grey) and 'sten'

56

(stone); and the Swedish word 'dovlarare' (teacher of the deaf), composed of 'dov' (deaf) and 'larare' (teacher). The elements in compounds can also be used as word pairs in phrases such as: deaf teacher, grey stone. To differentiate between compounds and their corresponding word pairs, Swedish uses different prosodic patterns: the compound is pronounced with 'accent 2' characterised by a certain combination of stress and tone.

In Swedish Sign Language, a compound is usually comprised of two signs. There are two ways of creating compounds in Swedish Sign Language. The first is analogous to the creation of compounds in the Swedish language. These compounds are Swedish-influenced and therefore considered 'loan translations'. In this way 'tecken' (sign) and 'sprak' (language) are combined into the compound 'teckensprak'. The compound sign TECKNA/SPRAK (SIGN/LANGUAGE) is formed in exactly the same way. Another example is 'sjukhus' (hospital). The Swedish compound and the Swedish sign SJUK/ HUS, are both comprised of the elements meaning 'sick' and 'house'. (For other examples, see Table 1.)

Table 1. Compounds created through loan translation

BLUE/BERRY	blueberry
DEAF/MUTE	deaf
DEAF/MUTE//CLUB	deaf club
FARMER/YARD	farm
PUPIL/HOME	boarding school
SICK/HOUSE	hospital
SIGN/LANGUAGE	sign language
SLEEP/ROOM	bedroom
TRAVEL/BAG	travelbag
VOCATION/SCHOOL	vocational school
YOUTH/CLUB	youth club

The second means of forming compounds in Swedish Sign Language (SSL) is not influenced by Swedish. These compounds may be called genuine compounds. Examples of genuine compounds are TANKA/DJUP ('begavad') – THINK/DEEP ('clever'); (see figure 1a–c) KAFFE/SKYLT ('kafe') – COFFEE/SIGN ('cafe'); and PAPPA/MAMMA ('foraldrar') – FATHER/MOTHER ('parents'). (For other examples see Table 2.)

In Table 2 some signs are represented by descriptions of the form rather than by glosses indicating the meaning (COLD/CLENCHED-HANDS-BEATING-EACH-OTHER; SEE/KNOCK-ON-PALM). Those elements of the compounds do not exist as single signs today. They may have been free forms when the compound was first created but Österberg (1916) has not been able to identify them and uses this kind of description without giving the meaning.

1a

1b

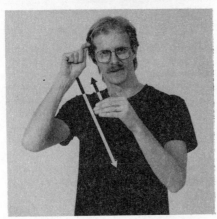

1c

Table 2. Genuine Compounds*

BROWN/FACE	Africa
COFFEE/SIGN	café
COLD/CLENCHED-HANDS- BEATING-EACH-OTHER	winter
EAT/PECK	hen
FATHER/MOTHER	parents
GOOD/APPLAUD	beneficial
GOOD/HEART	generous
HEAR/NAME	famous
LIVE/SIGN	hotel
LIVE/TOGETHER	living together (noun)
PROMISE/GIVE	permit
RED/COMB-ON-HEAD	rooster
RED/RIBBON-ON-HAT	station
RED/STREAMING-ON-ARM	blood
SEE/BORROW	imitate
SEE/GONE	disappear
SEE/KNOCK-ON-PALM	try
SEE/REFUSE	hate
SICK/STRONG	healthy
SMALL/GROUP	minority
TALK/AGAINST	protest (verb)
TALK/BACK	answer
THINK/DEEP	clever
THINK/EMPTY	forget
THINK/LIVE	lively
THINK/SAME	approve
THINK/TIRED	absent-minded
TOOTH/YELLOW	rat
WRITE/REMAINING-ON-PAPER	take notes

*Hyphenated glosses are single signs

The Recognition of Compound Form

In sign language a phrase and a compound, both with the same elements, can be distinguished from each other by the way they are signed. The initial element in a compound is somewhat different than the same element in a phrase, and thus the two constructions can be distinguished. The difference is found in a drastic shortening of the initial duration of the sign, as compared with the duration of the sign in a non-compound phrase. In order to analyse how the initial sign changes, and to see how the entire compound is signed, I videotaped several examples of compounds signed by a group of deaf people. They were also asked to sign the initial sign of a compound, both as a simple sign and as the first sign in a phrase consisting of the same signs as the compound. The videotape enabled me to see how the initial sign in a

compound was articulated (e.g. THINK in THINK/DEEP), compared with
the single sign (THINK) and its form in a prahse (THINK DEEP). I was also
able to compare the production of the compound (THINK/DEEP) with that
of the phrase (THINK DEEP). This difference and others dealt with in this
paper have been described extensively in the *Signs of Language* (Klima and
Bellugi, 1979), with examples from American Sign Language.

Using the timer which was superimposed on the sign, I could measure the
duration of a sign (a) isolated, (b) as phrase initial, and (c) as a compound
initial, as well as (d) the whole phrase, and (e) the entire compound.

Table 3. Duration of signs in compounds (centiseconds)

Signer No.	1	2	3	4	5	6	7
THINK	48	70	76	28	96	30	38
THINK DEEP	24	28	20	6	8	6	8
THINK/DEEP	16	10	16	2	6	4	4
THINK DEEP	112	76	118	52	126	60	58
THINK/DEEP	52	52	112	36	64	40	50

Using signer No. 1 as an example, we note that THINK isolated lasts 48
csec; in THINK DEEP it lasts 24 csec; in THINK/DEEP it lasts 16 csec. This
shows us that THINK in the compound-initial position is temporally
compressed as compared with the other two productions of THINK. The
production of the whole phrase takes 112 csec and the whole compound 52
csec. These measurements also show that the duration of the compound is
much shorter than that of the phrase. As one can see from the Table,
although times vary between signers, the pattern is always the same.

To find out whether the same sign is reduced both in first and second
position, several signs were produced, appearing alternatively in first
position in one compound and in second position in another compound.
Examples are LEKA in LEKA/SAND (PLAY/SAND) and LEKA/PLATS
(PLAY/YARD), and also in OVA/LEKA (PRACTICE/PLAY) and in
BARN/LEKA (CHILD/PLAY).

The results were as follows:

Table 4. Duration of signs in compound-initial and compound final
positions (centiseconds)

Signer No.	1	2	3	4	5	6	7
LEKA/SAND	22	34	38	14	8	6	24
LEKA/PLATS	24	34	32	12	10	8	34
OVA/*LEKA*	36	36	64	34	20	30	40
BARN/*LEKA*	32	34	68	32	24	34	46

Looking at the subject No. 1 again, one can see that the sign LEKA takes 22 csec in LEKA/SAND and 24 csec in LEKA/PLATS, both occurrences as initial sign. In second position, LEKA takes 36 csec in OVA/LEKA and 32 csec in BARN/LEKA. This indicates that the sign LEKA is more reduced in initial position than in second position. The results here correspond well with those obtained for compounds in American Sign Language, 'The position of the sign in a compound determines the degree of the sign's compression'. (Klima and Bellugi 1979, p. 213.)

Before we discuss how this reduction is possible and how we can in more detail examine what happens with the first and second sign in a compound, we shall first look at the structure of the sign.

The Three Aspects of the Sign

A sign's structure is characterised by its three aspects:
1. Articulator
2. Articulation
3. Place of articulation (Bergman 1977).

The articulator is the hand involved in performing the movement. The hand takes different hand shapes (e.g. flat, clenched, pinched, index hand). When two hands having the same hand shape are used in the movement, the term double articulator is used. The way the hand is held (e.g. up, forwards, left) is called the hand's *attitude*.

The action of the articulator is the *articulation,* which means any kind of movement (e.g. circular, forward, turning) with one exception: a sign whose articulation consists of contact only.

When the articulator is acting, it occurs somewhere in space. This aspect is called the *place of articulation* and as a rule is located at some part of the body.

The articulator can also act in the space in front of the body. This is called the neutral place of articulation. If both hands are acting in a sign with a single articulator, the second hand can function as the place of articulation.

The First Sign in a Compound

The reduction in a compound, which happens primarily in the first sign, can be described as a change in the three aspects. For the articulator, both the hand shape and the attitude can change. The change of the hand shape occurs through regressive assimilation. In a compound this means that the hand shape of the articulator of the second sign has an influence on the hand shape of the first articulator, resulting in the first articulator changing to resembling the second. Let us compare the first element of TALK/BACK ('answer') with TALK. The index finger hand of TALK becomes a flat hand in the first sign of TALK/BACK, taking the same hand shape as the sign BACK (G > B).

Now if we compare RED/COMB-ON-HEAD ('rooster') (see Figure 2c–d) with RED COMB-ON-HEAD, we can see that the index finger hand of the sign RED (see Figure 2a) in the phrase becomes a clenched hand with the middle finger, index and thumb extended in the compound (G > V̊). This is the same hand shape as in the sign COMB-ON-HEAD (see Figure 2b). In a comparison of DEAF/MUTE//CLUB ('deaf club') with DEAF/

MUTE, the index hand in DEAF/MUTE in the compound becomes a clenched hand with bent index finger and thumb $(G > \overset{\circ}{X})$. This is the same hand shape as in CLUB. Such changes occur also in LOOK/GONE ('disappear'), SEE/BORROW ('imitate'), COLD/CLENCHED-HANDS-HITTING-EACH-OTHER ('winter').

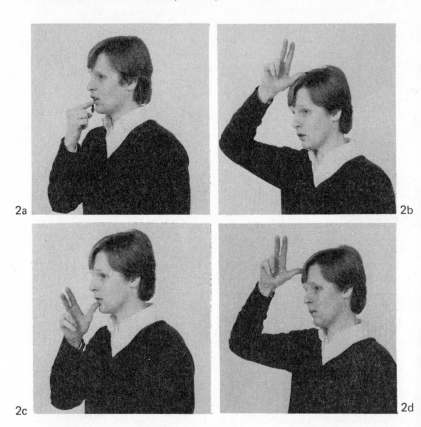

2a   2b

2c   2d

The attitude of the articulator changes compared with the isolated sign. If we compare THINK/DEEP ('clever') with THINK DEEP, the hand in the sign THINK in the phrase is held up with the palm towards the body. In the first sign in THINK/DEEP the hand is still held up, but with the palm away from the body. Compare also RED/COMB-ON-HEAD with RED COMB-ON-HEAD. In the phrase, the hand in the sign RED is held in front of the mouth with the palm towards the body. As the first sign in the compound, the hand is held the same way, but with the palm to the left.

In the articulation there are both temporal and spatial reductions. These reductions can be due to shorter movements, a decreased number of movements, the movement itself changing or the movement disappearing completely. Similar changes take place with compounds in American Sign Language:

> 'Movement components . . . are reduced and weakened . . . single movement, double contact alternating movement, repeated movement (bounce, twisting) all shorter in time, reduce in length, weaken in stress. . .'

Klima & Bellugi, 1979, p. 216.

Looking at HEAR/NAME ('famous') as compound with HEAR NAME, we see that the articulator of HEAR in the phrase is carrying out a movement from the ear out to the side. In the first sign of HEAR/NAME the length of the movement is reduced so strongly that the articulator is just held in front of the ear.

Examining COFFEE/SIGN ('cafe') and COFFEE SIGN, the articulator of COFFEE in the phrase makes circular movements above the other hand, the place of articulation. As the first sign in the compound COFFEE/SIGN, the circular movements have completely disappeared, and the articulator just contacts the place of articulation. The forward movements in the signs SEE and GOOD also disappear when they are signed in compound-first position as in GOOD/HEART ('generous') and SEE/GONE ('disappear'). Similar changes in articulation also occur in, for example: SIGN/LANGUAGE ('sign language'), SICK/HOUSE ('hospital'), SMALL/GROUP ('minority').

If there is any change in the place of articulation between the two signs in a compound, the initial sign will approach the position of the following sign. Let us compare, for example, FATHER/MOTHER ('parents') and FATHER MOTHER. In the phrase, the locations during articulation are: forehead-chin (FATHER) and chest-chin (MOTHER). In the compound, the positions are reduced to the lower part of the face.

If we compare DEAF/MUTE ('deaf') and DEAF MUTE, we find that in the phrase, DEAF is articulated at the ear and MUTE at the mouth. In the compound the position of the first sign is in the middle of the jaw nearer to the chin, which is the position of the following sign.

The Second Sign in a Compound

For the second sign no striking changes were observed in the three aspects. The sign in this position was signed in much the same way as its corresponding isolated sign. The only observed difference is that in some signs the articulation of the second sign is somewhat faster. Compare THINK/DEEP ('clever') with THINK DEEP. Here the articulation of DEEP is somewhat faster than when it is signed in the phrase as is EMPTY in THINK/EMPTY ('forget') compared with THINK EMPTY.

Another characteristic of the second sign is that when the first sign's articulator is beginning its action, the second hand is already in its position. This is always the case when the second sign has two hands involved, regardless if they have double articulation or if the hand is the place of articulation.

In a phrase, a following sign does not take its position until the first sign has completed its movement. (See for example SMALL/GROUP ('minority') and SMALL GROUP.)

When the other hand in the second sign is the place of articulation, it is brought closer to the first sign's position, thereby reducing the transition.

> 'Transition reduction may be accomplished spatially by making the two signs of a compound closer together in signing space than they would be in a phrase.'
>
> (Klima & Bellugi, 1979, p. 218.)

In the phrase, the other hand stays in its usual position when the second sign is signed.

If we compare THINK/DEEP ('clever') with THINK DEEP we can see how, in the compound, the other hand moves closer to the first sign's articulator, in contrast to what the other hand does in the phrase. Similar movements occur in THINK/EMPTY ('forget').

Constraints on Compound Form

In genuine compounds the first sign always has a single articulator. The only exception I have observed is PROMISE/GIVE ('permit') which has a double articulator. In loan translations, both single and double articulators can occur in the first sign. The second sign in either may be signed with one or two hands.

If the two signs have their place of articulation at different levels of the body (e.g. head and hand), then the sign with the highest level (head) will tend to become the first element in the compound (but not if both signs are signed at head level). This is true for both kinds of compounds.

One example of a genuine compound will illustrate this tendency. This example is TOOTH/YELLOW ('rat'). (See Figure 3a–b.)

3a   3b

In compounds where one of the signs is a colour, it normally is the first element (see for example compounds with RED and BROWN, Table 2). All colour signs, with three exceptions, are signed with one hand and at different places on the face. The exceptions use the second hand as place of articulation rather than the face. One of those is the sign for 'yellow'. The sign for 'tooth' is signed by pointing at the teeth. According to the above mentioned pattern, the sign for 'rat' should be signed YELLOW/TOOTH but because the sign TOOTH has its place of articulation on a higher level than YELLOW, the order of the signs is reversed, and 'rat' is signed TOOTH/YELLOW.

The tendency of compounds to appear with the higher sign first has also been observed in loan translations. Let us look at the sign of 'Bollnas' (a town in Sweden) as one example. The first part of 'Bollnas' looks like the Swedish word 'boll' (meaning 'ball'), and is therefore signed with BOLL (BALL), (double articulator; neutral place of articulation) – the second part 'nas' (meaning 'headland') looks like the word 'nasa' (meaning 'nose') which is signed at the nose. If one were following the original word order in the sign compound one would sign BOLL/NASA, but as the sign NASA is at a higher level (and has a single articulator) than BOLL, the order is reversed and 'Bollnas' is signed NASA/BOLL (NOSE/BALL).

This inversion occurs even when the signer is simultaneously mouthing the word 'Bollnas'. This demonstrates the perseverence of sign language over the influence from Swedish, and the tendency of signs to occur in the order: highest sign first.

The same tendency has also been observed in what has been called 'slips of the hands' (Klima & Bellugi, 1979) when a Swedish compound is mouthed and accompanied by an inverted compound sign. Thus the Swedish name 'Bergman, has been observed as MAN/BERG,where MAN ('man') is signed at the forehead and BERG ('mountain') in the neutral place of articulation. 'Hjärtfel' ('heart trouble') is another of these inverted compounds: Fel ('wrong') is located at the nose and HJÄRTA ('heart') at the left side of the body. Such mispronunciations also indicate that the tendency 'highest-sign-first' is a preferred arrangement in compounds.

The Historical Change in Compounds

When comparing the compound signs described by Österberg with their form today, one can discern certain tendencies in their historical development. Similar observations can also be made when comparing signers of different generations. The oldest signers often use forms like the ones described by Österberg.

One observed change is the already mentioned regressive assimilation in the articulator (hand-shape as well as attitude) which was discussed in the previous examples: TALK/BACK ('answer'), RED/COMB-ON-HEAD ('rooster') and DEAF/MUTE//CLUB ('deaf club'). The same kind of change can be seen in the sign for 'winter', COLD/CLENCHED-HANDS-HITTING-EACH-OTHER. In Österberg, COLD was formed with the clawed hand in front of the mouth, palm inwards. However, in the modern compound, COLD is signed with clenched hand (in front of mouth, palm inwards). The form of the second element, as can be seen from the above description, is the clenched hands hitting each other on the palms.

In the sign for 'try', SEE/KNOCK-IN-HAND, we can see another example of complete assimilation of handshapes. In the single form, SEE (see Figure 4a) is signed with the V-hand (extended, spread index and middle finger) palm inwards, moving away from the nose. In the compound the fingers of SEE have become bent and the attitude has changed so that the palm faces left (see Figure 4c). This shows assimilation to the second element's articulator, KNOCK-IN-HAND (see Figure 4b), which is a bent V-hand, knocking on the flat hand (the place of articulation). In the sign 'try', we can also see how the second element has changed as well in a movement towards symmetry of handshape. Frishberg, in a paper about historical change in American Sign Language, states that 'if both hands are acting in unison, and more particularly if one hand acts on the other, the hands will assume the same configuration' (Frishberg, 1975, p. 700). The place of articulation (the second hand) strives to achieve the same hand shape as the articulator. This has happened with the sign for 'try', where the second hand, flat with palm up, has become clenched, palm inwards (see Figure 4d). This is only partial assimilation in that the flat hand has become clenched, thereby approaching the form of the bent V-hand where all fingers are clenched except for the index and middle finger. Complete assimilation would result in the clenched hand having the same bent V-hand form as the articulator. This complete assimilation has been observed for some deaf students in the school for the deaf in Lund, where the first element has been completely reduced and TRY is a single, non-compound sign (see Figure 4e).

4a

4b

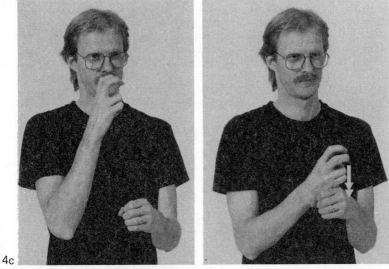

4c

4d

4e

Similar observations have been made for 'clever' – THINK/DEEP. The hand shape of the place of articulation in the second element is usually a flat hand. However, for a few signers the form of the place of articulation has changed and it resembles the form of the articulator.

The same tendency seen in 'try' can be observed in 'winter' and 'station'. The first element disappears when signed by younger signers and becomes a single unit. 'This tendency for signs to become single units, i.e. not remain compounds, is very strong.' (Frishberg, 1975, p. 710.)

Even when the signs become single units, the first element may not disappear completely. The first element often leaves some kind of trace behind. We can see this in the second element of the sign 'winter' (clenched hands hitting each other) for example. Before contact is established, one hand is held clenched palm to the left. This attitude is a vestige of the first element where the articulator moves down from the mouth towards the other hand before they hit each other.

One problem in the study of the development of compounds should be mentioned: there is a group of signs which seem to be compounds but which we have not been able to reconstruct, not even by consulting Österberg (1916). These signs are formationally similar to RED/COMB-ON-HEAD ('rooster') in that (a) they have a double contact and, (b) the two contacts are established at different parts of the face. Such signs are considered to be compounds because single signs tend to have just once place of articulation, not two. One such sign (meaning 'trade union') is identical in form to RED/COMB-ON-HEAD but for the hand shape ($\overset{\circ}{X}$). It is reasonable to assume that the first element comes from RED but the origin of the second part is not known to us. Another example of the same kind is FATHER; the index finger establishes contact first with the forehead, then with the chin. The downward movement is conceived as a transition movement not as a feature of the articulation of a single sign. (Popular etymologies of FATHER are compounds.) The history of these compounds is not likely to be revealed unless some now unknown descriptions of signs should be discovered.

Summary of Observations about Compound Form

In sign language a compound is usually composed of two signs. A compound is performed faster than a phrase consisting of the same signs. The reduction in performance time takes place for the main part in the first sign. While the first sign begins its action, the other hand of the second sign prepares its position, either as double articulator or as the other hand with the function of the place of articulation. If the other hand is the place of articulation in the second sign, it will be placed closer to the position of the first sign. There is a strong tendency for the sign with the highest place of articulation to become the first sign in compounds.

The research project on Swedish Sign Language in which this study was carried out is financed by the Bank of Sweden Tercentary Foundation (RJF 79/206). Brita Bergman is responsible for that work and I wish to express my gratitude to her for support and encouragement.

English translation: Anna Hein Nordling
                          Richard Schulman
Demonstration of signs: Mats Jonsson
                          Lars Wallin
Photograph: Johan Fogelquist

IS BSL AN SVO LANGUAGE?

Margaret Deuchar

The title of this paper, 'Is BSL an SVO language?' was chosen to remind us of one of the prevailing approaches to syntax in linguistics, and of how it might be applied to the analysis of BSL or sign languages in general. However, I wish to argue both against this prevailing approach in linguistics and against its application to the analysis of sign language.

One of the most important characteristics of twentieth century linguistics is its continual search for universals of language, i.e. features which are common to all languages, regardless of their genetic origin or geographical diffusion. This search has been extended to sign language as it has become an accepted object of linguistic research, and has led to controversy in ASL research as to which word order typology the language belongs to, if any. Fischer, for example (1975:5) states that "the basic word-order in ASL is Subject-Verb-Object", whereas others, such as Friedman (1976) dispute this.

In this paper I hope to show, with reference to BSL, not only that it is difficult to determine a basic sign order, but also that an approach which limits itself to sign order will account for less of the data than a more functional topic-comment analysis. Having argued for a topic-comment analysis of my data, I shall discuss the constraints on production of the data which might determine this kind of structure.

Let us assume for the moment that it is worth trying to determine a basic sign order in BSL. After all, a reputable introductory textbook in linguistics says, "We find in all languages that sentences contain a noun-phrase subject (S), a verb or predicate (V), and possibly a noun-phrase object (O)" (Fromkin & Rodman, 1978:335). This statement contains the common assumption that the sentence is the appropriate unit of syntactic analysis, but what is a sentence in BSL? (It is worth pointing out here that this question is not easy to answer for any language, spoken or signed, that does not have any written form, or for any spontaneously produced data, including spoken English (cf. Crystal, 1980a). Linguists generally agree that the verb is the basic constituent of the sentence (cf. Lehmann, 1978:8), so perhaps we should focus on BSL verbs initially, to see how they are related to the constituents surrounding them.

Since the search for basic word order generally involves establishing the relationship between verbs and adjacent noun phrases, I investigated the linguistic environment of verbs in a twenty minute film of spontaneous signing. Using mostly semantic criteria to identify the category of verb and noun, I found that the occurrence of a three element sequence of a verb and two noun phases was extremely rare in any order, but that a verb would sometimes appear before or after a nominal argument. (This parallels Friedman's (1976) finding for ASL.) Since Lehmann (1978:8) has suggested that all languages can be classified as either VO or OV, the absence of overt subjects in BSL might at first sight seem not to matter. However, there does not seem to be either a consistent VO or OV order in the data. Examples from the data with the nominal object after the verb include the following:

(1) CLEAN ALL   'I cleaned everything'.

(2) MOCK WELFARE-WORKER   'She teases the welfare worker'.

Examples with the nominal object before the verb are as follows:

(3) HOW-MUCH KNOW-(NEG)   'I don't know how much'.

(4) NUMBER TELEPHONE NUMBER HAVE 'I have the telephone number'.

(5) TEN p PUT-IN   'put in 10 p'.

At this point I had not only been unable to categorise BSL as a VO or an OV language, but I had also dealt with a very small proportion of the data that might be relevant to the syntactic analysis of BSL. I had only dealt with verbs, and of those, only those that appeared to be transitive. The categories of data that I had left out included utterances consisting minimally of (a) a noun phrase and an intransitive verb, (b) two noun phrases, (c) a noun phrase and an adjective, and (d) an adverb and a noun phrase. The following are examples of utterances falling into these categories:

Noun phrase and intransitive verb

(6) L. WILL CLOSE DOWN   'Lewisham (club) will close down'.

(7) FATHER FALL   'Father fell'.

Two noun phrases

(8) FARE THERE BACK TEN p   'The fare there and back is 10p'.

(9) b-i-n-g-o CROWD   'There was a crowd at Bingo'.

Noun phrase and adjective

(10) b THAT b-e-e-r PINT CHEAP   'That pint of beer is cheap'.

(11) BEFORE FARM THERE FARM HOUSE OFF (NEG) SAME CONTINUE   'The farm house which was there before hasn't been pulled down, it's still there.

(12) k-i-l-b-y BEFORE GOOD NOW GOOD?   'Is Kilby, who was good before, good now?

Adverb and noun phase

(13) NOW GOOD RIDER GOOD a-t READING?   'Are there good riders now at Reading?'

(14) THERE WE-TWO GO   'We both went there'.

None of these data will be referred to if we limit our attention to the order of constituents in constructions with a verb and object. I would argue that we might achieve a much more general description of the BSL data we have looked at so far if we analyse all utterances in terms of a topic-comment structure. A fairly conventional definition of topic and comment is as follows: "The topic of a sentence is the person or thing about which something is said, whereas the further statement made about this person/thing is the comment" (Crystal, 1980b:358). The important point about the notion 'topic' is that it is defined primarily on a functional, or semantic basis, rather than a structural, or syntactic basis. Li and Thompson (1976) provide a useful discussion of the notion of topic which inspired my analysis, and Chafe (1976:50) suggests that "the topic sets a spatial, temporal or individual framework within which the main predication holds."

We may see how this notion of topic applies to the BSL data. Following Li and Thompson (1976), we shall take as a working assumption that topics in the BSL data will be in utterance-initial position where they occur. (Non-temporal means of marking topic in BSL will be explored later.) Li and Thompson suggest that topic is more of a discourse than a sentence notion, so that its scope may be larger than the individual sentence. For this reason I suggest that the topic may not appear before every verb, though we may expect it wherever there is a change in the topic.

To begin with, the notion of topic may help to explain the different orders of what we called 'verb' and 'object' in data items (1) to (5). In (1)–(2) the order seemed to be VO, whereas in (3)–(5) the 'object' (which appears in initial position) is in fact topic, or the 'framework within which the predication holds'. This order was actually more common than the other: otherwise it might be argued that these are special, 'topicalised' constructions, comparable to English sentences of the type, 'It was 10p that I put in', where the normal word order has been altered to put special focus on '10p'. However, in BSL, the topic-as-'object'-verb construction seems to be basic in the data. In items (1) and (2) which have a different constituent ordering from (3)–(5), we may assume there is no overt topic because it has not been changed since a previous mention in the discourse. For (1) I do not have data from earlier in the discourse, but (2) was part of an utterance as follows:

(2a) WIFE TALK SIGN f-n-y GOOD SHE MOCK WELFARE-
    WORKER
    'My wife talks and signs in a funny way. She's good. She makes fun of
    the welfare worker'.

Here the topic is clearly WIFE, introduced utterance-initially. The topic remains the same over the rest of the utterance, so it does not need to be signed again before MOCK.

An important characteristic of topics (cf. Li and Thompson, 1976) is that they are definite. In data items (3)–(12), there is a definite noun phrase topic in initial position in each item. In (3) the topic, HOW-MUCH, is a question, but refers to a definite amount of money; in (4) NUMBER is made definite by the qualifying noun phrase which follows, TELEPHONE NUMBER; in (5) the topic is a definite amount of money again, this time 10 p; in (6) it is a particular deaf club, Lewisham; in (7) it is the signer's father; in (8) it is a fare to a particular place, 'there and back'; in (9) it is a particular event, Bingo (probably the last time that Bingo had been played at the deaf club); in (10) it is a particular pint of beer that the signer has just bought; in (11) it is a particular farm house, known to the addressee, that both of them had seen before; and in (12) it is a particular person identified by his name, Kilby. In (3)–(12), then, all the topics are definite noun phrases indicating referents known to both signer and addressee.

The topics of (13) and (14) do not appear to be noun phrases: instead they are a temporal and a spatial adverbial (NOW and THERE respectively). These also function as topics in that they refer to a definite time or place, and 'set the spatial or temporal framework within which the main predication holds' (cf. Chafe, 1976:50).

So far I have suggested that the BSL data we have looked at might be better analysed in terms of a topic-comment than a subject-predicate framework. However, the usefulness of the notion 'topic' does not preclude the existence of subjects in BSL. I would suggest tentatively that pronouns may be more likely to function as subjects, and noun phrases as topics, in the kind of data we have looked at. If subject and topic do not always coincide, then topic will be more salient in the analysis. The function and distribution of topic and subject in BSL seems a fruitful area for research, but cannot be considered in more detail here.

Assuming that the data can indeed be analysed in terms of topic and comment primarily, I should now like to discuss the constraints on the production of the data which might help to explain this structure. The constraints discussed will fall into two categories: those of the medium in which BSL is produced, and those of the communicative situation in which it is produced. First I shall consider the resources of the spatial-visual medium, and the ways in which they might determine a topic-comment structure. Until now I have almost ignored two aspects of the spatial-visual medium: the fact that it allows BSL to have a spatial as well as a temporal dimension, and the fact that various channels of activity have the potential to operate independently, including the two hands, the head, the eyebrows, the eyes and eye gaze.

While ignoring the spatial dimension of BSL, I have concentrated on the temporal dimension, on how relationships between signs might be expressed by temporal sequence, and I have suggested in particular that topic occurs sequentially before comment. Various aspects of the BSL data have been analysed to give support to the notion of topic in BSL, but no marking for the topic itself has been considered other than its sequential position, i.e. utterance-initially. But since the spatial dimension is also available to BSL, we might expect topic to be marked spatially as well as temporally, either by the simultaneous occurrence of a topic-marking signal in a channel other than the hands, or by the spatial relationship between signs representing topic and comment. Since marking for any syntactic function in both dimensions would seem to provide redundancy, but to require particularly fine co-ordination of the two dimensions, it seems likely that it would apply only to forms with functional constancy (cf. Li and Thompson, 1976:463), i.e. where there is a 1:1 relation between form and syntactic function. This is true of the notion of topic in a way that it is not true of other grammatical notions such as subject, for example.

To make this more concrete, we may look at some data where it seems that topic may be marked either by non-manual signals or by relative spatial positioning of the hands. Liddell (1980:22) states that in ASL, "Topics are accompanied by a slight backward head tilt and a brow raise". I did not find this kind of invariant marking in the BSL data, but did find some interesting non-manual marking. Data item (13) was actually part of a longer utterance, transcribed in more detail as follows:

Eyebrows	——————— raised ———————
Eyes	
Manual gloss	NOW GOOD RIDER GOOD a-t READING THERE GOOD (pause)

Eyebrows	—————————— raised ——————————
Eyes	Widened
Manual gloss	RIDER MARVELLOUS RIDER o-r m

Translation	"Are there good riders now at Reading? Are the riders good or mediocre?"

In this utterance the eyebrows are raised throughout after NOW indicating that this is a question, and in addition, the eyes are widened during the second occurrence of the manual sign RIDER. Earlier I suggested that NOW was the topic of item (13), but I think it is also the topic of the supplementary question, 'Are the riders good or mediocre?' The second occurrence of RIDER is then a sub-topic of the entire utterance, and I would suggest that its function is marked in two ways, (a) by the pause which occurs before it, so that it is temporally initial to the second question, and (b) by the widening of the eyes during this sign. Thus there seems to be both temporal and spatial marking of this sub-topic.

Another piece of data which is worth examining in more detail is item (12), transcribed below in more detail:

Eyebrows	—————————— raised ——————————
Manual gloss	k-i-l-b-y BEFORE GOOD (pause) NOW GOOD

Translation	"Is Kilby, who was good before, good now?"

Here I would argue that the entire topic is K-i-l-b-y BEFORE GOOD, or 'Kilby, who was good before'. BEFORE GOOD seems to function as a postmodifier (perhaps equivalent to a restrictive relative clause in English) which adds to the definiteness of Kilby by further identifying him. The idea that BEFORE GOOD may be included in the topic is given further support by both temporal and spatial signals: there is a pause after GOOD, and there is eyebrow raising (to mark a question) only over the last two signs, NOW GOOD.

Another non-manual signal suggesting the separation of the topic and comment is apparent in the following example:

Eyebrows	—————————— (invisible on film) ——————————
Head	
Manual gloss	OTHER THAT t-e-a-m GOOD RIDER COME v-i-s-i-t COME

Eyebrows	—————————— (invisible on film) ——————————
Head	nod —
Manual gloss	GOOD t-e-a-m ALL SAME?

Translation	"The other teams that come to visit, are they good teams or all the same (as before)?"

Semantic criteria suggest that the topic here is the entire first line, and the comment the second line. Some support for this is provided by the occurrence of a head nod over GOOD, the beginning of the comment. Liddell (1980) has done a detailed analysis of the possible rôle of the head nod in ASL, and concludes that one of its main functions seems to be assertion. In the light of his finding it is interesting to note that the head nod in BSL occurs at the beginning of the comment, since the comment is an assertion about the topic, generally providing new information in contrast to what is given. (But see, e.g., Chafe, 1976 for a more sophisticated discussion of these notions.)

The final possible way of marking topic and comment that I shall consider is by the relative spatial positioning of the hands. In item (5), what I earlier identified as the topic and comment are actually signed using different hands. We may transcribe (5) in more detail as follows:

Right hand	TEN P	
Left hand		PUT-IN
Translation	"I put in 10p	

It is interesting to note that TEN p (the topic, which is signed first) is made with the signer's dominant (right) hand. His right hand remains in the position it took for fingerspelling 'p' while the left hand signs PUT-IN. So the topic and comment are not only separated in space and time, but the relationship between them is also indicated by part of the end of the topic being held while the comment is signed. This process is also illustrated in item no. 10, which is transcribed in more detail and with more accuracy as follows:

Eye gaze			Towards addressee and away
	Right	b THAT b-e-e-r	PINT
Manual gloss	Left		CHEAP
Translation		"A pint of that beer is cheap"	

Here the comment, CHEAP, is signed with the left hand while the right hand is signing PINT beside the actual pint of beer. The intersection of the spatial and temporal dimension is shown particularly well here in that, in addition to the spatial difference of PINT and CHEAP there is a temporal difference: the sign PINT is begun before and finished after CHEAP. Non-manual signals also seem to play a rôle in that the signer's gaze moves towards his addressee as he signs CHEAP, and then back to his beer.

The importance of the medium of BSL in influencing its structure might be demonstrated not only by examining medium-related features in BSL data, as I have just done, but also by comparing its structure with other languages using the same medium. Some ASL researchers, for example, have suggested that a topic-comment analysis is appropriate for ASL (see e.g., Woodward, 1972; Ingram, 1978; and McIntire, 1980; for a useful review of various approaches, and support for the idea that old is ordered before new information in ASL). However, others (notably Fischer, 1975; Liddell, 1980) report that the basic order in ASL is SVO, although other orders can be derived from this by topicalisation. To take another sign language, some of the data from Danish sign language presented in Hansen (1975) looks rather amenable to a topic-comment analysis, e.g., the items glossed as HOUSE/OLD HOUSE//THERE MAN WOMAN// and translated as 'In an old house lived an old man and his wife' (Hansen, 1975:250–1).

So there is some indication that data from other sign languages may be analysable in terms of a topic-comment structure, and I shall now consider to what extent this is likely to be due to the constraints of the medium versus other factors. It has been suggested by some ASL researchers (e.g., Boyes, 1972; Kegl and Chinchor, 1975) that because visual short term memory is more limited in capacity than auditory short term memory, use of the temporal dimension will have limitations in sign language. Such researchers suggest that this indicates the importance of the spatial dimension for encoding information simultaneously in time. Kegl and Chinchor say that this will entail "a simpler mapping between visual sign and meaning than there is between sound and meaning" (Kegl and Chinchor, 1975:   ). If they are right, this is a possible explanation for a topic-comment structure, since, as I pointed out earlier, topics exhibit a 1:1 relation between form and syntactic function.

However, we should beware of overestimating the effect of the medium on sign language. Studdert-Kennedy and Lane (1980), for example, suggest that both spoken and signed languages use both sequential and parallel organisation, though in different ways. Levelt suggests that it is important to distinguish between "what is simultaneous or successive in the signal, and what is in the process" (-ing of the signal) (Levelt, 1980:141). His concern is with processing, and he suggests that "on-line processing is highly similar for spoken and sign language, and that the similarity increases from word/sign to sentence to discourse level" (Levelt, 1980:154).

Levelt's emphasis on the similarity of sign and speech processing at the discourse level leads us to a consideration of the kinds of data on which we are basing conclusions about sign language structure. I pointed out earlier the importance of the notion 'sentence' to the investigation of basic word order, and also the difficulty of identifying the sentence in any data which is spontaneously produced, whether speech or sign. The BSL data which I referred to were spontaneously produced, as were most of the data referred to by those ASL researchers who found a topic-comment analysis appropriate for ASL. However, it is interesting to note that those who are in favour of the notion of basic sign order for ASL tend to base their analysis on elicited sentences rather than on spontaneous discourse (cf. e.g., Liddell 1978:67). There are at least two possible ways in which elicited sign sentences may differ from spontaneous sign discourse: (1) they may be influenced by the structure of the dominant spoken language, and (2) the communicative situation in which they are produced may have an effect on the data.

I do not wish to discuss the possible effect of spoken language on elicited sign sentence production here (but see Friedman 1976), but I would like to discuss the effects of the communicative situation on the production of spontaneous language data in general. So far I have suggested, on the basis of my analysis of BSL data, that BSL might best be analysed in terms of topic and comment. The implication has been that some spoken languages, by contrast, English in particular, are best analysed in terms of subject and predicate (or subject, verb, object). However, analyses of English in terms of subject and predicate are based on very different kinds of data from the BSL data: the English data used are most commonly sentences produced in isolation by native speakers for the purposes of analysis rather than for the purposes of communication. Linguists working on spontaneously produced spoken English report finding something like a topic-comment structure there (cf. Ochs, 1979; Givon, 1979). This kind of structure seems to be particularly common in face to face conversations where speakers are exchanging information (or comment) on the basis of shared knowledge (or topic). An example of an English utterance which can be analysed in terms of topic and comment is given by Ochs (1979:64) from a conversation between students about an art course: "The twentieth century art, there's about eight books". Here, "the twentieth century art" is the topic, and the rest, the comment.

This suggests that any conclusions about the syntactic structure of a corpus of language data should not be generalised to the language as a whole before data from other communicative situations have also been analysed. So before classifying BSL as a topic-comment language, we should also consider data produced, for example, in more formal situations. One problem with data from formal situations is that it seems to be influenced by the structure of English (cf. Deuchar, 1978) so that it is not clear to what extent we are still dealing with BSL. However, it seems likely that the influence of English in formal situations may decline as BSL becomes more acceptable as a public mode of communication, and we may expect to see variation and change in the structure of BSL as it performs new functions.

Conclusion

I have tried to show in this paper that the question "Is BSL an SVO language?" is not a very fruitful line of enquiry for the data available. Instead I have suggested that analysis of the data in terms of a topic-comment framework may provide more insights into its syntactic structure. In attempting to explain this structure I have suggested that we should not limit our attention to the rôle of the medium, but should also consider the effect of the communicative situation. This should convince us that neither signed nor spoken languages are homogeneous or predetermined in structure, but that structure can vary and change according to the circumstances of language use.

SIGN LANGUAGE OF THE DEAF AS A COLLOQUIAL SYSTEM

G. L. Zaitseva

In the Russian community of the deaf, two sign systems are employed for communication. One of them, sign language (SL), is acquired by a young child if he or she is in immediate communication with members of a deaf community (family with deaf parents, school for the deaf, etc.). The second communicative system, Signed Russian (SR), is signed speech which develops in an essentially different situation. After reaching a definite level of verbal skill and when in a situation of comparatively official communication, e.g. speaking to a school meeting, a deaf child uses signs, ordering them like the words of an ordinary spoken sentence. Development of verbal speech is accompanied by continuous sign vocabulary increase, and in this way a sort of secondary sign system is gradually constructed in which signs appear as visual equivalents of ordinary words, and their order replicates that of verbal language. In the deaf community, signed Russian is used for official communication, public addresses, etc. This type of speech is also used by professional translators when translating public lectures, in educational institutions, etc.

The present paper is concerned with the analysis of SL. Functional characteristics of SL are determined by its role in unsophisticated communication, and this is where its functions are similar to those of verbal colloquial speech. Researchers define colloquial speech as the speech "which is found in conditions of immediate communication, when the relations between participants are informal and there is no aim towards a message of official character". (*Russian Speech,* 1973, p.17.)

Colloquial speech is considered to be a special linguistic system, differing from the codified normative literary language. We will compare SL with Russian colloquial speech (CS) as two communicative systems or languages. Such a comparison will permit the differentiation of the esssential features of SL, connected with its main function – providing unsophisticated, private communication.

Among the most important analogies are the following:

1. *Situation Involvement*

Both in SL and CS, situation is a component part of communication – it is implanted into speech. Consequently, presence or absence of the topic of the talk may directly influence the construction of an utterance. If the topics are "given" in the situation, they need not be expressed in verbal (sign) expression. This peculiarity is *situation involvement*.

Because of this, many ordinary oppositions, such as "completeness of utterance – ellipsis" acquire in SL and CS quite a different form from normative literary language meaning. That is why sentences like "I to the armchair", "Where you my pen yesterday" in CS, and N. UNDERGROUND, I BUS in SL are common structures which are not considered elliptical. The following system of notation is used here:

Signs – (Upper case letters) translated Russian language	MOVE
Words – (Quotation marks)	"move"
Meanings – (Single inverted commas)	'move'

2. *Spontaneousness*

Unpreparedness or verbal "hanging about" finds its expression in repetitions, self-interruptions and hesitations when choosing words (signs) and constructions – the characteristics of both CS and SL. We can compare for example, the following utterances:

"She lived somewhere in Moscow suburb her village was"
GIRL LITTLE FEED CHICKENS SIX YELLOW PECK

Situation involvement and spontaneousness of speech production are preconditions of such general characteristics of both SL and CS as syncretism and discontinuity (discreteness) – the two antagonist trends appearing at different levels of language – lexical, morphological and syntactic. In the following section we will focus upon the manifestation of these specific characteristics in their relation to the functional purpose of SL and peculiarities of signed speech where the main kinetic unit is a gesture, i.e. a movement act.

The Lexicon

Analysis of the SL vocabulary reveals the peculiarity of system functional purpose. It is necessary to stress first that there are fewer signs than words in the spoken language. There are several possible explanations. Among these are historical reasons: SL in Russian began to be codified comparatively recently – at the beginning of the 19th century when the first educational establishments for the deaf appeared, while the spoken language appeared twenty to thirty thousand years ago. The deaf, communicating through sign language among themselves, have always lived in the society of hearing people, so after receiving education and learning words, they began to utilise verbal speech in certain communicative situations, acquiring knowledge accumulated by mankind and stored in books, etc. Because of the absence of special terms to express some notions (educational terms, such as "differential equation", "classicism", "artistic image", etc.) the deaf, after reaching a certain level of education, usually employ words. Corresponding signs either appear or are created purposely, for example, as translations of words. Such signs belong to the system of Signed Russian (SR), while the vocabulary of SL, similar to that of the colloquial spoken language, is used for unsophisticated, non-official communication.

It has already been stated that both SL and CS are characterised by situation involvement and spontaneity. Many special characteristics of SL vocabulary are connected with these two features, so, for example, that which is "present" in the situation of talk is not specially expressed – such meanings as body parts (face, nose, hand, etc.) are always expressed by pointing.

Syncretism and discontinuity, the main characteristics of colloquial systems, may be seen particularly in nomination. Nomination is usually understood as the process of ascribing names to the objects of reality, i.e. to denote. The special characteristics of SL nomination may be characterised from the point of view of their relevance to this communication medium, serving the purpose of unconstrained non-official conversation.

(a) *Syncretism* of SL is found in denotative uncertainty, i.e. when the same sign is used to indicate different referents of the real *world*. This phenomenon has been described elsewhere as the "polysemy" of a sign (Boskis & Morosova, 1959). What is important here is that the same sign is used to denote different referents according to certain rules. The following examples illustrate the sort of polysemy occurring with one sign having two meanings:

   i. *action – instrument:* AXE – HACK, HANDLE – SWEEP

   ii. *action – agent – instrument:* TO DRIVE – DRIVER – CAR, TO FLY – PILOT – PLANE

   iii. *object – attribute:* STONE – STONY, WOOD – WOODEN

   iv. *premises – action* for which it is designed: BATHROOM – TO WASH, THEATRE – PERFORMANCE

It should be remarked that the denotative uncertainty of some signs is usually eliminated in the process of communication by the context. If the context is insufficient for disambiguation, a second determinative sign is added which makes the meaning of the first more precise. for example, to express the meaning AGENT (ii), the determinative MAN is added; to make the meaning of PREMISES (iv) more precise, the determinative HOUSE is added.

(b) *Discontinuity* of SL is found under conditions of nominative uncertainty. Thus, when it is necessary to express a meaning for which there is no "ready-made" sign in SL, e.g. to signify BILBERRIES, the following sign construction is used:

    BERRY EAT TONGUE BLACK

To impart the meaning of KITCHEN PINAFORE (as opposed to the apron of a uniform) the following construction is used:

    APRON GIRL BE ON DUTY CAFETERIA SAME

(What is meant here is that the kitchen pinafore looks like the one worn when on duty in the school cafeteria.)

In addition, there are regular ways to stress the sort of intermediate position of some meanings compared with those having an established sign. A good example here would be a way to express the meaning 'to take a seat', which we observed in an experiment with a deaf student:

    STAND – NEGATION – SIT – NEGATION – INTERMEDIATE

To express the colour turquoise, the following sign construction is used:

    FOR – EXAMPLE – BLUE – NEGATION – GREEN – NEGATION – MIX

Thus the intermediate character of turquoise is stressed twice; with the sign FOR-EXAMPLE and the sign MIX.

Discontinuity as a specific feature of the SL lexicon has also been commented on by many scholars and has been described as the 'loquacity' of sign (Boskis & Morosova, 1959). Meanings expressed in verbal language in a generalised form are separated in SL and have different sign expressions. Thus the word 'to fly' corresponds to different signs in 'bird flies', 'plane flies'; the word 'stand' has different signs in 'man stands', 'suitcase stands', 'dog stands', 'stands on one leg', etc.

In all these cases discontinuity is undoubtedly connected with the kinetic modality of a sign. In fact, the occurrence of different ways of expressing the meanings 'plane flies' and 'bird flies', 'stand on two legs' and 'stand on one leg' is the result of the possibility of characterising different actions by the manner of sign performance: the imitation of signs flapping or the special features of sign shape indicating to stand on one leg. In doing so, the above-mentioned meanings are "separated" for the receiver who perceives the information visually.

In the phenomenon of discontinuity, one can also include a good many multi-sign nominations in SL, for example, the meaning 'furniture' is expressed by the sign string:

TABLE – CHAIR – BED – DIFFERENT

The meaning 'vegetables' is expressed in the following way:

POTATOES – CABBAGE – CUCUMBER – DIFFERENT

Grammar

Morphological Features

In discussing the morphology of SL one can note the absence of specialised units to express oppositions such as object-action, object-quality, etc., already mentioned in the discussion of lexicon. This characteristic of SL morphology appears in the general tendency to syncretism characteristic of colloquial systems. For this reason in SL there are no sign classes comparable to parts of speech in verbal languages (noun, adjective, verb, etc.). Nevertheless, in SL there is a well developed system of grammatical categories and other grammatical phenomena providing for the expression of meanings and their relations.

Grammatical Meanings

Grammatical meanings are those which are obligatorily expressed in a given language. For example, in Russian the meaning of case is grammatical as well as the meanings of gender and number for nouns. In English the meaning of number is also grammatical because it must be expressed – absence of a morphological marker shows that a noun is singular – 's' shows that it is plural. Unlike Russian, in English the meanings of gender and case for nouns are not grammatical. The following meanings which are obligatory in expressing certain ideas in SL are therefore grammatical for SL:

1. *Object Number*

There are two ways of expressing plural:

(a) reduplication of a sign denoting an object; to express plurality a sign is repeated at least twice as in TREE – TREES; BOOK – BOOKS.

In fact, the meaning of plurality can always be expressed by the determinative. The result is that the sign-nominative, without re-duplication and without the sign MANY – MUCH, always is singular.

2. *Verb*

Two regular ways of expressing time of action are found:

(a) sign-determinatives forming a paradigm similar to that of the English verb "to be" – such as WAS, AM, IS, ARE, WILL BE ("am", "is", "are", in present tense are not used in Russian). To express the meanings WORK, WORKED, WILL WORK, the sign-nominative TO WORK is used, to which the sign WAS or the sign WILL-BE are added.

(b) signs expressing time – YESTERDAY, TODAY, TOMORROW, combined with a sign-nominative in strings of the type WORK – YESTERDAY, or WORK-TOMORROW mean 'worked' and 'will work' respectively.

It is clear that the meanings of number with object names and the meanings of tense with action signs are expressed with detached components.

3. *Subject-Object Relations with Predicates*

In constructions with predicates where the character of the action demands the specification of an agent and object of the action, they are both expressed. For this a special type of sign construction is employed which specifies the distribution of roles. If the signer is the subject, signs such as INSTRUCT, RESPECT, NARRATE, etc., are directed away from him/her (I instruct, I respect, etc.); where the signer is the object of the sentence, the sign is directed towards him and means, 'I am instructed', 'I am respected', etc.

These special features of signs are connected with the situation involvement of sign communication.

4. *Modality with Predicates*

The expression of modality is a feature of SL grammar; if one examines sign-nominatives denoting actions one finds a regular correspondence between a sign-nominative, a sign structure meaning 'imperativeness', and a sign structure meaning 'desirability'. For example, when expressing members of the paradigm "to buy", "buy", "I would like to buy" in SL, in the first example a sign-nominative is used; in the second, a nominative is preceded by signs expressing 'I ask' or 'I order', and in expressing desirability the following sign structure is used:

IF + the nominative BUY + the sign which can be interpreted as meaning 'luck' or 'good fortune'.

Thus, the meanings of 'imperativeness' and 'desirability' are also expressed analytically.

Further research will help to find other grammatical meanings, i.e. those whose expression is obligatory in SL as a communicative system.

Other Regular Grammatical Phenomena

Besides the meanings which should be considered properly grammatical in the SL there are a variety of regular ways to express different shades of meanings and relations between meanings. Some of these regular ways of expression are found with object names, others with predicates, still others have a broader range of use. The list of those having the greatest spread is given below:

1. *Characteristics of Predicates*

There are regular means in the SL of expressing additional features of a predicate, characterising it from the point of view of the action being perfect or imperfect. For this the following are used:

  (a) Special signs occupying the position after a nominative which can be translated as 'finished', 'ready'. For example, the meaning of 'to have read' is expressed by the following sign structure:

    nominative TO-READ followed by the sign FINISHED

  (b) Change in the manner of sign articulation. This is used to express recurrent and repeated actions. Thus, to express recurrent action, the sign is produced more slowly and is repeated several times, while the expression of a single action is realised by a single and more abrupt movement.

There are other ways of expressing general characteristics of the signer's attitude to an action; for example, the signer's description of an action as unfinished at the moment of speaking, but an action whose fulfilment is expected. This meaning is expressed by a special sign which can be interpreted as "not yet . . .". This sign usually follows a corresponding nominative. We can compare this with a conversation in a verbal language:

  A. "Have you had dinner?"

  B. "Not yet."

In SL this would appear as:

  A. YOU-DINE   PAST

  B. DINE NOT YET

In cases where the signer's action is described as one which took place a long time in the past, instead of the sign PAST, a special sign LONG AGO is used. For example, the meaning 'met' not specially marked as having occurred a long time in the past, is expressed by the signs:

  'to meet' + PAST

but if a speaker wants to stress the fact that the action took place a long time before the time of the conversation, instead of the PAST sign the sign LONG AGO is used following the sign-nominative. (Zaitseva & Frumkina, 1981).

2. *Characteristics of Relational Constructions*

There are regular ways of expressing relations between signs such as possession, correlative location and others.

Possession can be expressed by particular signs: the sign of POSSESSION (cf. Namir & Schlesinger, 1978); the sign DESTINATION found in the situation where possession is to be realised, and also signs corresponding to possessive pronouns such as "my", "your", etc. Examples will illustrate these sign structures:

  BOOK – GIRL – POSSESSION (girl's book)

  GIFT – MOTHER – DESTINATION (a gift for mother)

  PEN – YOUR (your pen)

Spatial relations of objects are expressed in two ways: to express the notion of the location of objects a signer alters the signs (compared with their forms in neutral positions) so that they model the correlative locations of real objects; for example if a signer wishes to sign that in the right corner of the room is a table, but it is situated not along the wall but at a certain angle to it, then, while preserving the shape of the sign TABLE, the signer will produce it in a somewhat different manner: his hands will be farther to the right than for the sign-nominative, i.e. the orientation of the sign is changed. To express the meaning "standard-lamp over the armchair in the left nearest corner of the room", a signer will produce two signs simultaneously – the sign ARMCHAIR with the left-hand and STANDARD-LAMP with the right hand. The position and orientation of the signs n this case are changed as compared with their nominative forms.

There are also special signs expressing the meanings 'far', 'near', 'among', 'in the centre', 'before-behind', 'near-next to', e.g. WARDROBE-TABLE-WINDOW-BETWEEN (the window is between the wardrobe and the table) (Zaitseva, 1969).

Syntactic Features

Syntactic characteristics of SL as a system of non-official private communication are more easily analysed when compared with examples of verbal colloquial speech. The syncretism, and discontinuity of syntactic phenomena connected with the function of both systems are then clearly revealed.

Firstly, it should be noted that the order of signs in SL utterances does not coincide with that in the codified verbal language (Boskis & Morosova, 1959; Zaitseva, 1969; Namir & Schlesinger, 1978). Nevertheless the structure of sign utterances can be compared with phrases of dialogue in spontaneous speech. A speaker when beginning an utterance does not plan it from beginning to end; it is processed temporally, and so is always open for addition. This is the source of the specific "freedom" of utterance structuring both in CS and SL. Both are characterised by 'loose connections' and syntactic interference.

The special interest of utterances with added loose construction appears in the fact that a loose construction may integrate closely with the main part of the utterance. This makes it possible to express a wide range of meaningful relations (of cause, effect, purpose, etc.) that is, such utterances are syncretic. A few examples will illustrate this. (The loose constructions are underlined):

CS: "Somewhere I cut my finger <u>bleeding</u>"
  "Going to the hospital <u>toothache</u>"
SL: BOY <u>FALL FROM THE FENCE</u> CRY
  MOTHER WINDOW WASH <u>MUST BE CLEAN</u> RAG

It is clear that grammatical relations in loose constructions remain unexpressed, the necessary information being obtained through situation involvement.

Syntactic interfacing is a type of blending of two predicate constructions. These constructions interface in so far as they have common members. Syntactic interfacing is the result of speech unpreparedness and makes use of the linear characteristics of an utterance. It occurs where a speaker uses the last element of an utterance as the beginning of a new construction without pausing.

CS: "I'll wait for you <u>at the station</u> we'll meet"
  I walk <u>in the woods</u> up two hours I spend"

SL: GIRL LITTLE FEED <u>CHICKENS SIX</u> PECK GRAIN
    BOY THROW <u>STONE</u> FALL FAR

Our data show a great number of such constructions in the colloquial sign speech of the deaf.

Our construction of syntactic structures is also influenced by the motor nature of signs and visual perception of sign language. An illustrative example in this relation is found in a class of utterances with the sign CONNECTION, which functions similarly to the conjunction in spoken Russian. For example:

1. BOY BE ON HORSEBACK FALL CONNECTION CRY
   "The boy fell from the horse and that's why he burst out crying"
2. BOY CRY CONNECTION BALL FLY AWAY
   "The boy began crying because the ball flew away"

In comparison with Russian conjunctions which express specific relations of effect (that's why) or cause (because) in complex sentences, the sign CONNECTION is syncretic. Lack of information (what is "cause" and what is "effect" in a complex sentence) is compensated for by the context. If a signer feels it necessary to make a remark more precise, he/she uses a particular type of sign construction. In the nominative the sign is performed without a marked movement, but when it is necessary to stress that the first part of an utterance is a "cause", and the second is an "effect" (example 1), the hands in the process of sign articulation move from left to right. In example 2 the fact that the "cause" is in the second part of the utterance is expressed by the sign being articulated from right to left. In other words, the kinetic nature of a sign and its visual perception allow the signer to stress the direction of causation by means of movement change. Thus, when it is necessary, the syncretism of sign structure may be overcome.

Conclusions

This paper has compared colloquial speech (CS) with the sign language of deaf people (SL). In many grammatical and lexical respects the two languages function similarly. It is hoped that further research in this direction will be fruitful for the linguistic study of the colloquial sign language of the deaf.

POSITIONS AND MOVEMENTS OF THE MOUTH IN NORWEGIAN SIGN LANGUAGE (NSL)

Marit Vogt-Svendsen

My interest in questions about language and language use is to a great extent motivated by my own experiences. Growing up in a bilingual environment, where sign language as well as spoken language was used, quite early gave me the experience of similar sociolinguistic norms found in both these languages: "Don't use those big signs! That is the wrong sign!" or "Don't speak with such a loud voice! Don't use that word!" were frequent examples of correction from grown-ups in my society. I did not like being corrected as to how to express myself in the languages which I felt were my own. Why wasn't the language of children good enough for grown-ups?

Another experience which made me curious about language use was when, for the first time at the age of twenty, I tried to combine speech and signs. The use of speech in sign language is, of course, rather meaningless. As a teacher of the deaf, however, this was expected of me. This combination did not work. Signs and words did not appear simultaneously, and some signs were impossible to combine with words. One of the reasons was given by one of my pupils.

Once, as an experiment, I tried to combine the manual component of a sign with a suitable word for it. The pupils in my class just laughed. The sign looked funny and strange to them. The reason was that the sign had a special oral component, different from a spoken word, which went with the manual component. Later I met Brita Bergman and Lars Ake Wikstrom in Stockholm who told me about similar signs in Swedish Sign Language. They supported my hypothesis on special oral components in signs.

Mouth positions in Norwegian Sign Language (NSL) is the topic of this paper, which is based upon a study of 37 signs in NSL. The oral components of these signs were analysed and described from recordings of both deaf children and grown-ups telling stories from their daily life, etc.

I will suggest why I think it is important for teachers of the deaf to have knowledge of the use of the mouth in NSL, by presenting some of the signs which I have been studying. Then I will give in summary my analysis and descriptions of the 37 signs in my study (Vogt-Svendsen, 1981).

NSL Mouth Positions in the Education of Deaf Children

NSL is generally not accepted for education purposes in Norway. Teachers have often considered NSL as insufficient both for stimulating normal development of language and for developing speech, reading and writing. This was one of the main reasons for constructing Signed Norwegian, a sign system which reflects spoken language in a one-to-one fashion. Teachers of the deaf are trained mainly in Signed Norwegian and told to insist on children using spoken words simultaneously with signs in order not to destroy the children's ability to use voice when speaking.

My experience as a teacher, however, has quite clearly convinced me that this approach to education does not work well. In order to teach the children spoken and written Norwegian as well as other subjects in an easy and natural way with satisfying results, I found it necessary to try to use their primary language, NSL, in the educational setting. Furthermore, it became clear to me that by insisting on the use of speech simultaneously with signing, I would not be able to learn or understand the language used among the children.

My study supports the contention that we, the teachers of the deaf, are bound to underestimate language as well as general knowledge among deaf children. Most signs in my study have a special oral component which belongs to the sign. As already mentioned, these signs cannot be used simultaneously with spoken words. A natural consequence of combining spoken words and signs will be that teachers neither learn nor are able to observe these signs as commonly used among the deaf. The teacher is then forced to spend a great deal of time in teaching children symbols for concepts they have already mastered and understood in their own language.

The following signs may serve as examples of how necessary it is for teachers to know more about mouth positions in sign language.

If we tell a hearing child to do his/her homework we will sometimes get the answer that the homework has been done. The answer will probably be given in a correct grammatical manner according to the norms of spoken Norwegian. If we sign the same request to a deaf child, he will give the same answer in signs as the hearing child provided in spoken language. But there will be a difference in symbols and syntax. If the deaf child makes a direct translation of his signs into spoken Norwegian, which is what the deaf child actually is compelled to do when he is expected to use spoken language and signs simultaneously, we usually end up hearing as a response to our command "Go and finish your homework!" the answer "ferdig før" which can be translated as "finished before". These two words are spoken and simultaneously accompanied by two manual signs. The phase, however, is ungrammatical in spoken and in Signed Norwegian. If we take a closer look at our example 'ferdig før' (finished before). we will observe some interesting nuances. The signing in this phrase is not even grammatical in NSL. The manual signs are the same, but in NSL they must go together with two distinct oral components. The point is that the use of these oral components will make the mouth look different from the way it looks in the production of the Norwegian words, although there may be some resemblance in features between the oral component and the face speaking the words.

The words "ferdig før" (finished before) combined with these manual elements has wrongly been looked upon as a typical example of the poor language of the deaf. It may, however, serve as an example of the child's unsatisfactory knowledge of spoken language as well as an example of the teacher's rather meagre knowledge of sign language.

For other signs in NSL it is not even possible to speak and sign simultaneously. An example of such signing is the sign HAR-IKKE-GJORT (HAVE-NOT-DONE) (Fig. 1).

It the deaf child uses this sign, and the teacher notices it, it is looked upon as, at best, a rather meaningless gesture, or as an indication of the child's incomplete mastery of language.

Figure 1
HAR IKKE GJORT (HAVE NOT DONE)

We are very often faced with situations where the teacher tries to explain a concept. The teacher explains in Signed Norwegian different aspects of what may be considered as crucial for understanding. For example, a teacher may describe the expression "in olden days" as meaning that there were no cars, no television and so on. After some time, sometimes hours or days, at last one pupil grasps the meaning. This pupil then turns around and facing the rest of the class he/she translates the expression from Signed Norwegian to NSL in a matter of seconds (Fig. 2).

Figure 2
I GAMLE DAGER (IN OLDEN DAYS)

Suddenly all pupils understand it in this way. Pupils with some knowledge of spoken and written language seem to be a necessary support for teachers of the deaf.

Another problem commonly discussed among teachers is how to teach deaf children to understand concepts which reflect emotional states. We do of course, observe that deaf children express joy and anger. We do not, however, believe that the children are able to express the finer nuances that lie in between.

In my recordings, however, I have found several examples where this is untrue. These expressions are very often symbolised by signs with a distinct oral component. But the children have not, of course, developed the ability to express these various moods in spoken or written language during the first years in school. Figures 3, 4 and 5 illustrate the point.

Figure 3
FORUNDRET (ASTONISHED)

Figure 4
FORBAUSET (AMAZED)

Figure 5
FORSKREKKET (FRIGHTENED)

Some of these mouth positions may resemble non-verbal components of these expressions (Baker, 1980). We all have an image of an astonished or frightened mouth or face. We do not, however, find among hearing people such fine nuances in mouth position as are found in NSL. The facial expressions in these signs do not seem to be mimetic or non-verbal expressions commonly used in all forms of communication, rather they may be looked upon as oral components which go along with the manual components.

Many of the signs in my recordings have some positions of the mouth which cannot occur in communication where spoken language is used. An example of such positions appears in the sign NETTOPP-NÅ (JUST NOW) (fig. 6).

Figure 6
NETTOPP NÅ (JUST NOW)

The oral component in this sign does not resemble the oral component in the spoken words. The facial expression is quite different. This may be one reason why signs with oral components have been classified as exaggerated mimetic expressions because the deaf lack language ability to express feelings, moods and so on.

For reasons like this deaf children have been told that they must not use such mimetic expressions. "You look funny", "deaf", and even "deviant" are usual expressions. Attitudes like these are also found within the deaf population despite the fact that these signs are commonly used among the deaf.

Another reason for this rather negative attitude may be that the signs, in my opinion, wrongly, have been looked upon as slang with low status. They have therefore not been accepted as symbols rightly belonging to a language. We find similar beliefs in other countries too (Hansen, 1980).

There is one sign in my material which, in my opinion, can be classified as slang. That is the sign SLØV (DOPEY) (Fig.7). SLØV (DOPEY) is a sign primarily used, as slang is in spoken language, among younger people.

Figure 7
SLØV (DOPEY)

In order to recognise NSL as a language in its own right teachers should be aware of the existence of oral components in signs, which do not match the oral components in spoken words.

Analysis of the Oral Components in NSL
In the video recordings there are many signs without any particular function of the mouth. Other signs may often be combined with mouth positions indicating the whole spoken word. Furthermore, there are some signs where the mouth seems to have an adjectival/adverbial function as in LITEN-BLOMST (LITTLE-FLOWER) (Fig. 8), and some signs where the mouth simply functions as an instrument to imitate specific actions, such as eating or drinking.

Figure 8
LITEN BLOMST (LITTLE FLOWER)

Those signs I chose to analyse, however, were signs which definitely belong to the established vocabulary in NSL. A change of the oral component in many of these signs will result in a sign with a different meaning or with no meaning at all. Consequently, the mouth definitely functions as a chereme in much the same way as handshape does. The change from one position of the mouth to another results in a change in meaning even when the manual component remains unchanged. Figures 9 and 10 illustrate this.

Figure 9
SUR (mat) (SOUR (food))

Figure 10
SUR (person) (SOUR (person))

When starting to describe the oral components in these signs, very often I found it rather difficult to decide whether specific positions were individual forms of expression, an expression of a specific mood, or the basic form of the sign (Figure 11).

Figure 11
I GAMLE DAGER (IN OLDEN DAYS)
(She smiles while signing)

If we examine figure 11, we see that the mouth of the signer is curved upwards. If we compare this figure with figure 2, it can be seen that this curvature is not the basic position of the mouth in this sign. This signer is just smiling while signing. But of course the smile might be important for the meaning, as it may add information to the basic form.

I have not found any satisfactory system developed for describing the oral component in sign language (Sutton's, 1977, system does not meet the requirements here). I tried therefore at first to adapt the different positions of the mouth to systems used for describing non-verbal expressions (Ekman, 1973; Argyle, 1975). (Author had no access to Ekman and Friescn, 1978.) A system for mimetic description of different positions of the mouth was not effective. Some positions could of course be described by using positions found when expressing spoken language. As an example the Norwegian sign SLØV (DOPEY) (Figure 7) has an oral component which can be described by two distinct letters used in describing spoken Norwegian. The letters are F and Ø. However, it is not possible to use such a principle for more than a few signs in my material.

A further system based on the same principles used to describe the hand in sign language (Stokoe, 1960), for the positions of the mouth, using the articulator's form, place and articulation did not work, but did give me important information on the specific parts of the mouth which were important to include in a descriptive system. For example, I found it necessary to describe the positions of the jaw because of its influence on the different shapes of the mouth (Figure 12). The extent of jaw opening was a delicate problem not easily solved.

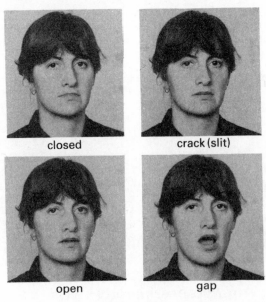

closed   crack (slit)

open   gap

Figure 12

Two positions of the mouth with the same opening of the jaw may not necessarily be visually similar. A description of the different forms of the lips seems to be of most importance. Many mouth positions include complex lip configurations. In the sign SUR (MAT) (SOUR (food)) in figure 9, we see that the lips are drawn together with a simultaneously upward curving.

An analysis of the cheeks was found necessary as the configuration of the cheeks influences the form of the mouth. In the sign TYKK (FAT) (Figure 13), we will observe that the cheeks are puffed out by air. In the sign MAGER (SKINNY) (Figure 14), the cheeks are sucked in.

Figure 13
TYKK (FAT)

Figure 14
MAGER (SKINNY)

The tongue is important in different ways in different signs. In signs such as NETTOPP-NÅ (JUST-NOW) (Figure 6), we can see only the tip of the tongue; in other signs a description of the surface of the tongue seems to be important.

In some signs the lips are extended by a stream of air as in the sign LEI (TIRED) (Figure 15).

Figure 15
LEI (TIRED)

This stream of air has an influence on the visual impression of the positions of the lips.

Air may also be expelled in puffs. This action does not alter the visual image of the lips alone, but also alters the positions and tension in this region of the face. The air in these puffs, unlike the silent stream of air in LEI, is not from the lungs, but is air pressed out of the cavity of the mouth through the narrow passage of the lips (similar to the explosives in vocal language). An example of such a position we can find in the sign IKKE-BRY-SEG-OM (CAN'T-BE-BOTHERED) (Figure 16).

Figure 16
IKKE BRY SEG OM (CAN'T BE BOTHERED)

Finally, there are a number of signs where the mouth has a distinct position, with the oral component as a static expression, for example, the sign GLEDE-SEG (LOOK-FORWARD-TO) (Figure 17).

Figure 17
GLEDE SEG (LOOK FORWARD TO)

For other signs a movement rather than static position of the mouth is important as in the sign IKKE-BRY-SEG-OM (CAN'T-BE-BOTHERED) (Figure 16). I have chosen to describe initial as well as final position of the movement by labelling these 1 and 2.

The full notation system is given in Table 1.

Let us take a closer look at some of the signs already presented, for example, GLEDE-SEG (LOOK-FORWARD-TO) (Figure 17). The mouth is closed, which means that the jaws are closed too. The strongly bent upwards position of the lips is described as stretched out and bent upwards. The cheeks are neither puffed out nor sucked in. The tongue cannot be seen and the mouth position cannot be influenced by air streams or puffs because the mouth is not open. Therefore the oral component in this sign may be described as closed, stretched out, bent upwards.

Another example is the description of the oral component in the sign NETTOPP NÅ (JUST NOW) (Figure 6). The jaw opening is described in the system as a crack. The lips are pursed. The tip of the tongue however can be seen. There is no use of the air stream. The oral component, therefore can be described as: crack, pursed, tip out.

The system has been devised specifically for the 37 signs notated. I do think, however, that there are many possibilities for extending the system. The system above may require future development to make it more precise. This will be important in order to give hearing teachers of the deaf, and others, information on the oral component in the sign language of the deaf.

Acknowledgements

This work is based on my master's thesis at The Advanced Teacher Training College of Special Education, Hosle, Norway. It is supported by the Norwegian Research Council for The Sciences and the Humanities. My thanks to Brita Bergman and Kjell Skogen for very helpful supervision on this work. The signs have been discussed with deaf people from different parts of Norway, especially with Anne Danielsen, who demonstrates the signs in the photographs, and Odd Inge Schröder, who has been of great help all through the study. Photographs are by Per Gran. This paper will also appear in Sign Language Studies.

Table 1. Notation system for positions of the mouth

Jaw opening	Positions of the lips	Positions of the cheeks	Positions of the tongue	Use of air
closed ●	neutral ‖	puffed out ( )	tip out ᴗ	air puffs ʅ
crack (slit) o	bent up(wards)	right cheek puffed out	tip left ᴄ	stream of air {→
open	bent down(wards)	sucked in	tip touching back of front teeth	
gap	stretched out		tip touching front of front teeth	
	pursed together		surface against back of lower lip	
	pushed forwards ‖			
	sucked in			
	lower lip stretched out			
	lower lip bent up against front teeth			
	stretched out, bent up			
	pursed together, bent up			
	pursed together, bent down			
	pursed together, pushed forwards			

MULTI-CHANNEL SIGNS IN BRITISH SIGN LANGUAGE

Lilian K. Lawson

This paper will focus on "multi-channel" signs in British Sign Language (BSL). Many multi-channel signs have been regarded as idioms, but this term has aroused controversy, in ASL as well as BSL. "The non-exact matching of signs and words and the difficulties in representing signs by words has led to the erroneous conclusions that ASL is telegraphic, simplified, or restricted." (Cokely, 1978a). However, like ASL, BSL is much more than just "telegraphic, simplified, or restricted"; it is a complex visual/gestural language of the British Deaf.

Problems with the term "idiom" were voiced by Brita Bergman at a sign language workshop in Edinburgh in 1980: she states that idiomatic signs are not unusual to users of sign language, but are signs used as frequently by deaf people as they would use other kinds of signs. The Swedish Sign Language researchers call them 'Deaf Signs'.

Others at the same workshop suggested that the term "idiom" was incorrectly used and should be replaced. We at Moray House thought that Baker's (1980) term "multi-channel signs" was a more appropriate term, covering both those signs previously called idiomatic and those other signs which had no idiomatic expression but had equally complex form and function. Both groups incorporate other channels as well as the manual channel: for instance facial expressions, mouth movements, cheek(s) movements and body movements. Some of the other channels are used in combinations giving specific non-manual signals (Baker and Cokely, 1980; Liddell, 1980).

Baker and Cokely (1980) include a brief section about idioms:

> . . . often, the mistake in the past has been to assume that since these and other signs are used frequently in ASL, but do not have an easy 'word for sign' equivalent – that they are 'idioms'. This is like saying that the English word 'run' is an idiom since it has so many different meanings and occurs so frequently in the language (English). However, by reviewing the three definitional criteria of idioms as stated above, we can see that such words and signs are not idioms but, rather, are frequently used, *multiple-meaning* words or signs. (p. 119)

This is exactly true for similar signs of BSL that are now called *multi-channel* signs.

Multi-channel signs are used frequently and interpreted with ease by native BSL signers. They are not easily understood by hearing people who do not have native competence in BSL. Multi-channel signs of BSL are too often not included in the dictionaries or manuals of British Sign Language, and were previously ignored by professionals in the education and welfare of deaf people – probably because they appeared to be so complex that their meanings seemed odd or peculiar, without "word for sign" equivalents. Multi-channel signs can rarely be translated into single words, but more commonly must be represented by phrases or complete sentences. From general observations it seems that multi-channel signs are most frequently made use of in informal situations, and appear to be less frequently used in formal situations such as conferences, meetings, classroom teaching and church services. These signs also appear to be used more often by native deaf signers than by deaf signers who have good competence in English or who may prefer to sign an English variey like Signed English.

Table 1. Non-manual features of British Sign Language

Head Movements		*Face/Facial Expressions*	
nod	up/down	Depends on emotion and/or	
nod	up and down	context: e.g.	
turn	right/left	smile	intense
shakes	sideways	grimace	frightened
tilt	right/left	sad	boredom, etc.
tilt	forward/back	severe/prim	

Eyes	*Eyebrows*	
gaze/stare	raise	up/down (brow raise)
ogle	raise	right/left only
almost closed (slits)	knitted	(brow squint)
tightly shut		

Cheek movements
puff out
suck in
right/left cheek out only

Mouth patterns	
open	wide open (o)
closed	pursed lips (oo)
tightly closed (m)	teeth showing through open
corners of mouth pulled tightly	mouth (e)
apart with teeth just showing	upper teeth on lower lip (f,v)
(ee)	lower teeth on upper lip
mouth pulled down at corners	smiling mouth
tongue fully extended	tongue protruding out of mouth (th)
lips vibrating (bbrr)	lips puckered forward (sh)
lips open briefly and shut	lips tightly shut and then open
tightly (um)	(po) (ba)

Shoulders		*Chest*
shrug	up/down	sigh
shrug	up and down	heave
hunch forward		
tilt	right/left	

Body movements	
twist	right/left
twist	sideways (as in negation)
tilt	right/left
tilt	forward/backward

Multi-channel signs incorporate non-manual activities. As seen in Table 1, there are many possible non-manual activities in BSL.

Non-manual Activities and Meaning

For some signs, special non-manual activities or non-manual signals appear not to be obligatory. Other signs must, in certain circumstances, obligatorily incorporate specific non-manual activities or signals. For example, the signs SHORTER-THAN-EXPECTED and WOULD-HAVE-BEEN always incorporate the mouth pattern "um". The sign NOT-HAPPENING (COMING)-FOR-A-LONG-TIME always incorporates the puffing-out of cheeks. Some other signs can use one or another non-manual activity such as the sign I-HAVE-NOT-SEEN-YOU-FOR-DONKEY'S-YEARS which can use either puffing-out or sucking-in of the cheeks. Three closely related signs meaning I-HAVE-NOT-SEEN-IT-AT-ALL contrast in their manual features.

	Hand Movement	*Non-manual Feature*
Sign 1	Supination	Mouth pattern "v"
Sign 2	Up and Down	Mouth pattern "th"
Sign 3	Sharply Down	Puffing-out of cheeks and shut mouth

Why three specific non-manual activities exist for this sign is not yet known, but the answer may possibly lie in slightly differing meanings. It seems that there is a connection between one or more specific non-manual activities and the meaning of multi-channel signs. For example, let us look at the last three examples of I-HAVE-NOT-SEEN-IT-AT-ALL. The first incorporates the mouth pattern "v" which may be simply part of *negative incorporation,* as the same mouth pattern "v" is incorporated in a number of signs incorporating negation. For example, I-HAVE-NOT-HEARD-OF-IT-AT-ALL and I-HAVE-NOT-THOUGHT-OF-IT-AT-ALL both use the mouth pattern "v" and the same manual activity of supination. The second sign meaning I-HAVE-NOT-SEEN-IT-AT-ALL has the mouth position "th" which may be related to function of time, as that sign specifies I-HAVE-NOT-SEEN-IT-AT-ALL-*YET.* The signs NOT-YET, I-HAVE-NOT-SEEN-IT-AT-ALL-YET, I-HAVE-NOT-HEARD-IT-YET, and I-HAVE-NOT-THOUGHT-ABOUT-IT-YET, all use the same non-manual features and manual activity of moving one or both hands up and down twice. The third sign I-HAVE-NOT-SEEN-IT-AT-ALL has the non-manual feature of puffing-out cheeks. This may be used to emphasise the negation as the meaning of this sign is I-HAVE-*NEVER*-SEEN-IT-AT-ALL. The same manual activity of sharp downward movement and non-manual feature of puffed cheeks are also used in signs like I-ABSOLUTELY-REFUSE-TO-DO-IT or I-ABSOLUTELY-DON'T-WANT IT AT ALL. Table 2 lists non-manual activities and their associated meanings.

Grammatical Function of Multi-channel Signs

It is possible to separate multi-channel signs into different categories according to their grammatical functions or other kinds of function they

Table 2. Multi-channel Signs

Head Movements	Meaning
Nod up and down	emphasis; yes
	Pretend to understand but do not know what he is talking about; or
	He never disagrees, he just follows you; he agrees with everything you say.
Nod down	true
	Proper.
Head shakes sideways	negation
	That is not the person/place I was talking about earlier.

Facial Expressions	
Astonishment	surprise
	I was flabbergasted.
Boredom	bored; fed up
	He repeats everything again and again.
Intense	just; recently
	That is the person/place I was talking about earlier.
Frightened	fear; scared
	I am so scared to go....
	Legs shaking like a leaf.

Eyebrows	
Eyebrows raised	wonder
	I was so astonished/my jaw dropped open wide....

Eyes	
Ogle	popping out eyes; wide open eyes
	Eyes like 'chapel hat pegs'!
Almost shut	tired; exhausted; bleary eyed
	I am suspicious of you.

Cheek Movements	
Puff out	huge; crowds; large masses
	I have not seen you for donkey's years.
Suck in	expensive; sore; thin; disappear
	I am brilliant/smart.

Mouth Patterns	
oo	expensive; thin
	Oh my God!
v	not in; not there
	You're kidding me!
bbrr	cold; vibrating machines; thunder
	Describing a story in detail.

bo (pah)	success; delicious
	I have been caught red-handed.
	I have been there.
ee	endeavour; determination; intensity
	He was ever so persistent.

Shoulders
Hunch forward

coward
It was really a terrible thing to do....

Chest Movement
Heave

relieved; phew
I have been caught red-handed.

Body Movement
Body tilt forward

fall; drive
My eyes popped out.

seem to perform in their role in BSL. Such categories are:

Negative Incorporation: As well as the non-manual activities of head shaking, corners of mouth pulled down, or in "v" contomation, pushing up of lower lip or raising of the upper lip, and/or narrowing of eyes, there is an additional manual activity incorporated within the sign itself, usually the twisting and supinating of the open hand (if the hand is closed, it opens at the same time as it twists). For example:

Meaning
I am not keen/
comfortable

Non-manual feature
Corners of mouth pulled
down

Figure 1. Negative Incorporation

Time-relation signs: These signs include the expression of duration of time, unexpectedness, or suddenness, lengthy duration of time, etc. They involve modulations such as repetition of manual movements as well as specific non-manual signals.

Table 3.

	Meaning	Non-manual feature
1.	I have not seen you for donkey's years.	Puff or suck cheeks
2.	He did not stay here very long.	Um
3.	His stay was much shorter than expected.	Um

Example 3.1 either incorporates the puffing out of cheeks and a relatively slow hand movement which suggests the meaning "really a long time"; or it incorporates the sucking in of cheeks and relatively rapid hand movement which suggests the meaning "not so long".

In Example 3.2 and 3.3, there is a sudden, tense closing of the mouth (um) which indicates suddenness or unexpectedness. A closing action of the hand is also incorporated, which again may relate to the brevity of time. Therefore, it may be seen that the sucking in of cheeks and the rapid movement of hand(s) are normally associated with the meaning of brief duration of time, while the puffing out of cheeks and the slow movement of hand(s) is associated with the meaning of a long duration of time.

When a mouth pattern of "um" is incorporated, the movement of hand(s) usually involves a closing action which may or may not be sharp. The meanings of signs which use one or more of these features: sucking in of cheeks, mouth pattern of "um" and closing hand(s), are related to suddenness, unexpectedness or brevity of time.

Demonstrativeness: Signs with this function are used to refer to some specific person or place or object. For example:

Meaning	Non-manual feature
That was the person/ place I was talking about earlier.	Intense facial expression, head nodding, mouth pattern: "ee".

This sign can only be used if a certain person/place has been referred to previously. The specific facial expression is intense and the brows are raised. Liddell (1980) describes this non-manual signal in ASL as a restrictive relative clause, and in this example too, its function may be a restrictive relative clause marker.

Meaning	Non-manual feature
He would have been killed but was not.	Head nod, "um".

This sign incorporates the specific mouth pattern "um" and a head nod, with no other non-manual activities. Its function may be similar to that of the existence/assertion marker "hn" (Liddell, 1980) the main activity of which is a slow head nod.

Meaning	Non-manual feature
There is/he is there.	Head nod, "sh".

Both incorporate the head nod and mouth pattern "sh" (puckered lips). The head nod is similar to that of the existence/assertion marker "hn". Liddell (1980) also mentions that the function of the non-manual signal "hn" is parallel to the English auxiliary verbs "be" and "do", which are predicates of existence in English. The translations of the BSL multi-channel signs above indicate that they also perform the function of verbs of predicates of existence.

Intensifiers: This category includes multi-channel signs which translate as adjectives and intensifiers. They incorporate closing of the mouth (um), and puffing out of and sucking in of cheeks. For example:

Meaning	Hand Movement	Non-manual feature
I am smart at . . .	Rapid	Sucking of cheeks; sucking of air, "oo" mouth pattern.
I am very brilliant	Slow	Puffing out of cheeks; "oo" mouth pattern.
I an very knowledgeable	Closes	"Um" mouth pattern.

Signing with Cognitive Meaning: This category includes signs whose meaning is related to cognitive functions such as memory. For example:

Meaning	Hand Movement	Non-manual feature
I never forget it!		Mouth shut, intense facial expression.
*It has remained in my memory ever since.	Slow	Blowing air through mouth. Puffing out of cheeks.

*"It" refers to some long past incident that could never be forgotten.

As already explained earlier in the section on Time-relation Signs, the above sign IT-HAS-REMAINED-IN-MY-MEMORY-EVER-SINCE has a slow hand movement and puffing out of cheeks whose features are certainly related to the meaning of lengthy duration.

Meaning	Hand Movement	Non-manual feature
I completely forgot all about it. My mind went blank.	Closes	Sucking in of cheeks, blowing air through pursed lips, mouth pattern "oo".

Because the hand articulates a closing action and the signer's cheeks suck in, we would expect the meaning of brevity of time or suddenness, and the non-manual features incorporated within the above sign, I-COMPLETELY-FORGOT-ALL-ABOUT-IT or MY-MIND-WENT-BLANK, show that the signer is surprised or aghast to find him/herself forgetting completely about something.

Expressions of Astonishment: This category includes signs which express different words or expressions of astonishment. A specific facial expression used by the signer expresses astonishment. For example:

Meaning	Non-manual feature
Oh my God!	Wide open eyes, mouth pattern of "oo" and
My mind is boggling!	sucking in of cheeks *or* mouth shut and puffing out of cheeks.
My jaw dropped wide open.	Wide open mouth and tongue fully extended.

The wide open mouth and wide open eyes of MY-JAW-DROPPED-WIDE-OPEN (and also of I-WAS-FLABBERGASTED, MY-EYES-WERE-POPPING-OUT and I-WAS-AMAZED-TO-SEE-THAT) indicate surprise (or fascination).

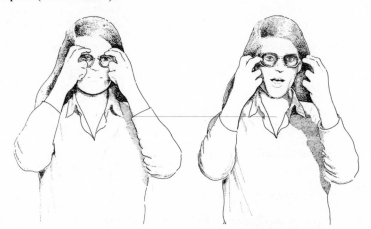

Figure 2. The Sign "MY EYES WERE POPPING OUT"

The obvious non-manual features illustrated here are wide open eyes and wide open mouth, with a "surprised" facial expression.

There are several more categories under the headings of specific non-manual features or grammatical functions and these are still under investigation.

Conclusion

In conclusion, the initial research concentrating on the non-manual features and multi-channel signs of BSL appears to show that signers are not just using body language to show their varying degrees of moodiness and emotion. The findings so far seem to show that non-manual features like those described in this paper have an important role to play in the grammar of BSL. Different non-manual features may perform specific grammatical functions, meaning that one type of non-manual feature may perform only one grammatical function. For example, the mouth pattern "sh" is only used in multi-channel signs whose meaning appears to be predicative. Similarly, the mouth pattern "um" is only found in multi-channel signs which express meanings of brevity, unexpectedness or surprise, and no other meanings.

As mentioned earlier, there are several more categories under the headings of specific non-manual features, and it will remain to see whether our assumption that non-manual features perform grammatical functions is also true in the other categories.

PART TWO: DEVELOPMENT

INTRODUCTION

The study of sign language development has important implications for developmental psychology, spoken language acquisition studies, linguistics and other disciplines. The papers in this section cover a wide range of aspects of sign language development which will be of interest to teachers, linguists and psychologists alike. Child language acquisition as a discipline arose in the 1960's following suggestions by Chomsky that research on how a child learned language would inform theoretical linguistics and provide evidence for specific theories of language. Since then, researchers have turned away from only looking at how children acquire linguistic rules, to examining the contexts of interaction in which language arises, the contribution of adults, and the social purposes for which language is used by children and adults. Language is thus seen as developing socially and fulfilling a range of functions other than simply the exchange of linguistic information.

In addition to descriptions of the paths of linguistic development, the acquisition of structural rules and the development of social interaction, the age at which children pass through various motor and linguistic milestones has been well described. With the development of interest in sign language, a number of researchers began to investigate sign language acquisition in deaf children. One early finding (Schlesinger and Meadow, 1972) was that children learning sign language appeared to be linguistically well in advance of children learning spoken language. These children produce simple signs from about 10 months of age, as compared to speaking children who produce single word utterances after the first year.

Other research (Bellugi and Klima, 1972) has shown that deaf children learning sign language are as systematic and productive in their language as hearing children, and that deaf children not exposed to a sign language input may be able to construct signs and develop a proto-language on their own (Feldman, Goldin-Meadow and Gleitman, 1978). The papers in this section provide further evidence in all these areas.

Volterra's paper suggests an hypothesis which may reconcile the opposing views on whether deaf children can create a sign language without an adult input by comparing hearing children who used gesture rather than speech for their communication, and a deaf child of deaf parents. She suggests that while hearing children can produce utterances which are combinations of deictic (pointing) and referential signs, only the child with access to an adult sign language model can combine two referential signs, and that this signals the beginning of syntax.

Bonvillian examines the relationship between cognitive development and sign language development. As children learn to sign in advance of learning to speak, the interesting issue of the relationship of general cognitive development to language development arises. Piagetian theories of development claim that there is a close relationship between various developmental stages. If signing children are linguistically advanced, are they cognitively advanced? Bonvillian explores this area by looking at hearing children learning to sign from their parents. He concludes that the close link between cognitive stages of development and language development must be re-examined.

Scroggs, through longitudinal observations of a number of deaf children both with hearing and deaf parents, is concerned with communication strategies, in social interaction, rather than with the development of linguistic structure. By focussing on an examination of facial expression, visual and tactile cues provided by the parent of a deaf baby, the richness of interaction in the absence of any auditory components can be observed. She suggests that if signing can be added to this rich system of communication it builds on previously existing interaction. She suggests that hearing parents can sign in productive ways even when their command of the language is poor.

These three papers lay the ground work for further research in this area; more specifically they point towards the important contribution sign language research can make to the broad area of development in both hearing and deaf children, and the role of sign language as a first language.

GESTURES, SIGNS AND WORDS AT TWO YEARS, OR WHEN DOES COMMUNICATION BECOME LANGUAGE?*

Virginia Volterra

Introduction

Recent research has indicated that gestural communication in hearing children plays a fundamental role in the language acquisition process (Bates, 1976; Bates, *et al.*, 1979; Bruner, 1975; Lock, 1980).

Two years ago at the Copenhagen Nato workshop, I presented a paper on symbolic development in spoken and gestural modalities. I stressed the striking similarities in content and sequence of development between words and gestures used by hearing children at one year of age. I now want to pursue the same line of research but with a more precise analysis of gestural communication in one to two year-old hearing children. More specifically, I want to compare their gestural communication with the communication of a deaf child of deaf parents who has been exposed to sign language since birth. The overriding question is: can we find differences between the gestural communication of a child exposed to a sign language and a child exposed to a vocal language and if so, at what point in development do they occur? This comparison will offer us the opportunity to discuss the role of linguistic input in prelinguistic communication and in language development.

Method

We collected data on the gestural and vocal communication of a hearing child named Luca from nine months to two years, three months, using both diary accounts by the child's mother and periodic videotaped sessions (Caselli, 1981).

To integrate these observations, data were collected with the same methodology on two other hearing children, Francesca (observed from twenty months to two years), and Giorgio (observed from two years, three months to two years, six months). These two children were chosen for this research because they exhibited a gestural communication much richer than their verbal production. They were children about whom their parents typically said: "He doesn't speak, but I can understand every thing he wants". As for deaf children, we had only one subject. Massimo, a deaf child of deaf parents, was observed from two years to two years, six months, always with the same methodology (diary accounts and periodic videotaped sessions).

Table 1. Ages of Observation for the children (years–months)

		Observed		
		from	to	
L	= Luca	0–9	2–3	
F	= Francesca	1–8	2–0	hearing, exposed to a spoken
G	= Giorgio	2–3	2–6	input
m	= Massimo	2–0	2–6	deaf, exposed to a signed input

Massimo had attended school with hearing children from the time he was two and received special oral training from a speech therapist three hours every week.

Massimo's data were collected and transcribed by Marilena Belfiore (Massimo's mother), Cristina Caselli (Luca's mother), Teresa Ossella (Massimo's speech therapist) and by the Author.

Data Analysis
The data can be analysed and discussed from many perspectives (for a complete report see Caselli, *et al.,* 1981). I will limit myself here to three major points, which I think are the most relevant for our analysis.

1. The difference between 'deictic' gestures, especially pointing, and 'referential' gestures produced by children from one to two years of age.
2. The form and content of the referential gestures found in our subjects.
3. The types of two-gesture combinations and word-and-gesture combinations produced by the subjects.

It is extremely important to distinguish between deictic and referential gestures. (I am not completely satisfied with these terms; I use them for want of better ones.) We describe as 'deictic' gestures those such as *showing, giving* and *pointing.* Deictic gestures appear at around 10 months of age and at the very beginning they are produced one at a time and often simultaneously with vocal signals. Elsewhere (Bates, *et al.,* 1975) we have called these gestures 'performative' gestures: they express only the child's communicative intention, to request or to declare, while the referential meaning is given entirely by the context in which the communication takes place. We have also described the developmental sequence from showing and giving to pointing. Pointing out an object to others, which is the last deictic gesture to appear, represents the final detachment from physical contact with the object (Camaioni, *et al.,* 1976), when the child acquires the capacity to refer to an object or an event without contacting it in order to communicate with others. The deictic gestures of course change their semantic content depending on the contexts to which they are referring.

Referential gestures, on the other hand, stand for or represent stable referents. Their meaning is conventionalised by the child and adults. Their basic semantic content is not changed in different contexts.

The referential gestures tend to appear a bit later than the deictic gestures and often specify what was previously referred to only through pointing or other deictic gestures. We have noted elsewhere that these referential gestures pass through the same decontextualisation process as words and that they become true symbols only at the end of this process (Volterra, *et al.,* 1979).

Table 2 contains a list of referential gestures observed in our subjects. The left hand column indicates which of the subjects produced the gesture (L = Luca; F = Francesca; G = Giorgio; M = Massimo). The upper-case words in the centre are glosses for the objects or the actions the children were referring to; English translations are given on the right. (For a description of the gestures, see Caselli, *et al.,* 1981).

Table 2. Referential Gestures Observed

Children				Referents	Translation
L	—	G	M	BRAVO	VERY GOOD
L	—	G	M	CIAO	BYE
L	—	G	M	PIU'	NO MORE
L	—	G	M	LAVARE TESTA	WASH HAIR
—	—	G	M	FARE GIRONTONDO	RING AROUND THE ROSY
L	—	G	M	NASCONDERSI	PEEKABOO
L	—	G	M	PICCHIARE	HIT
L	—	G	M	BERE	DRINK
L	—	G	M	MANGIARE	EAT
L	—	G	M	DORMIRE	SLEEP
L	—	G	M	APRIRE	OPEN
L	—	G	M	BUONO	GOOD
L	—	G	M	PRENDERE	TAKE
—	—	G	M	ELICOTTERO	HELICOPTER
L	—	G	M	AEREO	AIRPLANE
L	—	G	M	PIANOFORTE	PIANO
—	—	G	M	VOLARE	FLY
L	—	G	M	SCOTTARE – CALDO	HOT
L	—	G	M	COMPARE – SOLDI	BUY – MONEY
L	—	G	M	COLTELLO	KNIFE
L	F	G	M	TELEFONARE	PHONE
L	F	G	M	VENIRE	COME
L	F	—	—	OROLOGIO	CLOCK
L	—	G	M	PETTINARE	COMB
L	—	G	M	CAPPELLO	HAT
L	—	G	M	TROMBA	TRUMPET
L	—	G	M	PICCOLO	SMALL
L	—	G	M	GRANDE	BIG
—	—	—	M	PIANGERE	CRY
—	—	—	M	CAVALLO	HORSE
—	—	—	M	PALLONE	BALL
—	—	—	M	SCOPPIARE	POP
—	—	—	M	PESCE	FISH
—	—	—	M	POMPA	PUMP
—	—	—	M	ROMPERE	BREAK

There are important individual differences among hearing children: Luca and Giorgio produced more than 25 different gestures, Francesca only two. She, in fact, used pointing especially in complex combinations. On the contrary, there are striking similarities between the two hearing children and the deaf child, especially in the referents these gestures refer to. As for the form of sign production, we need to transcribe and analyse these gestures in greater detail, but at first glance they appear to be performed with the same formational parameters. In particular, Giorgio, the hearing child who used referential gestures most frequently and for a longer period, became increasingly precise and systematic in his gesture production.

Furthermore, the decontextualisation process also appears to be the same. In the first session, Massimo, the deaf child, performed the sign (gesture)

SLEEP holding in his hand a small toy bed. We know also from his mother's diary that at the very beginning he performed the gestures of DRINK and EAT always holding a container or a spoon to his mouth exactly as the hearing children did. Later he performed the same gestures without the object. (Massimo was also moving from a 'pantomime' version of the action gesture to a more codified execution of the same gesture: for example: 'eating' changes from the gesture of holding a spoon to his mouth to the sign EAT.) When we examine the origins of these gestures we find that some arise from routine play interactions with adults ('Say bye bye', 'No more' and so on). At first they tend to appear only in these play situations prompted by adults. Progressively they go through a slow process of decontextualisation from these first routines and they are used spontaneously by the children to communicate their requests or their comments on the world. For example:

BRAVO: asking for the adult's approval, clapping his hands

CIAO: describing that someone left; asking to go out

PIU: describing that something has disappeared or become invisible

NASCONDERE: asking someone to play peekaboo; describing that someone has disappeared

BALLARE: asking the adult to turn on the radio

Other referential gestures arise directly from the actions performed by the child on physical objects. For example:

BERE: asking for a drink

MANGIARE: asking for food

TELEFONARE: asking for his toy-phone; or describing that someone is phoning in the other room

PRENDERE: asking to take something or describing the action of taking

APRIRE: asking an adult to open a door, a box or some other object

PIANOFORTE: asking for his toy-piano that is in another room

CAPELLO: asking for his hat before going out

These gestures derive clearly from the child's recognition of the appropriate function of an object. None of these gestures imitates the form of the object.

Moving from a Piagetian perspective, we recognised these gestures as schemes of symbolic play. But at that time (Volterra, 1980) we did not realise that these gestures could be used as communicative gestures, at least by some hearing children. They could be combined with other communicative signals and form a genuine communicative system.

We have until now considered the various gestures in isolation, but in fact, children from around one year of age produce combinations of communicative signals. Continuing our comparison between the hearing and deaf children, let us now consider the combinations produced by our subjects. Table 3 shows only a few examples for each type of combination produced by our subjects.

As we can observe from this Table some of the combinations are exactly the same in the hearing and the deaf child:

DG + DG = deictic gesture + deictic gesture

DG + RG = deictic gesture + referential gesture

DG + W = deictic gesture + word

RG + W = referential gesture + word

Table 3. Combinations of Gesture by Type

Children	Types of Combination	Examples	Translation
L F G M	Deictic gesture +	QUELLO QUI	THAT HERE
L F G M	deictic gesture	TU QUELLO	YOU THAT
L F G M	DG + DG	QUI LUI	HERE HIM
— — G M		IO QUELLO	ME THAT
L F G M	Deictic gesture +	QUELLA *brr*	THAT *car*
L F G M	word	QUI *mamma*	HERE *mummy*
L — G —	DG + W or	QUELLO *ape*	THAT *open*
L F G M	W + DG	TU *ahm*	YOU *eat*
L F G M		*ahm* QUELLA	*eat* THAT
L — — —		*oh* TU	*seat* YOU
L F G —		*nanna* QUI	*nap* HERE
L — G M	Deictic gesture +	QUELLO BERE	THAT DRINK
L F G M	referential gesture	TU TELEFONARE	YOU PHONE
L — G M	DG + RG or	A ME PIANOFORTE	TO ME PIANO
L — G M	RG + DG	MANGIARE QUELLO	EAT THAT
— — G M		PRENDERE QUELLO	TAKE THAT
L F G M		VENIRE QUI	COME HERE
— — G M		CIAO IO	BYE ME
— — — M		MAMMA LI'	MUMMY THERE
L — G M		QUELLO GRANDE	THAT BIG
L — G M	Referential gesture +	PICCOLA *piange*	LITTLE *cry*
L — G M		NO *brrr*	NO *car*
L — G —	RH + W or	OTTO *buono*	*cookie* GOOD
L — G —	W + RG	*papa* CIAO	*daddy* BYE
L — G M		*mamma* SOFFIARE	*mummy* BLOW
L — — —	Word + word	*papa via*	*daddy gone*
L F G —		*papa piu*	*food no more*
L F G —	W + W	*da brrr*	*give car*
L F G M		*mamma apo*	*mummy open*
L — — —		*e mio tetto*	*mine that*
— — — M	Referential gesture +	POMPA PALLONE	PUMP BALLOON
— — — M	referential gesture	PALLONE SCOPPIARE	BALLOON POP
— — — M	RG + RG	PESCE MANGIARE BUONO	FISH EAT GOOD
— — — M		SOLDI CAVALLO	MONEY GO – HORSE

There are some differences, however. The combinations DG + W and RG + W that become progressively more frequent in hearing children, are less frequently produced by Massimo. He more often produced the gesture and the word that correspond to the same referent: he said *palla* and performed the sign PALLA at the same time; the most frequent combinations were those with *Mamma,* the only word he used from the first session without the corresponding sign. But the striking difference between the deaf and hearing children concerns the combination RG + RG. The deaf child is the only one to produce combinations of two referential gestures. The hearing children in this study, even those particularly prone to gestural communication, never combined two referential gestures. They combined instead either two words or one referential gesture + one word. This is probably the most important finding of our study, and I want to use it to advance a more general hypothesis.

Discussion

Linguistic capacity implies different abilities, in particular, the ability to use symbols and the ability to combine these symbols.

The child must, in fact, learn to separate different aspects or parts of the world (different actions, objects, people and events). He must learn to make direct reference to these parts in order to communicate this reality. He can reach this goal in two ways: by referring directly to these parts through deictic gestures such as pointing, and/or by using appropriate and different symbols (vocal or gestural) to represent these different referents. This is probably not a one-way process: the use of deictic gestures and the use of symbols may help the child to distinguish the different parts of the world around him.

Finally, in order to communicate progressively more complex messages the child must put the different gestures together. He can reach this goal by using two or more deictic gestures and symbols in a sequence. But, clearly, the combining of symbols implies a more advanced cognitive effort than the combining of deictric gestures: the child must reconstruct all aspects of the reality he wants to communicate at the representational level and with only very limited support. From our data it appears that hearing children, despite the fact they are exposed to a predominantly vocal input, demonstrate a capacity for using symbols in both modalities: vocal and gestural. Furthermore, they demonstrate a capacity for combining two or more signals in the gestural modality as well: they produce combinations of two or more deictic gestures and combinations of a deictic gesture and a symbol (gestural or vocal).

But they do not combine two gestural symbols: they combine two vocal symbols (i.e. two words) or a vocal and a gestural symbol. The final move toward the vocal modality takes place when they have to use the symbolic and the combinatorial capacity simultaneously.

The capacity for combining two symbols to communicate clearly depends on the linguistic input the child is exposed to. At this point, and only at this point do we note a difference between the child who has been exposed to a vocal input and the child exposed to a signed input: the first combines two vocal symbols and the second, two gestural symbols.

Indirect evidence that to combine two symbols it is necessary to be exposed to a linguistic input (spoken or signed) comes from the research conducted by Feldman, Goldin-Meadow and Gleitman (1977) on the gestural communication of deaf children not exposed to a signed input. In their data, I have found only complex combinations of two or more deictic gestures or combinations of one symbolic gesture (in their terminology a 'characterising sign') with one or more deictic gestures.

I have examined all the phrases reported by them, over 500, but could not find any combination of two symbolic gestures. This crucial point, apparently overlooked by the authors themselves, might lead to a different analysis and interpretation of their data.

In conclusion, linguistic capacity implies different abilities and in particular, a symbolic and a combinatorial ability. Both these abilities can be expressed in both modalities: gestural and vocal.

Because hearing children exposed to a vocal input and deaf children exposed to a signed input or to no input at all both use symbolic gesture and combinations of gestures to communicate, we can argue that these two abilities do not depend directly on the exposure to a linguistic input. What appears to depend crucially on the exposure to a linguistic input is the capacity to combine symbols, in other words the capacity to use both abilities (symbolic and combinatorial) simultaneously in order to communicate. This capacity signals that the child is passing from a general communicative ability to managing a real linguistic system.

Finally, we hold that research on gestural communication in hearing and deaf children can give us a special insight into the general process of language acquisition.

Acknowledgements

I would like to thank Francesco Antinucci and Alfonso Caramazza for their suggestions and criticisms in developing the general hypothesis of this paper.

*A modified version of this paper appears in *Sign Language Studies,* 1981, p. 33*ff.*

EARLY SIGN LANGUAGE ACQUISITION AND ITS RELATION TO COGNITIVE AND MOTOR DEVELOPMENT

John D. Bonvillian, Michael D. Orlansky, and Lesley Lazin Novack

In this paper, we discuss the findings of a longitudinal investigation of sign language acquisition in very young children of deaf parents. Along with maintaining records of the children's acquisition of American Sign Language (the sign language most widely used by deaf people in the United States) we measured the children's developing motor and sensorimotor skills. This approach of studying language acquisition in a mode different from that of spoken language afforded us the opportunity to re-examine many widely-held views about the interrelationships among language, cognition, and motor development. The results of this investigation suggest that many of these views may need to be revised, as they were not supported when examined from the perspective of the development of a manual language.

Previous studies of sign language acquisition in children of deaf parents, or with close deaf relatives, have shown that the acquisition process bears a close structural resemblance to the development of spoken language skills in hearing children whose parents have normal hearing. This conclusion is based on several longitudinal studies (Klima and Bellugi, 1972; Nash, 1973; Schlesinger and Meadow, 1972) of the acquisition of American Sign Language (ASL) by the young children of deaf parents. Clear similarities in the acquisition patterns were seen in the deaf and hearing children's acquisition of meaning for individual signs or words, in their combination of lexical items to express a wide range of semantic relations, and their acquisition of mature grammatical usage.

There does, however, appear to be at least one important aspect in which the two acquisition patterns differ: children who are learning signs have a generally accelerated pattern of early vocabulary development. According to Schlesinger (1978), a child growing up in an environment where ASL is the principal means of communication probably would begin to use signs at an earlier age than a hearing child growing up in a non-signing environment, would begin to use spoken words. It should be pointed out, however, that this conclusion is based on only a very few case studies, in which detailed records of the subjects' cognitive and motor development were not kept.

The acquisition of ASL by young children has provided a new perspective from which to examine the question of what cognitive skills are necessary precursors to language. Completion of the six stages of the sensorimotor period is widely believed to be a prerequisite to language. The importance of this level of cognitive attainment is attested to by Piaget, who maintains that the ability to use symbols is, in effect, an observable product of the completion of the sensorimotor period, and that 'the acquisition of language is itself subordinated to the working of a symbolic function' (1962, p. 1). Bruner (1966) and Sinclair (1971) also have pointed to sensorimotor development as basic to the acquisition of language. The position on the relationship between thought and language is most effectively summarised by Bowerman (1978):

The cognitive development most often proposed as the primary prerequisite to language acquisition is the capacity for mental representation. . . . The ability is the crowning achievement of the sensorimotor period of development, and emerges during its sixth and final stage, at about 18–24 months, as outlined by Piaget. . . . The capacity for representation is manifested in symbolic play . . ., deferred imitation, the ability to reconstruct invisible displacements of an object (the final test of the concept of object permanence), and other signs of memory for absent objects and events (p. 351).

Consistent with this position, a study of profoundly mentally retarded children (Kahn, 1975) found that the attainment of sensorimotor skills played an important role in the language acquisition of this population as well: a high correlation was shown to exist between completion of sensorimotor (or stage VI) cognitive skills and the language acquisition of the retarded children.

However, the view that children must complete sensorimotor stage six skills, or that object permanence must be developed prior to the acquisition of language, has recently been called into question. Some children show minimal language skills prior to the completion of the sensorimotor period (Folger and Leonard, 1978; Moore and Meltzoff, 1978). Indeed, the onset of single word use by Piaget's own three children occurred during the fifth stage of their sensorimotor development (Ingram, 1978). At the same time, it should be noted that for these three children, as well as for four other children whose records of sensorimotor and language development Ingram analysed, rapid vocabulary development did not take place until the sixth stage. Completion of the sensorimotor period thus appears to be related only to certain language scores or abilities (Corrigan, 1978).

One probable reason for the frequently reported divergent results in investigations of language and cognitive interrelationships is that many of the investigators employed differing criteria for assessing the same cognitive abilities or for determining the presence of language (Corrigan, 1979). Despite these difficulties, several measures of cognitive development have been found to be relatively good predictors of language and communicative skills. Strong correspondence between young children's symbolic play and their language development has been reported (Bates, *et al*, 1979; Nicholich, 1975, 1977). Two other measures of cognitive development have also been shown to be good predirectors of communicative development. Bates, *et al.* (1979) found that young children's scores on two of the scales (*means-ends* and *imitation*) from the Uzgiris and Hunt (1975) ordinal scales of psychological development were clearly related to communicative and language development. Interestingly, these children's performance on the scale of *object permanence* – the skill most frequently associated with the onset of language use – was not. Similarly, Snyder (1978) showed that the presence of stage VI means – ends abilities was a critical factor that separated very young children who acquired language at a normal rate from children who evidenced language delay. These latter two findings suggest that the ability to use symbolisation to achieve desired ends or goals may be more intimately related to language development than the mental representation entailed in object permanence.

Just as the investigation of sign language acquisition can provide a new data base from which to re-examine questions about language and cognitive interactions, sign language acquisition data can be used to re-examine previous findings on the interrelationships of language and motor development. The processes of early language and motor development traditionally have been seen as occurring in a synchronous fashion (Gesell and Amatruda, 1947; Lenneberg, 1967). Their acquisition followed an orderly progression, with advances in language and motor skills largely interlocked: progress in language occurred after a child completed a spurt in motor development. However, these conclusions were based on studies that examined only records of children's *spoken* language development. An additional variable of interest in the present study was the relationship between sign language and early motor development. It is generally accepted that early motor skills develop more rapidly than do early speech skills. Thus, because sign language is a visual-motor system, it might logically be inferred that the relationship between sign language and motor development would be substantially different from that between spoken language and motor development. The present study also addressed this issue by comparing the developing sign language skills of the children with their progress in motor skill development and with spoken language acquisition norms.

Method
Over a 16-month period the investigators (two adult males and one adult female) made regular visits about once every six weeks to the homes of 11 very young (first- and second-year) children of deaf parents. During each visit we obtained written and videotaped records of these children's early sign language usage. These records were supplemented by diary accounts of the children's signing, maintained by the parents, and by interviews with the parents regarding the children's sign usage. Along with these records, we took systematic measures of the children's developing motor and sensorimotor skills.

Subjects
The subjects were 11 young children from from nine families with deaf parents. In seven of the families both parents were deaf and residing at home. One family included a deaf mother and a hearing father, and one family was a single-parent household with a deaf mother. The initial focus of the study was on the nine children under one year of age (modal age = five months), but it was expanded to include two slightly older siblings on whom detailed developmental data were available. The children were selected according to the criteria that they (1) had at least one deaf parent, (2) were being exposed to a sign language as a first language, and (3) had no discernible brain dysfunction or physical handicap other than possible hearing loss. One of the subjects was found to be congenitally deaf, the other 10 apparently have normal hearing.

The parents in the participating families converse within their families and circle of deaf friends mostly in American Sign Language. The parents, however, when interacting with signing people who are not deaf, frequently use ASL signs in a manner that conforms more closely to English syntax. Thus, although the children were primarily exposed to ASL, they also observed English language syntax to some extent. Most of the parents made an effort to have their hearing children gain regular speech practice through interactions with hearing neighbours and relatives. Virtually all the children were also exposed to spoken English through television in the home.

Sign language usage

Information about the children's initial sign language usage came in part from their parents. We provided each set of parents with a notebook designed to assist in recording data on their child's sign language production. The parents recorded the following: the *date* a sign was first produced and the approximate English equivalent of the sign, the *context* in which the sign was produced (both the non-verbal situational context and the apparent function, together with the utterances of the parents or companions that immediately surrounded the child's sign), and any *irregular aspects* of the sign's formation (young children frequently make slight errors, or 'baby-talk variants,' in their early formation of signs). The information on context was necessary in order to decide whether a particular sign should be placed in the child's list of mastered vocabulary items.

Information on the children's signing was also obtained through our visits. Each visit lasted about an hour. We found that interviewing the parents about the written records they kept for the preceding month enhanced our knowledge of how a sign was used. Moreover, our probing about the signs in the interviews helped transmit to the parents what kinds of information we wanted, and supplemented their already thorough records. During each visit, the parents were asked to encourage their child to produce as many signs as possible, and we made written and both structured and unstructured videotaped records of the children's sign productions during each visit. The structured videotape records consisted of a two-minute 'normal play' and a three-minute 'communication' period which were relatively similar in setting across families. During these visits, we made an effort to maintain a casual and relaxed atmosphere. The videotapes also enabled us to check the reliability of our written records, as well as providing detailed recorded information of the children's sign productions. In calculating the children's sign language vocabularies, immediate imitations of the parents' sign productions were not included, nor were pointing gestures that were not themselves conventional ASL signs.

Measures of sensorimotor development

Our measures of cognitive development were the six scales of sensorimotor functioning from the Uzgiris and Hunt (1975) ordinal scales of psychological development. The six scales are: Development of Visual Pursuit and the Permanence of Objects; Development of Means for Obtaining Desired Environmental Events; Development of Imitation: Vocal & Gestural; Development of Operational Causality; Construction of Object Relations in Space; and Development of Schemes for Relating to Objects. Performance records were kept for the nine subjects under the age of one year across each of the scales. During the course of our visits, it was occasionally impossible to get a child to complete all six of the scales. For this reason, some of our calculations of the subjects' stage placements on the various subscales involved slightly different population sizes. In those cases where we were unable to complete the testing, we made certain on our next visit to examine the child first on those scales we had not been able to administer during the previous visit. We did not adminster the scales of sensorimotor development to the two oldest children; they were included in the study only because their parents had diary accounts of their early signing.

Results
Early sign language acquisition

In comparison with the norms of spoken language development, the subjects in the present study typically attained in sign language the equivalents of the corresponding spoken language milestones several months in advance. This general pattern of accelerated language development is in accord with the results of other studies of early sign language acquisition (Holmes and Holmes, 1980; McIntire, 1977; Prinz and Prinz, 1979; Schlesinger and Meadow, 1972). The subjects produced their first recognisable sign at an average age of 8.5 months, with six of the subjects producing their first sign by nine months. In the subsequent weeks the children gradually acquired other new signs, resulting in a mean vocabulary size of 10.0 signs at the age of one year. Investigators of spoken language development typically have placed the date of the appearance of the child's first word at between 11 and 14 months (Cattell, 1940; Shirley, 1933a, 1933b). There are, however, a number of difficulties involved in deciding at what age a child first 'uses' a word or a sign. For example, in several of our subjects, the signs for 'milk' (the opening and closing of the fist of one or both hands) and 'good-bye' (waving of the hand and arm) were the first signs mastered. Although these are the correct manual gestures, and were usually produced in the appropriate situation, it is not evident whether these 'signs' should be interpreted as fulfilling a linguistic function or as an action pattern simply associated with a specific stimulus or situation.

Because of the difficulties in specifying a date for the appearance of the first word, Nelson (1973) employed the age at which each subject in her study had uttered 10 different words as the principal initial measure of vocabulary development. This was accomplished by Nelson's 18 subjects at a mean age of 15.1 months. In the present study, the mean age at which the children had produced 10 different signs was 13.2 months – nearly two months earlier than Nelson's subjects reached the same milestone in spoken language development. This difference between the two groups in mean age of achievement of a 10-item vocabulary was statistically significant: $t(27) = 2.67$, $p<.02$. By the time the children in the present study were 18 months old, they had a mean vocabulary size of 48.7 signs, another indication of accelerated early vocabulary development (cf. Lenneberg, 1967). Moreover, those subjects who initially showed more rapid acquisition of signs continued in this capacity, as the size of the children's sign language vocabulary at one year of age was clearly related to their vocabulary size six months later $r=.97$, $p<.001$. At the same time, there were marked individual differences among our subjects in the ages at which they achieved the different milestones in vocabulary development. For example, the ages at which the subjects mastered their first 10 signs ranged from 10 months to 17 months. But overall, the subjects' individual sign production was clearly accelerated in comparison with the norms for spoken language production.

The children also showed slightly accelerated performance, in comparison with the norms for spoken language production, in the ages at which they began to combine signs. The mean age at which the subjects first combined signs was 17 months, with the range in ages extending from 12.5 to 22 months, whereas normal children typically join two spoken words at around 18 to 21 months of age (Gesell and Thompson, 1934: Slobin, 1971). As was the case in early vocabilary development, the ages at which the subjects began to combine signs varied considerably, with the range in ages extending from 12.5 to 22 months. However, there was no relationship between early vocabulary growth and the onset of sign combinations; the correlations between the subjects' vocabulary sizes at the ages of 12 and 18 months with the ages at which they first combined signs were small and non-significant ($r=.16$, $p=.69$, at 12 months; $r=.01$, $p=.99$, at 18 months).

Motor development

The subjects passed the different motor milestones at ages which closely approximated those of children in previously reported normative studies. The children in the present study began to sit at a mean age of 6.7 months, to crawl at 7.2 months, to stand at 10.1 months, and to walk at 12.8 months. These ages are similar to the values given by Stone and Church (1975) in their summary of previously published norms: seven months (sitting), eight months (crawling), 11–12 months (standing), and 18 months (walking). Overall, then, the subjects were very slightly accelerated in terms of the average ages at which they attained the motor milestones, but clearly within the expected age ranges. The children's acquisition of these motor milestones did not appear to affect their progress in sign language acquisition. Rather than pausing in their sign language development after achieving a new motor skill, the subjects exhibited steady progress in their vocabulary development, gradually increasing the size of their sign language lexicon.

language and sensorimotor development

The subjects' performance across the different scales of the Uzgiris-Hunt varied substantially, as is consistent with previously reported findings (see Dunst, 1980). The children in the present study typically were advanced relative to other scales on measures of object permanence, in line with previously established age expectancy norms. Not surprisingly, our subjects tended to progress more slowly through the scale of vocal imitation. This specific performance is probably attributable, in part, to the apparently reduced amount of recognisable vocal input from their parents, but also to the fact that this scale is typically more slowly traversed. Because of the substantial variability in the scale scores, an overall specific stage placement was not attempted for each subject. Rather, each subject's stage performance on the different scales was separately computed.

The interrelationships between the measures of the subjects' cognitive development and their language performance were relatively complex, and depended to a large extent on the criterion used in defining the presence of language. If the criterion were to be the children's production of their first signs, then most of the children would be performing in stage III (37.5%) and stage IV (37.5%) across the various subscales. If one were only to examine the subjects' performance on the *object permanence* and the *means-ends* scales, the scales most frequently associated with language and symbolic processing, then the children's performance on both these scales would extend from the middle of stage III to early stage V.

There may well be, however, good reasons for arguing that these initial signs are not particularly good indicators of true language ability. Many of the children's gestures appeared to be tied to actions (cf. Bloom, 1973), to occur as delayed imitations of a modelled sign, or to necessitate the presence of an object for contextual support. If one's criterion in defining the presence of language were to be the point at which the subjects used 10 signs, usually several months after their first recognisable sign gesture, one would have a more conservative measure of the children's language ability, since at this stage the children much more reliably named objects or events, although the signs were still often tied to the presence of an object or event for contextual support. Using the criterion of 10 recognisable signs, the children typically (50.0%) were at stage V on the measures of sensorimotor development, with the other half of the scores split about equally between stage IV and stage VI. In terms of the children's performance on the specific subscale of *object permanence,* 50% were at stage V, 50% at stage VI, although at intermediate steps of stage VI. The subjects' performance on the *means-ends* scale varied considerably more, extending from stage IV through stage VI (IV = 42.9%, V = 42.9%, VI = 14.3%).

Another perspective on the point at which children demonstrate language skill would be that of the combination of words or signs. Piaget, in fact, distinguished between the use of single words (which he placed in stage VI) and true capacity for language. If one were to examine our subjects' two-sign combinations as the point of onset of language (this event typically occurred several months after the presence of 10-sign vocabularies), one would find that most of our subjects were showing overall sensorimotor performance in stage V (36.8%) and stage VI (44.7%). [Stage IV performance on vocal imitation accounted for the large majority of scores below stage V and stage VI.] If one were to look a the scale of *object permanence,* one would find that half of the subjects had completed the entire scale (stage VI) at the time they first combined signs. Still, one subject was only in the middle of stage V, and the remainder of the subjects were successful at completing only intermediate steps of stage VI. Again, the performance on the *means-ends* scale was more variable; although the majority of children scored in stage VI, the range in performance extended from stage IV through stage VI.

The above findings cast doubt on the position that completion of the sensorimotor period, or of the scales of object permanence or means-ends abilities, is a necessary prerequisite for linguistic behaviour. Rather, the ability to name present objects or recent events probably entails cognitive skills already available to the normal child before the end of the first year. These skills appear to include the ability to recognize or identify an object over time or an event, a skill that Brown (1973) noted was a stage IV phenomenon, and that often occurred around eight months of age (cf. Cohen and Strauss, 1979; Fagan, 1976). Even when the production of sign combinations is employed as the criterion for the presence of language (Ingram, 1978), half of the subjects failed to show full mastery of object permanence, let alone completion of other scales from the sensorimotor period. One possible explanation for the wide individual variability on the sensorimotor scales in association with the three levels of the subjects' sign language output is that the criteria used to assess the presence of language may not have been specific enough. Perhaps, for example, in future comparisons of initial language productions and cognitive abilities, it might be wise to separate those signs that were made only in the context of a specific object or event and those signs that did not appear to be context dependent. The finding in the present study of accelerated acquisition of language milestones by signing children also suggests that using productive spoken language skills as the measure of linguistic behaviour, as in many previous studies, may well underestimate many children's true language abilities and result in correlations between language skills and cognitive development that are largely artifactual. Indeed, Huttenlocher (1974) noted that language comprehension typically preceded productive skills by several months, and that studies which employed only productive spoken language measures were likely to underestimate their young subjects' linguistic abilities.

General Discussion
One factor that probably played an important role in our subjects' accelerated acquisition of language skills was that they were learning a language in a mode different from speech. Children learning a visual-motor language, such as ASL, can readily have their hands moulded into the proper configuration and guided into the proper movement by their parents, siblings, or others. Comparable input and control by the parents would, of course, be impossible in an auditory-vocal language. Children learning to sign are also able to benefit from direct visual feedback of their production of many signs. Another reason why ASL may be more readily acquired is that the motor system in the young child appears to develop more rapidly than the speech system. Sperling (1978) observed that motor control of the hands matures before comparable control of the vocal system in the young child. Relatedly, the motor centre of the brain is ahead of the speech centre in neural development at birth, and in the ensuing months continues to develop at a more rapid pace. This pattern of relatively more rapid development can be seen in de Crinis' finding that measures of cellular maturation in the motor area of the brain at nine months were still ahead of those in Broca's speech area at 14 months of age (de Crinis, 1932; cited in Carmichael, 1964).

Because a number of signs in ASL are iconic – that is, they have a clearly recognisable tie to their referent – it has been suggested (Brown, 1977) that this may account for the finding that sign languages are more easily learned than spoken languages. When the signs that the children acquired in the present study were examined, it was found that about one-third (33.2%) of the signs that the children produced were iconic. Although the iconic aspect of these signs may well have assisted in their acquisition, the finding that two-thirds of the signs did not have a clear tie to their referent suggests that iconicity did not play a critical role. It appears unlikely that such young children would frequently be able to discern the etymology of the signs they acquired.

The absence of a clear relationship between the sizes of the children's sign language vocabularies (both at one year and at 18 months) with the ages of their initial production of sign combinations suggests that factors other than motor, visual, and iconic ones may be instrumental in the production of multi-sign utterances. Rather, the combination of signs may reflect more highly developed cognitive and memory skills, as the children express more complicated semantic relations. If this is true, then we would expect that future comparisons of the children's developing sign language skills would more closely parallel the norms for spoken language development, as both systems would be substantially reflecting underlying cognitive abilities.

In light of the present findings, it is apparent to us that at least a couple of widely-accepted notions and procedures in developmental psycholinguistics need to be reconsidered. One is Lenneberg's (1967) view on the limiting role of cognition in very early language development: 'The retarding factor for language . . . must be . . . a cognitive one and not mechanical skill' (p. 131). Although we believe that cognition plays a central role in the course of language development, other factors such as mechanical skill or the specific language modality also appear to be important in the acquisition process. This point is further underlined by recent findings (e.g., Bonvillian and Nelson, in press) that many previously non-speaking children, such as autistic children and mentally retarded children, can make substantial strides in communication skills when taught language in a different modality. A second aspect that we believe needs to be re-examined is the frequently employed experimental methodology of obtaining measures of subjects' productive vocal language and then correlating these scores with the subjects' performance on scales of sensorimotor development. Clearly, if we were able to obtain very different results in this area principally by shifting the language modality, then previous studies probably were measuring factors (e.g., speech production skills) not entirely related to the interaction between language and cognition. Of course, the approach of tying in specific linguistic skills and measures of object permanence has been challenged before on theoretical grounds. Indeed, Bates and her associates (1977, 1979) have argued that both linguistic behaviours and object permanence are probably surface manifestations of deeper underlying cognitive skills, and that one would not be justified in claiming that one was the prerequisite for the other. Similarly, even if future studies reported that some cognitive variables were good predictors of language and cognitive development, it would remain unclear as to whether these skills were necessary precursors to language, or were associated with a more general cognitive capacity that has language as one of its manifestations (see Miller, *et al*, 1980).

Acknowledgements
This research was supported by University of Virginia Research Policy Council Grants 5-23572 and 5-23802 to the senior author and by National Science Foundation Grant BNS-8023114 to the first two authors. We would

like to express our appreciation to the parents and children for their participation in the study.

AN EXAMINATION OF THE COMMUNICATION INTERRACTIONS BETWEEN HEARING IMPAIRED INFANTS AND THEIR PARENTS

Carolyn L. Scroggs

This is the description of a project that is in its very initial stages. The purpose of this project is to carry out a longitudinal study of the language development of a group of hearing impaired children starting at the point of identification.

A grant was obtained to begin preliminary research in conjunction with Infant Hearing Resource, a parent/infant program for hearing impaired children at Good Samaritan Hospital in Portland, Oregon, U.S.A. At this point we have four infants in our project on which video-taping and analysis has begun. The design of our project uses these four children as 'pilot' children – with these children we will develop observational and coding strategies and hypotheses for application to a group of 'main study' children who will be recruited later.

Subjects
Some comments concerning our children and their program are needed before any details of the study are discussed. First of all, obtaining (for study) hearing impaired infants who are truly pre-lingual is quite difficult due to the nature of early communication and the identification of deafness. The vast majority of hearing impaired children are not identified until around two years of age. They are identified at that time because they do not start talking. And our experience at Infant Hearing Resource is that the children coming in who are two years old have developed some very sophisticated communication strategies. Their communication is clearly not like the pre-language child. There are generally two groups where identification is earlier than two years. Where there is deafness in the family the parents are looking for possible deafness. These babies generally come into the clinic with few other health or developmental problems. The other group are those children who have serious, overt health problems which may be associated with deafness, so early diagnostic procedures are carried out. The children in our preliminary study reflect just such an array. In order to observe pre-lingual children, children who are younger than 10 or 11 months, we decided to include children who might have other health problems. And in fact two of the four children do have problems other than deafness. The third child in the study has hearing impaired parents, so the parents were aware deafness was a possibility. The fourth child does not have other obvious health problems, but was identified at six months of age. The children's hearing losses are in the severe to profound range and they have all been fitted with ear level aids. The youngest child at the beginning of the study was four months old, the oldest, 18 months old but at about the six months developmental level. None of the children were walking when the study began.

It is important to note the type of input system to which the children are being exposed. Infant Hearing Resource views itself as a total communication program – that is, the parents are urged to communicate to the children with their voices and to sign simultaneously. The signing being taught is called Oregon Sign Language, the sign language system being used at the Oregon State School for the Deaf. This system is somewhat similar to a Pidgin Signed English system, except that a limited number of inflectional markers are used and a sign is used for every spoken word. The signs are used in English word order.

Procedures

The procedure that is now being undertaken with the children is to video-tape them for about a half an hour once a month in their homes. They are video-taped in play sessions with their parents. What we are observing at this point in their development are the communication strategies used by the children and their parents. Later on we will video-tape the children communicating with their peers.

The strategies used for examining the parent/child interactions are those that have been developed for examining the pre-speech dialogues of hearing infants and their parents.

Before the research begun in the early 1970's, the communication of infants usually had been described in terms of noises made by the baby (Lenneberg, 1967). With the work of Bruner (1975), Brazelton (Brazelton, et al., 1974), Trevarthen (1974) and others, it became clear that these early descriptions were clearly inadequate and that parents and their babies use very complex strategies to communicate with each other. These strategies include not only vocalisation but facial expression, eye glance and movement of the head, trunk, legs, arms and fingers (Tronick, et al., 1979).

It was found that not only did the youngsters use these movements to communicate but the manner in which they used them resembled in many ways conversations that take place between adults (Collis, 1979) – that is, there appeared to be rules for starting, sustaining and closing the conversation and rules for turn taking. These dialogues, called proto-conversations, are heavily embedded in rhythmical patterns (Fridman, 1980). Three very apparent elements of these conversations are repetition on the part of both the mother and infant, mutual imitation, and joint action.

There has always been some question as to why hearing impaired infants are identified so late. The lack of growth of spoken language is the usual trigger for identification but the question has always remained why the lack of auditory response did not lead to earlier identification. It could be postulated that auditory response must play only a relatively minor role in the child and parents' interactive behaviour, but then the question is how communication can take place. The infant interactive studies seem to provide clues as to why the profoundly deaf infant and toddler can participate so fully with the parent without the parent realising the auditory component is missing. These studies made it apparent that communication behaviour between hearing infants and their parents was not limited to vocal/auditory responses but included very large visual and tactile components. It is possible that these visual and tactile components carried enough conversational cues to enable the child to participate very effectively in these early dialogues. However, to determine whether this conjecture is true or not it is necessary to observe hearing impaired infants with their parents. It will then be possible to see whether the hearing impaired infant does communicate successfully with the parent, whether the infant does participate in proto-conversations, and whether any differences are apparent between the hearing and hearing impaired infant. This then is the initial purpose of our project – to observe and describe these early interactions.

The second purpose of our research is to examine what happens to the parents' interaction patterns with the child as the parents begin to include signing in their communication strategies and to see what relationship exists between the signing system used by the parent and that used by the child.

Preliminary Observations

What is being examined at the present time in our project is the kind of behaviour used by the parents or the child to initiate a proto-conversation, the kinds of simultaneous and sequential and turn-taking behaviour used to sustain conversation, and the kinds of procedures used to end conversations. Recorded behaviour includes facial expression, eye gaze, head movement, arm and trunk movement, general body orientation, hand and finger movement, leg movement, and vocalisation. In the case of the parent, all of the above are included as well as the parent's use of spoken word and signs.

There are several stages to the analysis. The first stage consists of recording the observed behaviour in a paper and pencil format. This, of course, has proven to be a formidable task. To carry this out we have had to have two observers working together and have often had to call in a third and fourth party when we could not agree on what we observed.

The next step will be to code the observed behaviours. The preliminary work to carry out the coding for the prelingual infants has not yet been completed, so coding has not yet begun. What I will be reporting to you are some preliminary observations concerning how hearing impaired babies and their parents communicate.

Let me say at the outset that the proto-conversations between the parents and the children in our project are incredibly rich and productive. These conversations do not appear to differ much from the conversations between hearing children and their parents except when certain kinds of behaviour are being looked for. In watching these rich communications it becomes apparent why parents do not discover their babies' hearing losses.

The first thing that is very noticeable when viewing the video-tapes was how rhythmical the behaviour is when the parent and child are communicating. The following is an example of just such behaviour. The mother took a block and banged it on a box six times, very rhythmically. Then the baby swatted at the box using the same rhythm as the mother had used. The mother, while the baby was swatting at the box, again started banging the block in rhythm with her child's movement. This type of rhythmical movement and rhythmical imitation is a very frequent occurence. Another example was when one father began singing 'ba ba ba' and the child began to simultaneously imitate the movment she observed and then continued the movement after her father had stopped the movement. The youngster, after mimicking the movement four times, also began to vocalise with the movement.

This rhythmic behaviour appears to play an extremely important role in the conversations. It was used by our parents, as it is by other parents, to engage the child's attention (e.g., by tapping the youngster), to cue the child into a familiar play sequence (e.g., by bouncing a toy across the table), to check whether the child is interested in a specific game and to continue the conversation through imitating the child's behaviour. Rhythmic behaviour was sometimes started in one mode, such as vocalising, and then imitated by the other partner in another mode, such as tapping.

In addition to this type of rhythmic behaviour is the kind of coordinated rhythmic behaviour that takes place within the individual. For example, the parent may tap, vocalise, and nod her head all at the same time. A hearing impaired child who cannot hear such vocalisations, will often get more than one cue that meaningful, rhythmical communication is taking place. The parent may be looking intently into the child's face, smiling, moving her mouth and tapping the baby's arm all at the same time. The child, though deaf, becomes so familiar with this pattern that he will often wait until the mother is finished, watching his mother's behaviour before he begins his own movement. When given so many cues the child seldom interrupts his mother's movement, waiting until she has finished if he's really watching his mother. One exception to this is when the child begins to imitate the mother's behaviour. The child may begin in the imitation pattern while his mother is still talking (as the mother may do with the child). In observing these patterns it seems quite clear why the parent may never realise that the infant has a hearing impairment, not appreciating how many conversational cues are being used besides auditory ones.

One example of how sensitive the child is to these visual cues is a pattern we observed with our one child who has hearing-impaired parents. The parents nearly always signed to the baby when talking to her. If they had the baby's attention she would watch them intently when they were signing to her. Both of the parents, when they had finished whatever they were signing to the baby, would drop their hands into their laps, accompanied by a slight lowering of the shoulders. The youngster by six months of age was so in tune to this cue that she would instantly drop her eyes to her toy or whatever she was playing with when she saw the parents drop their hands into their laps.

It is probably worth noting that we saw one example of turn taking failure, which was a real irritant to the parent. One of the mothers would from time to time begin to talk to her child, calling his name fairly sharply, but out of the child's visual range. The child, because he was not attending to his mother auditorily or visually, would continue what he was doing and from time to time would even begin to vocalise midway through the mother's utterance. The mother would react to this interruption with annoyance. It is unclear to me if she realised what was annoying her.

The fundamental role of this rhythmical behaviour as the basis for successful communication just can't be over-estimated. It is reminiscent of the story of a hearing person turning on the radio listening to the news and the deaf person begins to tap to the rhythm, thinking what he is hearing is music. The rhythmical aspect seems to be fundamental to human communication functioning, no matter what mode of communication is being used. While there are learned aspects to this behaviour, some researchers such as Trevarthen (1979) feel that the rhythms are apparent so early that they must be built into the baby in one way or another.

We made another observation concerning our youngsters that rather surprised us. When infants are very young (up to three months of age), although they interact with objects, these do not play a very large role in conversations with their parents. As a colleague of mine stated, what the parent and infant at this stage do is play with each other's faces. However, as the child grows older, objects do begin to play a very large role. The incorporation of objects in play had a very unexpected effect on the communication pattern. On our very first night of video-taping, very early on the parent began to play with the child while sitting behind him. I thought that the parent was trying to sit so both she and her son were facing the camera so I suggested to her that this was not necessary and that she could sit face-to-face with the youngster, as I was concerned that the mother would be out of the child's line of sight. In no time, however, we discovered the mother back around behind the infant. That time I left well enough alone. The next day, in going back and looking at the literature on early communication behaviour, we found just such a pattern described (Collis, 1979). Sure enough, as infants become heavily involved with objects, parents often sit behind the youngster. The parent communicates to the baby by talking to him, and then by leaning forward and peering into the baby's face to figure out where the child is in his communication. The pair then can become engaged in parallel movement with the mother helping the youngster as he plays with the toy rather than mirroring the child's play behaviour as she might if she sat face-to-face with him. The unfortunate outcome for the hearing-impaired child is that a good deal of the mother's rhythmic communication behaviour is then lost to the child, as often when the mother is communicating in this position she is out of the child's line of sight. Two of the parents, interestingly enough, solved this problem by putting a mirror on the floor so that they could handle objects in a parallel fashion but the child could also see the mother's movements. Of course the mother did not always sit behind the baby when communicating, but it was a common pattern.

One area we have been interested in looking at is the parents' incorporation of signing as part of their communication strategies. We have been particularly interested in determining if such incorporation interferes with the rhythmical communication pattern. Two of the four families were new signers, one family decided not to use signing with their child, and the fourth family, because the parents were hearing impaired, had used signing for some time. The two mothers who were new signers were quite different in the ease with which they incorporated signing. One mother seldom got flustered. Signs that she knew generally she included easily and freely in her play. When she did not know a sign she did not worry about it. She just used nothing and continued talking and playing with her youngster. On the whole, the signing on her part did not seem to interfere with her conversation. As for the child's response to the mother's input, we saw that about the time he first started pointing, he also began to occasionally use a twisting movement with his hand when he was in conversation with somebody, a movement I have never seen a hearing child produce.

The other mother appeared to be much less easy with signing, using signs much less frequently at least while she was being video-taped. When she did use signs, they were not always well-cordinated with her on-going dialogue. What would happen would be that a look would go across her face as if to say, 'Uh oh. I'd better use a sign'. Then she would tend to rear back a little, get a very serious look on her face, and then use the sign. She would then lean forward, soften her face into her communication mode, and carry on with her communication. This was not the only time when we saw this particular movement. The parents in the program have been told that one way to encourage their children to vocalise is to imitate the child's vocalisations. Most of the time the parents did this very unconsciously and the imitation was very much integrated with their other play imitation patterns. However, every so often one would see that the parent 'remembered' that she/he was supposed to imitate. We'd see the same kind of slight rearing back and stiffening of expression for this contrived, non-conversational imitation. Another place one can see a similar movement is when teachers are using a pattern for correcting a hearing-impaired child's utterance. The teacher's face will become expressionless, she will rear back a little, and give the pattern she wishes the child to imitate. When she is satisfied with the child's utterance she will relax her shoulders, and soften her face, letting the child know it is now all right to go on with the conversation.

The children all seemed to be attentive to the signing in one way or another. The child with the deaf parents paid the most attention, usually looking at the parent's face or hands until the signed message was completed. The other two children would not always wait until the signed communication was completed. We often saw, however, that if the child were looking at the parent's face and the parent started signing, the child would very briefly glance at the moving hands. We did not often see the children watching the hands through an entire message. They may, however, watch the face or at least keep the signs within their peripheral vision.

One part of the transcription caused us a number of problems. The two hearing impaired parents are in fact more or less bi-lingual. They both have, as part of their linguistic repertoire, a considerable amount of English. When they signed directly to their baby, at least while we were video-taping, they talked to her and used for the most part Oregon Sign Language. I might point out that this youngster also appears to use her hearing quite a bit. However, when the parents signed to each other, they did not vocalise and used primarily a type of American Sign Language. However, the ASL was not textbook ASL, but rather communication between two married partners with all the abbreviations and shared knowledge that is common between couples. Moreover, our camera angle was not ideal and there were some signs that not even our deaf assistants could figure out. The language was just too shorthand and too private.

To sum up our observations to this point, it appears that the communication strategies used by hearing-impaired infants and their parents differ little from those of hearing infants. The communication is very successful and appears very normal. Conversations that are rewarding and fun take place between the parent and the child. While all the children vocalised, vocalisation was simply not the major carrying factor in these conversations. After observing the tapes, it became quite obvious why the absence of the auditory component did not, at this stage of development, cause serious disruptions in the communication process. Most of the communication took place face-to-face with the child, with a few notable exceptions. Moreover, the parent does not talk to the baby with a *bland* face. The parent gives many visual and tactile cues to the baby each time she/he says something. Significantly when our mothers wished *not* to become engaged in a conversation with their babies, they did so by avoiding eye contact. While the introduction of signing does cause some interference in the communication process, this interference does not overwhelm conversation. The parents and the children in our study all had established very complex, rich, and rewarding conversational routines. It appears that if signing can be successfully introduced to the parent, it can simply be applied to a very successful, already established communication system.

Acknowledgements

Research for this paper was supported in part by Medical Research Foundation of Oregon Grant No. 8033, 'Study of the Development of Language of Hearing Impaired Infants'.

PART THREE: COMMUNITY

INTRODUCTION

We have used the term 'community' here to describe the whole community both hearing and deaf, and this is a section which deals with the attitudes and practices of the community. It is perhaps here more than anywhere that change is taking place, and it is here that we would hope for most change. The treatment of deaf people through history has ranged from outright rejection and concealment by families with deaf children, to tacit acceptance and provision, but only as handicapped members of the community. While this acceptance is important, it may often attract the stigma of special provision and this is often society's way of refusing to understand the needs of the group under consideration.

The surge of interest in human rights has almost certainly raised the status of deaf people, and the interests in minority languages and cultures throughout the world has raised our consciousness of sign language. Linguistic study attempts to identify the pure form of the language and preserve it by naturalistic observation. Deaf people may now find themselves more accepted than ever before in many countries. However, at the same time there is a pressure to understand the deaf world, there is a corresponding pressure to integrate people within the majority hearing culture in which they find themselves. The greatest part of the deaf community have hearing parents whose major goal is that their children should understand and live in the wider community of the parents. Educators in special education, therefore, have a task which is almost impossible from the outset. They must understand and accept their pupils as they are, but yet must provide 'special' education to make them more similar to the community. They must aim towards the goals of development within the community, but yet communicate with their children in a language which they understand but which may not be understood by the community. In this pressure situation, educational practice tends to become informed not by research, but by attitudes and beliefs.

Too often in the past these attitudes have dictated an 'either-or' approach to deaf children's education and meant that teachers must speak *or* sign. The fact that some compromise in total communication may be possible, is probably an important breakthrough in the attitudes to and relations with the deaf community.

Bernard Tervoort has studied the status of signing in education in European countries by questionnaire, and indicates a more positive attitude towards the use of sign language than one might have expected even only 10 years ago. The responses to his study indicate, of course, a wide range of different provision and a varying level of control by authorities of the official methods. Many countries appear to be strictly oral, though most have a provision for 'handicapped' deaf children, whereby other methods usually involving sign, will be used. In practice this type of use of sign may well reinforce the stigma of signing for adult deaf people. It also assigns sign language to a place in the 'second division' of languages.

It is this position which is explored in the two papers following – Edwards and Ladd for the U.K., and Loncke for Belgium. Despite cultural differences and differences in living patterns, it seems there are many similarities in the language situations of West Indian people and deaf people in the U.K. Generally speaking, attitudes devalue each of these community's languages to the extent that they convince the users that their own use of it is 'bad'. In terms of grammar Edwards and Ladd show some very strong similarities which they claim as support for a view that BSL can be understood in terms of its similarity to this Creole. Their plea is for greater tolerance to the language of both communities and greater acceptance of its power as a first language.

Loncke, in a short exploratory paper, indicates how Sign has developed in an already bilingual hearing community. Historically, the two languages of the hearing community have not enjoyed equal status, and it is only recently that Flemish use has been acceptable. Perhaps because of this and certainly as a result of greater mobility among deaf people, there has been a growing awareness of Flemish Sign Language. Loncke shows how research in Belgium is developing and the research programme he outlines will be of particular help in the greater understanding of Flemish deaf people.

The last two papers in the section deal with the education side of the problem in a country where the language attitude barrier has been broken to some extent. In the U.S., it is now meaningful to consider the different results of the use of Manual English as opposed to ASL in educational settings. Research on educational method is unfortunately difficult to carry out, and we can only be in the early stages of appreciating the impacts on achievements of the use of signing. Gustason's paper is therefore an important one in setting out the state of use of ASL and Manual English in the U.S. What is striking is that she can now show, even for her small sample, that deaf children have begun to benefit and appear to out-perform their peers of a few years ago. Some negative feelings towards ASL can still be seen among some deaf teachers, but her conclusion is that attitudes have become more positive towards the use of Sign in the classroom, and that this must be of benefit to other educators and parents.

Hamilton tackles the awareness of the differences between ASL and manual English. He studied deaf children's judgements of a signers' social group membership, i.e., whether they could be termed deaf or hearing on the basis of perception of their style of signing. He shows differences in awareness according to age of the child, but also highlights the complexity of such judgements.

The section is particularly powerful in showing how the attitudes of the community influence our treatment of the sign language of deaf people. There are no simple ways of changing or controlling attitudes, and it is clear that there will always be a balance to be struck in education between respect for the native language and the need for achievement of the community's goals. The fact that these papers begin to demonstrate we might soon reach this balance, makes them particularly valuable.

THE STATUS OF SIGN LANGUAGE IN EDUCATION IN EUROPE AND THE PROSPECTS FOR THE FUTURE

Professor Dr. Bernard T. Tervoort

It seems to be more than just a good idea not to concentrate only on theoretical issues of sign language research, but also to consider some of the consequences this research is going to have in practice; such considerations seem to be a necessity if theoretical research is truly worth-while. I shall concentrate on one of these applied contexts in this paper, namely on the status of sign language in education in Europe and the prospects for the future. To deal with such a broad theme in a limited space implies that choices have to be made, that many details have to be left aside, and that arriving at a few general conclusions is all that can be hoped for.

This paper consists of two parts: (1) a description of the present use of Sign in countries of Europe and (2) the prospects of such use for the future.

1. The Present Situation

Although the present-day situation certainly reflects historical development, I can not discuss fully within this paper the history of signing in the context of the education of the deaf in Europe. The most recent short overview, and a very good one as far as I can judge, is the one given in Savage, Evans and Savage (1981). The most extensive study known to me remains Schumann's 'Geschichte des Taubstummenwesens' (1940).

It is common knowledge that from the very beginning of regular education of deaf children, some two hundred years ago, the two opposing philosophies (signing versus speech) have been present. The influence from De l'Epée's school in Paris and from Heinicke's school in Leipzig spread over Europe as the French versus the German Method. That was two hundred years ago; a century later, the Congress of Milan, after having listened to two other antagonists, Edward Gallaudet and Thomas Arnold, carried almost unanimously the famous resolution in favour of the oral method, thus creating the conditions for a victorious development of oralism all over the continent. Most European representatives voted in favour of the resolution, thus demonstrating that oralism was already spreading more rapidly than the French method, even in the decades before Milan. The resolution set the scene for an even faster growth thereafter, both of oralism and of the oppression of Sign, even in France, as Lane (1980) has described.

We have to pass another full century to find the beginning of a more moderate standpoint, namely at the World Congress in Hamburg, August 1980, where Otto Kröhnert, its principal organiser, rejected the Milan resolution not for its incorrectness but for its incompleteness. The deaf, he stated, live in two worlds with two languages, and it is about time that educators acknowledged that fact. Unfortunately, not enough educators in Europe have reached that point today, as we shall see.

The historical perspective is of interest to our theme, and it is fairly easy to study the development of European teaching in handbooks. But it proves to be very difficult to find out more precisely about the present-day situation and about subtle changes in attitude. Therefore, apart from using existing information from different sources now and then, I have decided to try and arrive at a uniform source of recent data by mailing an extensive questionnaire to representatives of all European countries. I shall deal with its structure and the response to it briefly first, and with the content of its information at length thereafter.

The questionnaire consists of three parts: (1) an introduction. (2) a section asking for general, and (3) one asking for specific information. The introduction just enquires about the country's official name in English, its language or languages, its schools for the deaf and their enrolments, and, finally, the estimated number of adult deaf. The section on general information was deemed necessary in order to establish the general context of signing in each country as background information for the description of educational philosophy and practice. This section tries to establish whether a true sign language similar to ASL as the best known prototype does exist, as opposed to an analogue of Signed English, and whether the two blend or interfere. Furthermore, in this section information on both sign language research and the characteristics of the communication of the deaf adults is sought. In the section on specific information, the focus is on the philosophies and practices of the educational system of the country and of the different schools. The pertinent way of questioning is: is sign used at all, and if so, in which ways and under which conditions.

As far as the response to the questionnaire is concerned, the following remarks are in order. The questionnaire was sent to representatives of the different countries of whom an unbiased answer could reasonably be expected; their names were taken from lists of participants of recent conventions. Of the 28 countries, the following 20 answered the questionnaire in full: Austria, Belgium*, Denmark, Finland, West Germany, East Germany, Bulgaria, Hungary, Ireland, Luxembourg, The Netherlands, Norway, Portugal, Rumania, Scotland, Sweden, French Switzerland*, German Switzerland, the Soviet Union, the United Kingdom and Yugoslavia. From correspondents of three more countries I received letters with extensive information instead of the questionnaire. Namely French-speaking Belgium*, Italy and Czechoslovakia. In spite of repeated letters of reminder, no answers came back from Albania, France, Greece, Iceland, Poland and Spain. I have tried to overcome this handicap as well as I could, by obtaining additional information from alternative sources. This was especially successful as far as France is concerned, thanks to the bimonthly *Coup d'Oeil: Bulletin sur l'actualité de la langue des signes et la communication*. Furthermore, I am still trying to find other addresses for the questionnaire in the countries that did not answer so far. The closing date for the answers was June 1, 1981.

In the meantime I would prefer to limit myself at the moment to giving information in terms of some trends that emerge from the answers given, rather than presenting exact figures and tables for some countries with empty spaces for others. An extensive report on all details would go beyond the

---

*I have counted Belgium and Switzerland each as one country, but due to their multi-lingual situation, there were more answers, or the possibility thereof.

limits of this presentation anyway, even if I had all the information at hand; it will be completed in a separate publication.

A final remark concerning the responses to the questionnaire is that most correspondents used the opportunity given in the last question to volunteer a considerable amount of useful additional information.

I now come to the information itself from the questionnaire. Following its line of questioning, the first focus will be on the general information concerning true sign languages versus signed spoken languages and the modes of communication of the deaf communities.

True sign languages are reported to be in existence in Austria, Denmark, Finland, France, East and West Germany, Hungary, Norway, Portugal, Rumania, Sweden, French Switzerland, the Soviet Union, the United Kingdom and Yugoslavia. They are reported explicitly to be non-existent in Bulgaria, Luxembourg, German Switzerland and Czechoslovakia. The others are silent about it. Additional information was requested on the existence of a sign language dictionary, about ongoing research, about courses taught, and about officially acknowledged use, e.g. by interpreters.

Eight countries report having one or more dictionaries: Belgium, Denmark, West Germany, Finland, France, Hungary, Norway, the United Kingdom and the Soviet Union; Yugoslavia states: 'in preparation' the same goes for The Netherlands. The same countries report ongoing research, together with Rumania. Courses in sign language are given in Denmark, Finland, Norway, Sweden, the Soviet Union and Yugoslavia; the United Kingdom notes: 'Yes, but only beginning'. Finally, officially acknowledged interpreters are reported for Austria, Denmark, Finland, the Germanies, Norway, Scotland, Sweden, and the Soviet Union, whereas unofficially they are available in most other instances.

We now come to the answers to the questions concerning the signed spoken languages; in summary, they read as follows: (1) Does your country have a manual system based on the grammar of the spoken language and comparable to Signed English, and if so, does such a system follow the spoken language's morphology or syntax; does it incorporate fingerspelling or speech and speech reading? (2) If such a well defined manual system does not exist, is there some actual occurrence of manualism that could be termed unofficially signed spoken language? Finally, as far as a mixture of the two is concerned the questionnaire limited itself to two questions: (3) How do the deaf adults in your country communicate as a rule under different circumstances, followed by a listing of these circumstances, with the deaf club on the one hand and communication with hearing persons not knowing signs on the other hand as the two extremes? and, (4) How do hearing interpreters communicate with the deaf as a rule, specified over the different modes, from official sign language all the way to speech-only? I shall try to summarise a great amount of information from the answers and comments in a few paragraphs.

Six countries acknowledge the existence of a well defined signed version of the spoken language that follows its morphology and syntax and incorporates speech and, sometimes, also fingerspelling, viz., Finland, Ireland, Norway, Rumania, Sweden and the Soviet Union. The Belgian correspondent reports: 'Not yet, but a workgroup is constructing a proposal for it. Among the more educated deaf, there is a growing awareness that some kind of signed Dutch should be adopted.' Ten countries state only that no such system exists, whereas five mention an unofficial existence with so many words, namely: East Germany, Hungary, Switzerland, Czechoslovakia and the United Kingdom. Regarding the existence of such an unofficial version, some interesting comments are made, of which I would like to quote a few. The German Swiss answer reads:

> Die Gehörlosen brauchen unter sich neben Sprechen und Ablesen ihre Einzelgebärden. Von einem gebärdeten Deutsch kann kaum gesprochen werden.

> (Apart from speech and speech reading, the deaf among themselves use single signs. One can hardly speak of a signed German.)

In other words: using signs with some speech does not warrant the conclusion of the existence of signed German. From Czechoslovakia comes the answer:

> We do not have our own sign language, and therefore also no dictionary. What we do have is unofficially signed Czech or Slovak learned by the deaf in the schools as a matter of course. The signs are different in the different schools. Included in part are fingerspelling and speech and speech reading.

The Portuguese answer reads:

> As far as I know, only once has some kind of signed Portuguese been systematically employed . . . a deaf person . . . used to teach deaf adults to read and write at the National Deaf Association in Lisbon. He is no longer teaching now. We have recorded some sentences in signed Portuguese but we have never analysed them carefully.

As far as the communication of the deaf amongst themselves and with the hearing is concerned: where a true sign language is reported to be in existence, it is obviously used among the deaf. This is the case in Austria, Belgium, Denmark, Finland, France, Norway, Rumania, Sweden, Switzerland, the Soviet Union, the United Kingdom and Yugoslavia. As an alternative, e.g. for more formal occasions or in communication with hearing interpreters and so on, these countries report the possible use of the signed spoken language with speech. In Bulgaria, Belgium, the Germanies, Hungary, Ireland and the Netherlands this latter type of communication is reported to be the usual mode for all communication of the deaf. All countries report the use of speech-only, or of speech with some signs or gestures in the communication with the hearing: a few add that in some instances the help of an interpreter is desirable. The only exception is Luxembourg, where the questionnaire was forwarded by the addressee to an anonymous speech therapist who claims that the adult deaf always use speech only even amongst themselves. I have written asking this person to please identify her or himself and to verify that this is not a mistake, but have received no answer. From other sources I am quite sure that the answers given about Luxembourg are biased; this is the only instance where this assumption had to be made.

As far as interpreting for the deaf is concerned: this is done in the country's own sign language or in the signed version of its spoken language, depending on the circumstances, in Denmark, Finland, Norway, Rumania, Scotland, Sweden, the Soviet Union, the United Kingdom and Yugoslavia, probably also in France; whereas the signed spoken language, usually with speech, is used for interpreting in Austria, Belgium, Bulgaria, the Germanies, Hungary, Ireland, The Netherlands, Rumania and Czechoslovakia. In The Netherlands research has been initiated to improve the status and quality of the interpreting. Again Luxembourg reports that interpreters use speech-only; obviously this can hardly be taken seriously. The other countries leave this part of the questionnaire unanswered.

This concludes a short survey of the information regarding the first, general part of the questionnaire on the status and the situation of Sign in the different European countries. I would like to try and come to a few conclusions, as follows:

Firstly, I would like to come back to the distinction between a true sign language and a signed spoken language. This distinction was explained briefly in the questionnaire, with reference to ASL and SE. For most linguists this distinction is clear; I am not sure it was clear to all those who were confronted with it for the first time, and from some of the answers I am quite sure that the recognition of the actual presence of the two as separate phenomena is even more difficult. There appears to be a relation between research and the recognition of the presence of a true sign language; in other words, only careful study of the structure of the communication of the deaf can establish whether the presence of true features of visual communication warrant the distinction between the two: an ASL-like and a SE-like system. From the evidence given, the presumption must be that the more research is carried out, the more evidence for the presence of a true sign language is found, or – the other way around – little or no research can lead easily enough to the statement that only some sort of signed version of the spoken language exists. I shall come back to the possibility that this might be true in some instances after all, due to the sign-suppressive influence of oral education, while dealing with part two of the questionnaire.

My second conclusive remark on this first part is closely related to the first one, and concerns the actual blending of features of visual communication with those of the spoken language, or – if one prefers – the interference between the two. There is a gradual transition in fact between true sign languages and the spoken language of the country involved; in most instances the two extremes prove to be theoretical constructs in fact; very rarely, or so is my impression, do European deaf use either one in a pure way. The fact that almost all the deaf use a mixture of the two seems to me to be the most challenging feature of future research, and certainly not one to be dismissed as impure and uninteresting. Theoretically oriented research in monolingual systems had to come first, no doubt, but applied research should turn to the complicated facts. I fully agree with Jean-Noel Dreillard who writes in *Coup d'Oeil* of December 1980:

> Je suis frappé par le nombre de personnes préparant des mémoires, thèses ou rapports sur les sourds, leur communication, leur vie, . . . et qui n'ont jamais mis les pieds dans un Foyer de Sourds, jamais assisté à une séance de langage gestuel. On reste dans le domain de l'intellectualisme, on ne descend pas dans la réalité de la vie des sourds. (83)
> (I am struck by the number of people preparing studies, theses or reports on the deaf, their communication or way of life, who have never put a foot

into a deaf club, never attended a talk on sign language. They remain in a domain of intellectualism and do not come down to the realities of the life of the deaf.)

This is hardly the moment to start delving into the problem of bilingual interference from a linguistic, psycho- or neurolinguistic point of view – the basis for such an approach was laid at the Dahlem Conference in Berlin last year (Bellugi and Studdert-Kennedy, 1980). I shall confine myself to the remark that, psychologically speaking, interference occurs at every point where psychological organisation takes place, and that it does not have to be negative in itself at all. Only when interference remains unsolved is it harmful, but where it is functionally integrated in the organism, it is a positive and enriching feature. The ways adult deaf solve their communicative problems should be a matter of study with this in mind.

Finally, I would like to conclude this section by quoting a very concise description of an actual situation, viz., the one in Scotland. Mary Brennan reports:

A recognisable type of signing called 'Signed English' is used, but it may be used in different ways by differing people. Signed English generally uses speech and speech reading and incorporates fingerspelling. Deaf people might use it without speech. Generally, English word order is followed, but the morphological changes are ignored.

I believe this to be an exemplary description of a great number of actual practices. It certainly fits the Dutch situation, the one I obviously know best. I might add: Dutch word order is usually followed, but apparently rule governed simplified syntactic registers are used, such as omitting function words. Some of you will term this a spoken language-biased approach, so let me continue by saying that it stands to reason to hypothesise that these rules originate in the basic principles of visual communication, for example, the replacement of grammatical items used in speech by systematic manual, facial and body symbols.

I now come to the second part of the questionnaire, specifically investigating present-day educational use of sign in Europe. I shall have to leave undiscussed the employment of a number of other manual techniques and devices, reported upon in the questionnaire, such as fingerspelling, cued speech, Mund-Hand Verfahren (Mouth-hand system), Paget-Gorman-like artificial systems, and the like, to concentrate on the use of Sign in a strict sense only.

The organisation of this specific part of the questionnaire is as follows. First, a short introduction explains that its sole purpose is the correct assessment of the educational situation as related to Sign. The correspondents are asked to disregard possible negative attitudes towards signing because of its alleged interference with language learning and speech proficiency, and not to pass judgement in any way, but to make their inventory of existing practices as complete as possible.

The first set of questions enquires about the official standpoints either of the departments of education or of the schools, concerning the following alternatives: (1) strict oralism with no signing accepted, (2) moderate oralism with signing ignored or tolerated, (3) acceptance of both oralism and combined methods, including signs, and, finally, (4) both positive acceptance and use of sign.

Lastly, all the following questions of the questionnaire work out these options in greater detail, asking more or less exhaustively for the specific circumstances under which Sign is used and the techniques involved, and, about any recent changes in attitude. Since most correspondents elaborate more extensively on the first set of questions regarding the standpoints in general, and since these answers are best suited to give an overall picture, I shall concentrate on a summary of these answers, and only occasionally deal with the details of the rest, leaving most of it for a longer publication later on.

There appears to be some sort of a continuum of possibilities between the two extremes: strict oralism for all deaf education on the one hand, and incorporation of Sign throughout the whole educational system for everyone on the other, with Luxembourg at the one end and the Scandinavian countries at the other. Leaving aside the Luxembourg answer, the strictest oralism is found in the German and Dutch speaking countries, all of them with a long oral tradition. Generally speaking, in those countries signing is used only for the multiply handicapped deaf child and sometimes reserved for the mentally retarded only. The correspondent of East Germany writes:

Bei der Bildung und Erziehung gehörloser Kinder (ausser bei gehörlosen Hilfsschülern) spielt die Gebärde keine Rolle. Die Lautsprache wird hier durch das Fingeralphabet unterstützt.

(In the education of deaf children, except the multiply handicapped deaf, Sign does not play any role. Here, speech is supported by fingerspelling.)

West Germany: 'The officially documented standpoint in the Federal Republic of Germany is oral and relates negatively to signing.' The correspondent of German speaking Switzerland reports the exclusive use of the classical German speech method, notwithstanding the fact that German Switzerland has many regional dialect varieties which make speech reading for the deaf a very difficult task. He continues:

Die Kinder in den Gehörlosenschulen . . . haben auf Gebärden aufbauende Verstäbdigungssystem entwickelt die höchstens toleriert, aber keineswegs studiert, gefördert, and festgehalten werden.

(The children in the schools for the deaf . . . have developed systems for mutual understanding based on signs: these systems are at best tolerated but in no way studied, promoted and documented.)

Belgium: 'There is no standpoint of the Department of Education but most schools pretend or try to be strictly oral.' The situation is more or less the same in the Netherlands. Apart from the German speaking countries and the Low Countries, a similar situation is reported for Hungary: 'There is strict oralism for teachers. Body language is accepted; the traditional Hungarian signs are used by the pupils only out of the classroom among themselves.' The same goes for Ireland: 'All the schools are strictly oral, however, the two major schools (one for each sex) in Dublin each have a small number of pupils with additional handicaps who are taught by combined methods.' Also Bulgaria and Portugal: 'All schools are oral; one of them is beginning to change now.' And – finally – Italy, although the information given for that country is somewhat vague.

Next in line on the contimuum are a number of countries where oralism is not viewed as the only means for normal deaf pupils and Sign is not reserved for spastic, autistic, dysphasic or mentally retarded deaf only. To begin with, there is a noteworthy difference between the other German speaking countries and Austria, where moderate oralism prevails, but 'no school is oral-only, and Sign with speech is used in secondary school'. A striking difference is the one between the two Switzerlands, as reported by the French-Swiss reporter; she characterises the attitude towards Sign 'plutôt positive' (rather positive), and notices some changes to which I shall come back shortly. Czechoslovakia reports officially moderate oralism with signing ignored, but 'in fact signs are used in different ways by different teachers'. The Soviet Union's standpoint reads:

> The system of education of deaf children in the USSR envisages the use of the spoken language (oral, written form and fingerspelling) as the main means of teaching. Sign language is an auxiliary means in the process of education.

Unfortunately, most of the detailed questions remain unanswered. A similar standpoint, but in greater detail, is reported for Rumania: 'Sign language and signs are auxiliary means used by our teachers in different ways, underlying the oral language for an efficient teaching.' '. . . the indivudual particularities of the pupils challenge the selection of the best ways to communicate with them.' The Rumanian report goes on to say that signs and fingerspelling are always used in relation to speech and that all schools use combined methods. The same is true for Bulgaria. The United Kingdom reports no official standpoint, but an encouragement towards moderate oralism. 'Individual schools, particularly head teachers, decide. Just under 42% of the schools for the deaf have some manual classes, but only two are exclusively manual.' Yugoslavia just states briefly: seven schools are strictly oral, seventeen are combined. As stated before, the most advanced standpoint is taken by the Scandinavian countries, including Finland. To start quoting the latter:

> All methods of education are approved of. Individual teachers have a wide latitude of choice in methodological matters and can neither be forced to use Sign nor be forbidden to do so. The use of Sign is supposed to be an aid in teaching Finnish and Swedish.
>
> While teachers of the deaf are not formally required to have any knowledge of manual communication, nearly all of them have at some time received instruction in manual skills and use signing to some extent. Sign language is at present also taught to future teachers of the deaf.

Finally, let me quote Denmark's Britta Hansen for the best summary of this standpoint:

> All schools for the deaf have education in the use of Sign Language and Sign for the teachers and the parents. Teachers of the deaf today recognise Sign Language as a language. Only a few hearing teachers know Sign Language fully enough to use it for teaching Danish, but most learn to master a pidgin form of Sign Language/Danish, and that is used all over Denmark. Research and courses in Sign Language are fully supported by the schools and the teachers.

I shall have to leave my description of the continuum from oral-only to Sign here, coming back to some countries in the context of other points, and regretting in passing, the fact that I did not receive enough information from some others as yet to make the picture a complete one.

The next point I want to discuss is that of a change in attitude emerging from the data. There is no change in favour of oralism, and there is an atmosphere of change in the other direction all over Europe. Let me again support this with some quotes from the answers. Loncke from Belgium writes:

> For one or two years some schools are beginning to consider combined methods while others are examining their oral standpoint. Three schools are studying the principles of TC without yet practising it. A real change is going on.

I can testify to a similar tendency in some schools in Holland. West Germany states:

> Sign Language is discussed at present. About July 1981 there will be a statement by representatives of the deaf, of the teachers and of the parents.

and furthermore:

> In Hamburg there is a movement in which the unofficial standpoint is relating more neutrally or positively to Sign.

Clear-cut changes are reported by Madebrink for Sweden. She writes:

> The basic educational-political approach changes in 1969 from the predominantly oral to a combined system with the introduction of new curricula. At that time, mostly Signed Swedish was used. From 1975 there has been a change in the direction of true bilingualism.

This fits Hansen's statement for Denmark:

> Teachers of the deaf today recognise Sign Language as a language, and bilingual education based upon sign language and Danish is being started in some of the schools, especially where deaf teachers are employed.

In French-speaking Switzerland, things are also changing:

> Jusqu'en 1978, l'enseignement . . . relevait de l'oralisme "tempéré". Création en 1975 . . . d'une commission d'étude de la langue des sourds et en 1978 ouverture d'ateliers dans lesquels des enseignants sourds apprennent aux entendants la langue des signes et la Française signée propre: aux diverses régions de la Suisse Française.

> (Until 1978, the teaching reflected moderate oralism. In 1975 a commission was founded to study the language of the deaf; in 1978 workshops were started where deaf teachers teach sign language to hearing people and the signs used in the different regions of French Switzerland.)

Even German speaking Switzerland reports a noticeable tendency towards more manualism in the schools. Yugoslavia's Zvonko states briefly: 'We follow the new philosophy of total communication.' Five countries list specifically a total of 38 schools which recently have changed their methods towards total communication: besides Yugoslavia, also Denmark, West Germany, Scotland, Sweden, French Switzerland. Concluding the discussion of the change of atmosphere, I would like to quote Mary Brennan of Scotland again at length:

> . . . There is no official policy. Decisions on policy are taken by the head teacher, usually in conjunction with the local authority and sometimes

after discussion with the Scottish Education Department." "Before 1977 all schools (except one using Paget-Gorman) used oral methods. The change to TC occurred as follows: 1977, one school; 1978, one school; 1979, two schools; 1980, one school; 1981, one school. Of these, two had previously used some manual methods." "The schools which have been using TC for some time tend to be more flexible in their use of BSL in some contexts. Most schools accept the use of BSL by the children, but the teachers themselves do not use it. . . .

There remain a few short points to be mentioned, before I can summarise the final section of the questionnaire and also the first part of my presentation. First: there appears to be a growing influence from the adult deaf communities and organisations: five countries volunteer this information, viz. Belgium, France, West Germany, The Netherlands and French- and German-speaking Switzerland. Typical in this respect is the remark that the better educated adult deaf who have been abroad are demanding better solutions. Another example: the adult deaf in The Netherlands are increasingly very assertive in claiming their rights, including improved communication with some of the schools. A similar standpoint and growing influence of parents are noted for a number of countries. Secondly, many correspondents point to the fact that often the situation differs from school to school and even from teacher to teacher, so as to make it almost impossible to talk about a generally accepted standpoint in all instances. As Loncke puts it for Belgium: 'It is impossible to give a consistent view of "the" schools in Belgium'. Thirdly, and finally, there remains the difficulty of the distinction between a true sign language and a signed version of the spoken language, as discussed in the first part. In evaluation the answers on this point in this section the same caution must be taken again. Some correspondents do not seem to be too familiar with the distinction itself, and even if some others are, they are unable to supply exact information. A true bilingual situation in which an authentic sign language is actually used is reported only for Denmark and Sweden. In all other instances, Sign – if used at all in an educational context – is either explicitly affirmed to be the signed version of the spoken language or implicitly presupposed to be only that.

I would now like to come to a few conclusions about this section which may also introduce the next one, on perspectives for the future. Many conclusions are evident enough from the information given so far. There is definitely some historical influence, there are great extremes in European attitudes towards Sign, there is a tendency away from pure oralism, there is pressure on schools from outside, specifically from deaf adults and parents of deaf children, and there is a preference for the type of manualism which closely parallels the spoken language. Two concluding remarks need a little elaboration.

The first remark runs parallel to the conclusion of the previous section. There appears to be a close relation between sign language research on the one hand and changes in educational attitudes towards the use of Sign. Wherever research finds out facts about Sign, its status is heightened, and its possible usefulness in overall educational contexts – not only the ones related to the multiply handicapped – is explored. Scandinavia leads the way, followed closely by the United Kingdom, and then by a great number of other countries where some research people are beginning to have their influence upon educators. Such influence can only be fruitful if the communication comes from both sides. I shall raise this point in the next section. The second remark concerns the more or less essential role of speech and speech reading as a function of the communication of the deaf adults among themselves. It is clear that some countries and schools are more oral than others; this has its consequences for the combined use of speech and Sign as opposed to the use of Sign-only. Deaf people in the Germanies and the Low Countries cannot communicate without also using speech as a rule; it is evident that the situation is different in countries with a well developed sign language. This relates closely to decisions in the future in favour of true bilingualism versus compromises in the form of signed versions of spoken languages.

2. The Prospects for the Future

Regarding the prospects for the future of Sign in the European education of the deaf, I would like to confine myself to making the following observations: In many places educators are beginning to have their doubts about the absolute value of the oral approach and are showing an increasing willingness to accept some sort of manualism throughout, but most of them are uncertain as to what to choose. On the one hand, speech proficiency undoubtedly remains a high priority for integration in adult society for most of their pupils, on the other hand, speech-only is clearly inadequate as the only communicative mode, not only later on but also during school years in a majority of the cases. Because they want the best for their charges, teachers do not like to take risks and therefore shun sudden changes. Schools do better as a rule with gradual evolution than with a revolution under outside pressure. Gradual changes in the educational systems can only be realised by close cooperation between educators themselves and outside help. Leaving aside the growing influence of parent associations, adult deaf organisations and other groups, I shall concentrate on the communication between school and research only.

One of the fields of recent research which will influence the teaching of deaf children in the near future is the study of pre-speech development and the beginnings of language, including the role of early interaction and communication between the child and his caregivers, usually his mother. This has been studied extensively for hearing children (see, e.g. Bates, *et al.*, 1979, Bullowa, 1979), and also for the deaf (see, e.g. Goldin-Meadow, 1977). As far as the latter are concerned, there is no doubt that during the first three years of life a visual communication system with features of a true language comes into being between a deaf child and his parents at home. Valuable communicative skills, a vocabulary and grammar thus developed are thereafter neglected, frustrated, and left unused by preschools practically everywhere. At some places, however, home training programs are being developed in which deaf children and their parents acquire a system of linguistic communicative skills based on a first vocabulary and simple syntax, using Sign or Sign plus speech in a well organised and uniform way. In close cooperation with these programms, preschools can take over, continue and expand them. This way schools have the opportunity to start renewing their educational program gradually and from the lower level up.

The basic choice for the more distant future is probably not the one between oralism and a system like total communication; it might well be the one between a monolingual versus a bilingual approach. It would take more than another presentation such as this to do justice to all the aspects of such a basic choice. The day-by-day choices for tomorrow, next term and next year are not as clear-cut. There appears to be a tendency to go from oral-only to speech with speech-supportive means such as fingerspelling or cued speech; from those there is a movement in the direction of the use of Sign to better disambiguate the spoken word; next comes a signed version of the spoken language either with speech or without it, depending on the circumstances; and, finally, the continuum develops from signed Danish, Swedish, English and so on to Danish Sign Language, Swedish Sign Language, British Sign Language, etc. At that final stage, the choice in favour of a bilingual educational philosophy is a fact. Most educators are weary of the consequences involved; it will take a long time before they get that far, if they ever will. Schools need assistance in deciding what is best for the individual child and what should be adopted as their general educational philosophy. Early identification, differential diagnosis and the like are research supported tools not in question here; others that are equally important are. Use of a signed version of the spoken language and courses in Sign, for example, need such basic tools as a well organised dictionary and fundamental knowledge about the interference and the integration of Sign and word. Use of a true sign language in educational contexts is simply impossible as long as such a language remains unidentified and its grammar and lexicon unaccounted for. Only a few countries in Europe are reaching that point now as we can hear from them at this congress. From their pioneering efforts and their beginning cooperation between research and classroom work we, the others, hope to be guided and helped in working out our short term and long term choices.

BRITISH SIGN LANGUAGE AND WEST INDIAN CREOLE

V. Edwards and P. Ladd

Introduction

The present paper explores some of the many similarities between two minority languages in British – British Sign Language (BSL) used in the normal social interaction of deaf people, and West Indian Creole spoken by migrants who arrived from the Caribbean in the 1950's and 1960's. Until very recently sign languages have received remarkably little attention and there has been great reluctance to accord them linguistic status. Yet comparison with creoles, another class of languages seriously neglected by linguists in the past, shows many striking parallels in structure, development and sociolinguistic variation. Of particular interest is the fact that many of the areas of structural similarity between BSL and West Indian Creole have traditionally been considered obstacles to assigning linguistic status to sign languages. Similarities in attitudes towards the two varieties will also be considered and it will be suggested that the low status of sign languages, and the reluctance of linguists to study them, can be explained more properly in social rather than linguistic terms. Equally important, developments in the education of West Indian children provide a useful point of reference for the assessment of certain aspects of educational practice in schools for the deaf.

The linguistic status of West Indian Creoles and BSL Popular attitudes

There is a long tradition of negative attitudes towards non-standard varieties and only in recent years have people tried to explain different varieties in terms of social and historical development rather than as a result of laziness and stupidity. Chambre (1858) describes the speech of West Indians of African descent as a 'barbarous idiom' and, even today, popular opinion still tends to be misinformed. One report on West Indian children in Birmingham (ATEPO, 1970) describes their language as 'babyish', 'careless and slovenly', 'lacking proper grammar' and even 'very relaxed like the way they walk'. In an experiment reported in Edwards (1976), 40% of the teacher sample agreed with the statement that 'West Indian English does not provide an adequate basis for abstract thought'.

A perusal of the literature on sign language reveals some striking parallels. Cochrane (1871) suggests that when the deaf mute expresses his thoughts and ideas in writing, there follows a 'violation of the rules of syntax; an utter disregard of grammatical forms, the inversion of different elements . . . a jargon of words'. More recently, Van Uden (1970) has expressed the opinion that sign language 'keeps the thinking slow', is 'much too concrete and broken in pieces'.

Attitudes of West Indians and the deaf

It is interesting to note the effect which such negative attitudes have had on Creole and BSL users alike. Hymes (1971) comments with reference to Creole speakers, 'Not the least of the crimes of colonialism has been to persuade the colonised that they, or the ways in which they differ, are inferior – to convince the stigmatised that the stigma is deserved'. One of the common prejudices transmitted to West Indians through an English modelled education system is that the way they speak is 'bad talk' and that they will never amount to anything if they 'talk like Quashie'. It is therefore not surprising that West Indians, and particularly educated West Indians, are among the severest critics of their own speech. Many deny all knowledge of Creole.

Similarly negative views are found among the deaf community. Many deaf people, particularly deaf professionals, consider BSL as 'broken', 'ugly' and 'telegraphic'. Deaf people educated at the country's only deaf grammar school frequently deny that they need, know or use any form of sign language. Some have been observed to studiously avoid using their hands in public places and on public transport, even at the expense of not being able to understand each other. It seems highly probable that such negative attitudes towards BSL will have a profound effect on the self-concept of deaf people. This is certainly suggested by the reaction of some deaf people in London, 1979 to seeing the first ever English film sub-titled for deaf people. They commented afterwards that they had never realised that hearing people talk rubbish too.

It soon becomes apparent that the deaf, West Indians and many other non-standard English speaking groups tend to have very ambivalent attitudes towards their language. On the one hand, they recognise the prestige of the standard and the low status of their own speech; on the other hand, they feel their own speech is more sincere and socially attractive than the standard. Thus in the West Indian community, Creole remains the language of sincerity and is reserved for expressing strong emotion. It is something very personal and private and can be used most effectively for excluding outsiders. There is evidence emerging that BSL is also viewed as a language of sincerity. Comments about the truthfulness, trustworthiness and lack of pompousness of BSL users have been elicited by Llewellyn-Jones, *et al* (1979) from deaf subjects who viewed video recordings of the same monologue in BSL and Signed English.

Attitudes of scholars
Deep seated popular prejudice has had an extremely damaging effect on attempts to look objectively at either creoles or sign languages. Until the 1960's many young linguists were advised 'not to waste their time on such peripheral subjects, but to study "real languages" if they wished to get on in the academic world' (De Camp, 1971). Reluctance to research into sign language can probably be traced back to the syllogism which permeates the work of Sapir and Bloomfield that (i) all people use gestures; (ii) gestures iconically reveal meaning and therefore; (iii) 'The Sign Language' (sic) is universal. Sapir (1921:21) classes deaf sign languages together with Indian sign systems and signalling at sea as 'vague symbolisms'. Bloomfield (1939:39) goes further and suggests that sign languages 'are merely developments of ordinary gesture, and that any or all complicated or not immediately intelligible gestures are based on the conventions of ordinary speech'. One of the consequences of scholars as influential as Sapir and

Bloomfield denying linguistic status to signing, was that research in this area was seriously neglected for the next thirty years or more.

Although language scientists throughout the forties and fifties recognised the validity of all language varieties, serious study of pidgins, creoles and non-standard varieties of English finally got off the ground only with the realisation by American linguists of the potentially damaging effect of statements being made in the sixties by educators and psychologists about Black English Vernacular (BEV). The findings of Labov (1976), Wolfram (1969) and others leave no doubt that, although BEV does not follow the rules of standard American English, it is none the less a perfectly adequate rule-governed system. In other words, we are dealing with a question of difference, not deficit. The arguments proposed by American linguists have since been applied to a number of other situations, including West Indian Creole (V. Edwards, 1979; Sutcliffe, in press) and non-standard British dialects (Trudgill, 1975).

Similar developments have started to take place in the study of sign languages. Bellugi (1976), for instance, reports that the research undertaken by various linguists in the U.S.A. 'shows that American Sign Language is indeed a language in every sense of the word'. There is now a clear understanding that grammatical features like copulas which are missing from sign languages are by no means universal in spoken languages and cannot therefore be used in denying linguistic status to signing. It is also widely accepted that adequacy should be discussed in terms of syntax rather than lexis. The fact that BSL borrows technical vocabulary extensively from English, in the same way as English borrows from Latin or Greek is no longer felt to suggest that BSL is in any way inferior (cf. Crystal and Craig, 1978:149). There remains, however, a certain 'audiocentric' bias in the approach of a number of scholars to sign language which suggests that the full implications of 'difference not deficit' have not yet been fully explored.

The question of iconicity represents an excellent case in point. Whereas spoken language is essentially arbitrary, with little or no relationship to the form of what it is said to represent, sign language is often described as iconic or pictorial. There is a limit to what can be represented pictorially in signs and this is therefore felt to restrict the potential of signing as a language. This assumption of iconicity, however, can be shown to be false. Although we would expect a greater degree of iconicity for visual signs than auditory words, signs tend to become more arbitrary as times goes by (Frishberg, 1975). The fact that hearing people do not understand sign language and frequently make wildly inaccurate guesses at the meaning of individual signs (Bellugi, 1976) also throws great suspicion on the notion of iconicity.

Nonetheless many discussions of sign language are based on the a priori assumption of iconicity. Crystal and Craig (1978:149) point to the difficulties of retaining an 'unambiguously iconic relationship between referent and sign' as sign language vocabulary increases. Tervoort (1961) argues that the imitational iconic, syncretic or concrete meaning of signs impedes the evolution to abstract usage, and points to the rarity of metaphorical uses of signs. Various writers are also preoccupied with the extent to which sign languages are context dependent, a state which they presumably consider to be a function, in part at least, or the iconic nature of sign language lexis.

Crystal and Craig (op.cit.) for instance, draw on examples of what Cohen, *et al.* (1977) call 'covariance' to illustrate their assertion that 'many signs are dependent on the immediate context for a correct interpretation' (p. 147). Among the examples of covariance cited are the variation of the sign 'carry' with what is being carried a feature which is in fact to be found in the Amerindian language, Hopi; and the dependence of certain sign senses on facial expressions, although kinesic features are now widely recognised for syntactic functions such as the modification of verbs.

Examples such as these point to areas of misconception about natural sign languages such as ASL and BSL. It is an object of concern that much work had led to inaccurate conclusions, and that these conclusions have been widely published and seldom challenged. Major research projects which resulted in a detailed description of BEV were necessary in order to justify linguists' assertions that non-standard languages and dialects should be judged on their own terms rather than in comparison with standard varieties. By the same token, considerably more research into the structure of sign language will be necessary to bring into question assumptions so deeply entrenched that they are thought to be fact.

Social parallels

The discussion of the previous section can leave no doubt as to the low status of either BSL or West Indian Creoles as linguistic varieties. In view of the widely reported findings that attitudes towards a particular variety tend to reflect attitudes towards users of that variety (Giles and Powesland, 1975; J. Edwards, 1979), it should come as no surprise to find that both deaf and West Indians constitute extremely low status groups within society.

The low status of West Indians in Britain

West Indians in Britain suffer discrimintion at the levels of recruitment and promotion. Their median weekly wage is substantially below that of white workers and they are concentrated in low status jobs. Their poor economic situation inevitably affects the kind of housing in which they live and sharing, overcrowding and a lack of basic amenities are the norm for disproportionate numbers of black people (Smith, 1976).

Certain British psychologists have suggested that the low level of achievement of black people can be explained in terms of a genetic deficiency, but by and large, the reactions of the academic community to the question of possible racial differences in intelligence have been rather muted. This is in marked contrast with the response of various American psychologists and educators. Herskovitz (1957), for instance, reports that until the late 1930's the most common hypothesis proposed to account for Negro speech was that it was 'the blind groping of minds too primitive in modes of speech beyond their capabilities'. Writers like Hess and Shipman (1968) recommend intervention aimed at the 'resocialisation' of black children, thereby imputing that their family life is inadequate. The ethnocentricism contained in statements such as these, and the unsound methodology which allowed their formulation have been widely commented upon (see, for instance, J. Edwards, 1979).

The low status of deaf people
Figures relating to the employment of the deaf do not exist, a fact which some commentators have taken to reflect the lack of concern at government level (Loach, 1978). From all informed estimates, however, a 10% white collar figure (compared with 8% of black people and 40% of the rest of the population) would appear to be an absolute maximum. Furthermore, jobs are sometimes refused deaf people for reasons which employers or trade unions mistakenly think must be as a result of deafness itself. Such a case is the decision to withdraw HGV licences from deaf people, although the level of noise inside a heavy goods vehicle is such that a hearing driver may have no advantage over the deaf (NUD unpublished report to Department of Transport, 1978).

Society obviously does not discrimate against deaf and black people in the same way, although the net effect may not be very different. There is certainly widespread evidence of the same kind of patronising and insensitive behaviour towards the deaf as there is towards black people. In the late nineteenth century Bell strongly discouraged deaf people from marrying each other (Bruce, 1973), a position endorsed as recently as 1974 by Van Uden, the head teacher of the biggest deaf school in Europe (*British Deaf News,* 1974:342). The same head teacher also proposed closing deaf clubs and making the use of sign language in public illegal. Firth (1966) unconsciously compared the deaf with animals – 'The dog knows when we are going out for a walk, and the deaf know when someone is upset or up to something'. There are frequent reports that deaf parents of deaf children have been completely ignored and excluded from National Deaf Children's Society branches, from school PTA's and from deaf children's mother and toddlers' groups. But undoubtedly the most disturbing example of the disregard for deaf people as full and feeling human beings is the recent discovery of operations to sterilise deaf women without their knowledge or consent (Montgomery, Hay and Holmes, 1979).

Sign Languages as Creoles
Many of the misconceptions about sign languages can be attributed to their comparison with English and other European languages. If, however, sign languages are compared with creoles many striking similarities become apparent. We will begin this section with a comparison of the structural similarities between BSL and West Indian Creole. We can usually follow the framework proposed by Namir and Schlesinger (1978) in their discussion of the problems of sign language grammar, since it is clearly of interest if those features of sign language traditionally considered problematic are in fact shared by spoken languages. Having established structural parallels we will go on to discuss the historical development of both varieties in an attempt to explain why such similarities should exist.

Linguistic parallels
The discussion which follows is restricted to BSL and West Indian Creole and aims to present illustrative evidence of our claim that BSL should be recognised as a creole rather than simply cataloguing all the similarities which can be found. Examples can, however, be multiplied by reference to

other creoles and we hope that in this respect our description will complement that offered by Fischer (1978a) of the parallels between American Sign Language (ASL) and Hawaiian Creole. We shall adopt the convention of quoting West Indian Creole in lower case and BSL in upper case.

Inflection

Both West Indian Creole and BSL are almost entirely inflection free. Plurality in nouns is either indicated by context –

de bwoy got two car
BOY TWO CAR HAVE

or by the use of the plural marker de . . . dem or ALL – Them

de people – dem; de bwoy – dem
PEOPLE ALL – THEM; BOY ALL – THEM

By the same token, possession is indicated by the relative positions of possessor and possessed rather than inflectionally as in English

de girl book; de man hat
GIRL BOOK; MAN HAT

Verbs do not inflect for tense or person, and meaning is usually dependent on context

De bwoy walk to school yesterday
YESTERDAY BOY WALK SCHOOL

De girl come now
NOW GIRL COME

However, both varieties have a well developed aspect system which differs significantly from that of English. Both can make a perfective/non-perfective distinction:

De man *en* go home
MAN GO HOME *FINISH*

Both can also make a continuative/non-continuative distinction

Me *a* read de book
ME BOOK READ (*circular movement*)

In addition, BSL makes use of a wide range of aspect markers which have been identified in ASL as predisposition, susceptive, incessant, frequentative, intensive, approximative, resultative, iterative and protractive (Bellugi and Klima, 1979:250–260).

Parts of speech

Namir and Schlesinger (1978) point out the frequency with which the same sign will be used for different parts of speech in spoken language. It is interesting to note that this is also a feature of West Indian Creoles. Take, for instance,

me a ready
ME READY (circular movement)
(I am getting ready: here ready/READY is a verb)
me ready
ME READY (short sharp movement)
(I am ready: here ready/READY is an adjective)

By the same token thief/THIEF can be used as a noun or a verb.

Omissions
Namir and Schlesinger also point out that when comparing signed utterances with their English translations, many words in the English sentence do not have a corresponding sign. They show, for instance, how various predicates can be omitted, and it is interesting to note that copula deletion is a regular feature of both BSL and West Indian creoles.

de policeman shouting; de teacher happy
POLICEMAN SHOUT-SHOUT; TEACHER HAPPY

Similar 'omissions' can be explained when it is recognised that neither BSL nor West Indian creoles have a passive voice –

De party postpone; de building use all de time
PARTY POSTPONE; BUILDING USE ALL-THE-TIME.

Not all of the omissions listed by Namir and Schlesinger are paralled by West Indian creoles. Function words like 'if' and 'because' occur regularly, as do predicates like 'come' and 'see'. It is interesting to speculate, however, on the extent to which these omissions are due either to the visual modality of signing, or the imperfect glosses which are often provided for the sign language translations (cf. Cicourel, 1978:281).

Other areas of similarity
Several other areas of similarity between BSL and West Indian Creoles are sufficiently striking to be commented upon briefly at this point. Concatenation of verbs, for instance, is a regular feature –

Me see old people running, going, panting fi catch de bus
ME SEE OLD PEOPLE RUNNING, 'RUNNING WITH DIFFICULTY', PANTING BUS CATCH

Topicalisation of verbs can be achieved structurally rather than through intonation as is generally the case in standard English –

A run im run mek im fall down
RUN RUN WELL FALL DOWN
(He fell down because he *ran*)

Reduplication, a feature widely observed in pidgins and creoles all over the world, is to be found in both BSL and West Indian Creoles –

talk – talk; pretty – pretty
TALK-TALK; PRETTY-PRETTY
De plane for ever going up, going up, up, up
PLANE-GO-UP, PLANE-GO-UP HIGHER, PLANE-GO-UP HIGHER STILL

Finally, it is intereting to note that both BSL and Creole treat negation in the same way as non-standard dialects of English and multiple negation is the rule –

Me never see nothing
ME NOT NOTHING SEE
Nobody never see nothing
NOBODY ALL-THEM NOT-SEE NOTHING.

Pidginisation and Creolisation
Pidgins are to found in all parts of the world and arise from contact between people who speak mutually unintelligible languages. They can be said to be

marginal languages which allow certain restricted communication between speakers of different languages. Their vocabulary is a great deal smaller than that of the native languages of their speakers, grammatical structures are more limited, and inflection of nouns and verbs tends to disappear altogether. A creole develops when a pidgin becomes the mother tongue of subsequent generations. It is characterised by a rapid expansion of vocabulary and structures which allows it to meet the communicative needs of its speakers.

The role of children in the creolisation process is critical. Bickerton (1974) argues that when a child is exposed to a pidgin it is logical that he or she should consider this to be a well-formed fully fledged language. He or she may also assume that there is more to the language than is immediately apparent and so may guess at the 'real grammar', creating in the process a language whose grammar is far more complex that that of the pidgin. The similarity between various creoles is thus accountable in terms of the characteristic ways in which young children process their language (Slobin, 1971; Fischer, 1978a). There is certainly a strong match between the kinds of structure which children can cope with from the point of view of cognitive development and the kinds of structure which frequently occur in creoles, and this presumably can be attributed to the absence of adult models.

The development of West Indian Creoles

Good examples of pidginisation and creolisation are to be found in the language varieties spoken in the Caribbean. Large numbers of Africans were transported from West Africa in the seventeenth and eighteenth centuries. They came from many widely differing geographical and linguistic backgrounds and slavers adopted a conscious policy of isolating Africans from the same background. It was essential therefore to develop a common means of communication. The vocabulary base on which they drew was primarily English, but there was marked African influence on both phonology and syntax. Even more interesting in terms of the present discussion, there were features which owe nothing to African or European languages, but are common to pidgins and creoles all over the world.

The situation in the West Indies today can best be described in terms of a continuum between standard West Indian English (a variety very similar to standard British English) and Broad Creole. Individual speakers will command a span of the continuum rather than a point on it. The speech of older, rural West Indians with little formal education will be situated nearer the Broad Creole end of the continuum than that of younger, urban, more educated West Indians. All speakers will use more Creole features in informal than in formal speech. The continuing use of English as the medium of education and government has led some writers (e.g., De Camp, 1971) to speculate that islands like Jamaica are moving towards what might be described as a post-creole continuum. The continuing poverty and high degree of social stratification, however, make other writers (e.g., Cassidy, 1970) think that the situation is likely to continue unchanged for the foreseeable future.

The development of British Sign Language

There are unmistakable parallels between the development of West Indian Creole and the development of sign language used by the deaf. Ferguson (1971) points to the fact that probably all speech communities have registers of a special kind for use with people such as babies, foreigners, and deaf people who cannot readily understand the normal speech of the community. We suggest that the attitude of a person addressing a foreigner, which is a prerequisite of any pidgin development (cf. Ferguson and Debose, 1977) is the same as the attitude to a deaf person.

Documentation on the development of BSL is either sparse or remains to be studied in depth. Any attempt at reconstruction thus involves some degree of speculation and simplification. Nonetheless it would seem reasonable to suggest that the eighteenth century marked an important turning point in the development of a widely understood British sign language with the establishment of the Braidwood schools in various parts of the country. Although they followed an oral modality only policy, they served a very useful social function in bringing together a deaf population which had been very sparsely distributed up to this point. The hearing teacher is likely to have addressed the children in simple pidgin-like structures following the Ferguson pattern outlined above. After school the children would inevitably have turned to signing, and to creolising the pidgin structures which arose from the contact situation of deaf pupils and hearing teachers. This would probably have been frowned upon with the same kind of severity which attended upon Africans trying to remake contact with their own language groups. Nevertheless the language grew and by the time the Church started missions for deaf adults in the 1840's there was probably enough similarity between the various dialects which had grown up for them to achieve mutual intelligibility. Deaf children of deaf parents would obviously have played a critically important part in this creolisation process.

In the nineteenth century there was a growth of schools using a contrived sign language, usually referred to in the literature as Pidgin Signed English (PSE) (see, e.g., Woodward, 1973c) as the mode of instruction. In this variety the syntactic structure follows English but the lexical items are drawn from British Sign Language. As deaf pupils became teachers and even head teachers it became clear that this was the language of upward mobility, and consequently it became the prestige variety to the extent where a diglossic situation could be said to obtain. PSE was used in formal situations, teaching conferences, church services and the like while BSL remained the language of informal conversation. From the 1880 Congress of Milan, however, sign language was once again banned in schools for the deaf and the idea of English as the only language worthy of learning became more and more deeply entrenched.

The current situation is more complex still. The twentieth century has witnessed the formulation of two further contrived sign languages for use in educational settings in Britain. The Paget Gorman Sign System (PGSS), named after its inventors, has very few lexical items from BSL, while Signed Systematic English (SSE) uses many lexical items from BSL but like PGSS, has invented affixes, suffixes, and new signs for articles, prepositions, conjunctions, etc., so that any sentence in English can be exactly mirrored in visual signs. The crucial difference between PSE, on the one hand, and PGSS and SSE, on the other, is that, although all follow English word order, PSE does not use the affixes, suffixes and other additions developed by educators for deaf children. Wherever it does feel the need to mirror spoken English, PSE uses finger spelling to fill the gaps.

A close examination of the signing used by deaf people reveals a continuum which can best be explained diagrammatically:

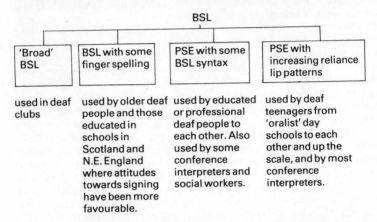

BSL

'Broad' BSL	BSL with some finger spelling	PSE with some BSL syntax	PSE with increasing reliance lip patterns
used in deaf clubs	used by older deaf people and those educated in schools in Scotland and N.E. England where attitudes towards signing have been more favourable.	used by educated or professional deaf people to each other. Also used by some conference interpreters and social workers.	used by deaf teenagers from 'oralist' day schools to each other and up the scale, and by most conference interpreters.

It might be imagined that the all pervasive influence of English would have resulted in the decreolisation of BSL by the late twentieth century. The special situation of deaf people, however, strongly militates against such a development. As Woodward (1973c) points out, if only 5–10% of deaf children have deaf parents, 90% will learn sign language in deaf clubs or school dormitories. Most deaf people are thus forced to recreolise BSL in every generation (cf. Fischer, 1978a).

Education
Given that the same distribution of intelligence would be expected in both deaf and West Indian communities as in the rest of the population, the level of underperformance in both communities is disturbing. Educational statistics over the past ten years have consistently shown that West Indians as a group are under-represented in upper streams and exam classes and over-represented in lower streams and non-exam classes (Townsend and Brittan, 1972; Rampton, 1981). The first major analysis of the level of achievement of deaf children was Conrad's (1979) survey of all profoundly deaf school leavers (i.e., children with a hearing loss of more than 85db) in schools for the deaf in the United Kingdom. He found in addition to a low rate of clarity of speech and ability to lip read, a low level of literacy.

It is possible to argue that many of the problems which face both deaf and West Indian children are a function of an educational system which is totally predicated upon the use of standard English. Black children are felt to be less intelligent, less well-behaved and less valuable when speaking a West Indian dialect than when they use British speech (V. Edwards, 1979). Many teachers of the deaf see the use of sign language as indicating slowness or stupidity and some of those who decide that it is useful in the classroom use it only with the classes with greatest learning difficulties. The literature on the education of West Indian children also reveals that teacher reactions are often paradoxical. On the one hand, children are labelled as non-verbal and inarticulate; on the other hand, teachers complain that they talk too much. It is interesting that many teachers of the deaf make similar observations about the children with whom they work – on the one hand, the children are non-verbal and, on the other, they never stop signing.

Attempts at curriculum reform

The recognition of non-standard varieties of English as valid linguistic systems in their own right has been slow in British education. There is nevertheless a growing feeling that the language or dialect which children bring with them to the classroom is more likely to facilitate than hinder the acquisition of standard English. The ILEA, for instance, in a radical appraisal of its policy on multicultural education, advocates the use of Creole in drama and poetry. And writers like McGuigan, Hoyle, Richmond and Griffin (see V. Edwards, 1979, 1980) have demonstrated how dialect can be used to some considerable effect in motivating reluctant readers to both read and write. The early reaction of teachers towards West Indian and other ethnic minority children was to minimise any differences which might exist by pursuing assimilationist policies. Now, however, there is a recognition of cultural and linguistic diversity as a source of enrichment on which the school can build and the presence of black children has stimulated discussion of a range of subjects including the status of non-standard dialects and 'language across the curriculum' which affect the education of all children and not simply those of immigrant origin.

The reservations which have long been expressed about allowing signing in deaf education are generally rationalised in terms of the negative effect which this would be likely to have on children's speech development. Numerous studies have shown, however, that children with a manual background prove better at oral skills than children with an exclusively oralist background (Mindel and Vernon, 1974). It is also interesting to note that deaf adults have long stressed that the use of sign language in education provides a base for motivation of deaf children to use more speech and auditory input, and thus to improve skills in reading and writing English (Ladd, 1978).

Conclusions

It is not difficult to understand the striking similarities between BSL and West Indian Creole if we consider the contact situation which gave rise to them and their subsequent development. The classification of languages such as ASL and BSL provides many interesting insights for linguistic theory on questions as basic as the creation of language, language acquisition and language change which have not been considered in this paper (see Fischer, 1978a; Edwards and Ladd, 1981). Most important for present purposes, however, we find that many of the areas which have long been considered problematic for the analysis of sign language occur quite regularly in spoken language.

We hope that this paper will represent a small contribution to the growing recognition of natural languages developed by the deaf as adequate linguistic systems in their own right. There is obviously an urgent need for a great deal more research before we can begin to come to terms with a linguistic system which demands methods of analysis sometimes very different from those necessary for the spoken languages with which we are more familiar. The need to guard against glottocentric bias is of considerable importance if we are to understand the underlying principles of sign language, and the lessons learned from the 'difference-deficit' debate which surrounded the issue of non-standard dialects of English need to be applied very carefully.

While we would not wish to argue that the situation of deaf children precisely mirrors that of West Indian children there are sufficient social and linguistic similarities for us to suggest that deaf education might very well learn a great deal from the philosophy of tolerance towards linguistic diversity which is developing in British schools largely in response to the arrival of West Indian and other ethnic minority children. Nor should we forget the very positive effects of using children's first language as a means of enhancing self-concept and motivating learning.

THE SPECIFIC SITUATION OF THE FLEMISH DEAF PEOPLE AND THEIR ATTITUDES TOWARDS SIGN LANGUAGE

Filip Loncke

In the last two decades a great deal of change has occurred in opinions about sign language. This change of attitude can be observed at the same time in the academic world, among teachers and among parents of deaf children.

The most obvious of the changing tendencies are undoubtedly these:

1. A decrease in the generally negative public opinion towards sign language and sign communication.
2. An increase of interest by linguistic scientists in previously less well-known communication modes.
3. A greater self-assertiveness in the deaf themselves.

However, one does not find these tendencies in the same degree everywhere. There are clearly many variations depending upon the specific situation of each country. The question to what degree we find them in the Flemish deaf people's situation in Belgium is particularly interesting, because in Belgium the Flemish language itself has also had a rather peculiar sociolinguistic history. The Flemish Language does not exist in fact: rather, it is the way Dutch is spoken in the North of Belgium. This means only some differences in phonological and lexiciological elements. There is no substantial difference between the written language of the North (The Netherlands) and of the South (Flanders in Belgium).

There is a linguistic boundary in Belgium from the East to the West (through Brussels, a bilingual area): the North of which is Dutch-speaking (Flemish), the South is French-speaking. Some people consider this language boundary as being a cultural boundary, between the Roman-inspired and the German-inspired cultural areas in Europe.

However, historically for most of its past, Flanders has been politically dependent upon France. This is why the language of the South (France) gained a higher status, and why it became the language of the aristocracy, the clergy and the new rich.

At the beginning of the 19th century, Dutch (Flemish) in Belgium was banned from all official usage. In the last hundred years, thanks to political action, it has slowly regained an officially equivalent status. Now, in Belgium, the Dutch language is recognised as having the same value as French.

However, some interesting sociolinguistic hierarchial factors still seem to play a role: in bilingual areas there is still an easier switch from Dutch to French than vice versa. In Brussels – the bilingual capital – this is in fact one of the most important political problems.

Flemish politicians in the Brussels area have tried to change this sociolinguistic situation by an active language policy. It has taken a very long time to accept the idea that Dutch (or Flemish) is a language of full value. Only a few decades ago the common opinion about Dutch was low; it was not fit for cultural or scientific purposes. The first Flemish-speaking university only opened in 1930! These old attitudes also had repercussions on everyday education: in some secondary schools, the pupils were forced to communicate in French, even during recreation times. If they dared to speak Flemish, they were reprimanded or even punished.

For anyone who knows the treatment of sign communication in some oral schools, there are clearly certain parallels with the Flemish situation of fifty years ago. In many deaf schools sign communication is still considered to be inferior.

One might expect that the social- political developments in Belgium would have had implications on educational philosophy in schools of the deaf, because there is a general view in Belgium that it is a social crime to make a hierarchy of languages. In fact, it seems it did not. Most schools for the deaf still maintain an extreme oral point of view, including a rejection of sign communication.

The same arguments that were used years ago to demonstrate the inferiority of Flemish in education and culture, seem to be considered still valid for sign language.

One might wonder how it is possible that in Flanders – an area with such a special sociolinguistic background – these opinions about signing are still alive.

We see three reasons for this:
1. Historically in the schools, there is a strong oral tradition with connections with some of the most oral schools in The Netherlands.
2. There is still great general ignorance about the findings of sign language research in other countries.
3. There exists almost no modern psycholinguistic research in the area of sign language. If there is, there is little influence of it on the everyday practice in deaf schools.

It seems that this unfavourable situation need not be necessarily permanent. In Flanders a few changes can be seen:
1. We see a very assertive elite deaf group coming up, as a result of their contacts with deaf people abroad.
2. For the last two years, in some schools for the deaf educators have tended to take a less absolute point of view. There is a realisation that oral education in its purest form cannot be adequate for every deaf child.
3. Collaboration has begun between deaf associations and some psycholinguists. In 1980 a working group of linguists and deaf people started an inventory study of communication in the daily life of the deaf in Flanders (family, work recreation).

As in many other countries, the first concern of deaf people is to gain higher status for sign communication. At this moment, their main effort is directed towards the standardising of the signs in use. This effort remains restricted to a kind of lexicographic description of the signs – standardised signs – that are edited in small dictionaries. It is not the aim that these standardised signs replace the signs that are in use at the moment. What one is trying to do is create a variety of signing that might be called a high-level variety. Clearly there is some similarity to concepts of diglossia (Ferguson, 1959) that was adopted for ASL by Stokoe (1969) (see also Loncke, in press). Stokoe stated that the H-variety of sign communication is very close to the syntax of the spoken language (in the case of ASL: English). In fact, the Flemish deaf who are devising this standardised sign system, use a philosophy that is rather sympathetic towards the H-variety. Rather than a real sign language, they intend a kind of Signed Dutch (or Signed Flemish).

The crucial question is if the aim of the Flemish deaf is realistic. The Flemish deaf state that a pure sign language is less accceptable for a high-level variety, because they think the grammatical rules of the spoken language should be respected. It is clear that this attitude must be understood as a compromise in a country with a strong oral tradition. In Flanders it still appears to be unacceptable to argue for a pure sign language. It seems that this is the real reason why the deaf propose a kind of Signed Dutch, presumably hoping that this will be more easily accepted among educationalists. But implicitly, the inferiority of pure sign languages seems to be assumed. With this whole project, one is in fact doing a kind of language planning. However, merely prescribing a language or linguistic elements such as signs is too simple a conception of language planning. Inherent to visual systems are some psycholinguistic principles which the language planner should respect (Deuchar, 1980). Therefore, language planning should be preceded by sign language research. If new signs are to be proposed, one must respect the formational aspects of the sign language or the sign system already in use. Some newly proposed signs are linguistically acceptable within the existing sign language, while others are not (Battison, 1978). At this moment, however, in Flanders we have no sign language research at all. With what hypotheses, therefore should we work for beginning sign language research in Flanders?

In the following, the term Flemish Sign Language (FlSL) must be considered as a theoretical construct. At this moment, we cannot demonstrate an autonomous and specific Flemish linguistic sign system. But of course the Flemish deaf use signing for their communication amongst themselves. It is very reasonable to assume the existence of FlSL

A research programme could consist of two main items:

1. What are the roots of FlSL?

    We have some evidence that FlSL is, like ASL, the product of creolisation of old French Sign Language, and its grammatical rules (having a higher sociolinguistic status) with the previously existing sign systems (Woodward, 1978). We know that the schools for the deaf in Flanders (most of which were started in the beginning of the 19th century), took their educational inspiration from the Institute for the Deaf in Paris.

    We can take as a working hypothesis that FlSL – once it has originated out of a creolisation process – remained under the strong influence of French Sign Language (FSL). In Belgium, schools for the deaf were built in the bilingual area of Brussels. These schools accepted children from both the North (Dutch-Flemish speaking) and from the South (French speaking). If we take into account the general Belgian cultural orientation towards France in the 19th century, then it is probable that FlSL even more than ASL has kept its relationship with FSL.

    Flemish deaf people say that contact with deaf people from the

South in Belgium does not cause many difficulties. They feel that the influence of FSL is very clear. However, they report many more communication problems with the deaf of France.

The Flemish deaf also say that it is much harder to communicate with Americans. When I told them that there are historical relationships between ASL and FSL, they answered 'We don't see similarities with FSL. Or, if there are some, they are difficult to see'.

2. How can FlSL be characterised linguistically? For this question we can take advantage of the more extended knowledge of ASL and use it as a reference point for the formulation of a number of hypotheses. As first topics of research, we propose examining:

   (a) the degree of iconicity and its psycholinguistic role in sign production and perception;
   (b) the principles of sequentiality (eventually compared with the principles of simultaneity);
   (c) a comparison of (a) and (b) with ASL.

A central issue is the question of how the hundred years' oppression of sign language in Flanders has yielded a sign language with a remarkable lower level.

In summary, FlSL requires considerable research effort to inform the language planners in Belgium. There are a number of similarities between FlSL and Flemish spoken language in their historical suppression, and changing attitudes towards Flemish should be helpful in the greater development and acceptance of the sign communication of Flemish deaf people.

MANUAL ENGLISH AND AMERICAN SIGN LANGUAGE: WHERE DO WE GO FROM HERE?

Gerilee Gustason

Since the publication of *A Dictionary of American Sign Language* in 1965, there has been a growing interest in the United States in the vocabulary and structure of American Sign Language. Much research has taken place on the semantics of that language. This recognition of ASL as a language in and of itself has had a profound impact on the self-image of deaf persons, and on the preparation of teachers to work with deaf students.

At the same time, in the 1960s, concern was growing over the poor educational showing of many deaf students. Research had documented the fact that the intelligence range of deaf persons was comparable to that of hearing persons (Vernon, 1969; Schlesinger and Meadow, 1972), that the visual cues presented for speechreading English were grossly inadequate for a comfortable learning of the language (Lowell, 1957, 1958), and that the average graduate of a public residential school for the deaf had poor reading skills (Babbidge, 1965). Accordingly, it is not surprising that many schools and programs for the deaf in the United States began looking for a clearer mode of communication. American Sign Language was being proved a language distinct from English at the same time the search was on for clearer ways of representing English so deaf children in school could achieve to a degree commensurate with their intelligence and take their places with their hearing peers in a society largely dependent on English for upward mobility.

This called forth, in the early 1970s, several books of signs designed to represent English vocabulary and inflections – *Seeing Essential English* (Anthony, 1971), *Signing Exact English* (Gustason, *et al.*, 1972) and *Preschool Signed English* (Bornstein, *et al.*, 1972). These spread rapidly throughout the country, and by 1976 two-thirds of the classes in the United States reported use of some form of manual communication in the classroom (Jordan, Gustason and Rosen, 1976). This was a great shift from the formerly oral-dominated elementary years, and the rapidity of the change can be seen in Figure 1.

This rapid change is understandable in view of the research findings noted above, especially if we remember that a major task of most teachers has been to make children literate in the language of their country. In addition, 90% of the parents of deaf children are hearing (Office of Demographic Studies, 1968–72), and hearing parents when expecting a baby expect to speak their own language with the child, not learn a foreign language to communicate with their infant.

It is also understandable, however, that the development and spread of such systems to manually encode English should come under attack by those interested in the integrity of American Sign Language. The initial reactions of many deaf adults to Manual English systems seemed to depend in part on their own English skills and on the ASL skills of the person who introduced the concept of Manual English to them. If rapport was established, a common reaction of deaf adults with weak English skills was 'wonderful for

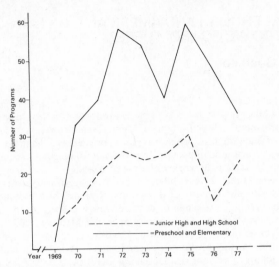

Figure 1. Total number of program changes each year (*not* cumulative)

children – too late for me.' Deaf adults with good English skills, on the other hand, often saw less need of manual English systems – unless they themselves were teachers. As research and promotion of ASL grew, however, and as Manual English systems were adopted and used by persons with no background in ASL, some conflict was probably inevitable.

Many persons and programs new to manual communication often seem to hope they can locate a 'package' which they can take home, plug in, and have instant clear and appropriate communication. It makes life difficult for such persons to realise that it is important to respect both the communication styles of the adult deaf in their locality and the communication needs of deaf children in educational settings. Many teachers in training seem to feel that the use of signs guarantees communication, or that the use of ASL guarantees comprehension, or that once communication of concepts has been established English is sure to follow, or that signing in English ensures the comprehension of concepts. Life, unfortunately, is quite a bit more complex than that.

It is now nine years since the publication of several Manual English sign books. In this time many school programs have adopted one of these as their chief source, with *Signing Exact English* the most widely used, and the Gallaudet *Preschool Signed English* series also widespread. (See Jordan, Gustason, and Rosen, 1976.) It takes time for teachers to develop skill, for parents to be taught, and for children to progress through the early language learning years to reading and writing skills. Even supposing instant fluency on the part of teachers and parents, and immediate consistency within a school and between home and school, children exposed to one of these manual English systems from infancy can now be only about ten years old. Over the same period of time, the number of multiply handicapped children moving through the schools has increased, due to the rubella bulge. Preschool programs have spread. More materials have come on the market for the teaching and testing of English with deaf children. The move to mainstream has placed many children in integrated school programs and made them hard to locate for statistical surveys. It is, in short, very difficult to isolate any given factor and say this has caused, or not caused, an improvement in the English skills of deaf children. Yet it is perfectly reasonable to ask whether such an improvement has occurred since the publication of the Manual English texts.

There are several studies that give food for thought. Moores headed a project to study preschool programs over a period of several years comparing those that used total communication, those that were oral, and those that used fingerspelling in addition to speech. It is interesting to note that his early findings indicated that the more structured programs did better, regardless of the communication mode, while over the period of years the total communication programs pulled ahead (Moores, 1970–74). Crandall (1975) reported that what the mother of a preschool child used at home had more impact on what the child used than what was used in school.

Few other studies seem to have been undertaken recently to evaluate English skills attainments. We are all familiar with the studies of former years indicating the superior performance of deaf children of deaf parents to those of hearing parents; however, these studies almost all took place prior to the onset of total communication. There have been no comparable studies comparing deaf children of deaf parents with deaf children of hearing parents who began total communication while the children were infants. One unpublished study of this nature was done by Babb in 1978, using Quigley's Test of Syntactic Abilities (Quigley, 1978); however, his age group duplicated the 10–18 age group of the TSA normative sample and thus utilised children who were already at least four to twelve years old when the manual English texts took the country by storm, and the results were inconclusive.

In the fall of 1978, a study was conducted at five school programs across the United States whose stated communication philosophy was Signing Exact English. There was, in fact, great variation from school to school in within-program consistency and fluency among teachers, and no attempt was made to assess teacher or parent fluency or how long a child had been in that specific program. Nonetheless, the findings are interesting in that younger children were, on the whole, performing at a higher level of English proficiency as measured by the TSA than were older children. In addition, although the TSA have norms for deaf children aged 10 to 18, children younger than 10 were performing better than the normative group's average (Gustason, 1981), Table 1 indicates the average percent correct on the TSA for several age groups, compared with the 53% of the 10–18 year old normative group.

In addition to the TSA scores, writing samples were collected from the children in these programs. These samples were then rated by readers in the English Department at Gallaudet College on a five point scale. In that program, a rating of 3.5 is considered equivalent to college freshman level. It should be noted that the only children to obtain 3.5 level were 11 and 13 years

Table 1. Mean percent correct by age group for all students with 80+ IQ, no additional handicaps, and hearing impairment before age two

Age range	% correct	N
7 – 9	56.4	8
10 – 12	63.4	15
13 – 15	58.1	16
TOTAL GROUP	59.8	39

old, and that a four year old received a rating of 2.83. The average rating of all the children in this study was 1.87. It must be borne in mind that the comparison is of children 7–18 years old with college students, and that a comparable rating of the average 7–18 year old deaf child in the United States is not available.

Another factor complicating the possibility of pure research on the impact of Manual English systems is the fact that these systems, and the results of ASL research, are more and more widely available, and many teachers are using an eclectic approach. The authors of *Signing Exact English* advocate the utilisation of ASL, and ASL principles, in promoting communication, through a bilingual approach, including translation and comparison, and through the incorporation of ASL elements into manual English signing – as, for instance, in the placing of the sign 'bow' in the hair to indicate a hair bow, at the neck for a bow tie, in the air in different positions for a bow and arrow and a rainbow, respectively. This becomes more, then, than simply a manual representation of an English word.

The biggest question in effective use of Manual English or of ASL, other than skill, is that of attitudes. If a modality, a system, or a language is not respected, it will not be effectively used. With the surge of interest in ASL and the growing self-respect this has engendered in deaf individuals, attitudes have at times seemed somewhat polarised concerning ASL and Manual English. Sometimes this has been related to ignorance: on the part of ASL advocates, of the principles and rationale of Manual English; on the part of Manual English users, of the features and possibilities inherent in ASL. The deaf teacher of the deaf has seemed to be the 'man in the middle' and as such has a perspective which we should consider.

In an attempt to discover what hearing impaired teachers of the deaf feel about both ASL and Manual English, a study was done during the winter 1980–81 of hearing impaired teachers who had graduated from the Gallaudet College graduate level teacher preparation program since 1962 – the year when that program first opened to deaf students. This study was done in conjunction with a larger study covering questions of curriculum review of

Table 2. Responses to checklist of forms used in classroom

	Profound before two (n = 17)	Profound after two (n = 13)	Severe, Moderate, Mild (n = 21)	Total n = 49
ASL	13 (77%)	12 (92%)	12 (63%)	37 (76%)
Sign English	14 (82%)	13 (100%)	16 (84%)	43 (88%)
Manual English	8 (47%)	7 (54%)	12 (63%)	27 (55%)
use suffixes or endings sometimes	9 (53%)	10 (77%)	10 (53%)	29 (59%)
use suffix or endings constantly	2 (12%)	1 (8%)	4 (21%)	7 (14%)
use -ing	11 (65%)	10 (77%)	14 (74%)	35 (71%)
use -s	5 (29%)	9 (69%)	11 (58%)	25 (51%)
use -ed	4 (24%)	8 (62%)	7 (37%)	19 (39%)
use -ly	4 (24%)	8 (62%)	6 (32%)	15 (31%)
use -ment	5 (29%)	4 (31%)	7 (37%)	16 (33%)
use -ness	5 (29%)	3 (23%)	7 (37%)	15 (31%)
use -ive	3 (18%)	0	2 (11%)	5 (10%)
use -ous	3 (18%)	0	2 (11%)	5 (10%)
use English as a second lang. methods	9 (53%)	6 (46%)	4 (21%)	19 (39%)
use invented signs	6 (35%)	5 (39%)	8 (42%)	19 (39%)
feel ASL is native lang. for all deaf children	9 (53%)	6 (46%)	7 (37%)	22 (45%)
feel hearing parents find it easier to learn a manual form of English than ASL	10 (59%)	9 (69%)	13 (68%)	32 (65%)

the teacher preparation program, and utilised an attitude questionnaire which was adapted from a language attitude scale developed by Pietras and Lamb (1979) for use with Black English. The forced-choice situation was difficult for a number of teachers; however, the results provide a good insight into general attitudes concerning ASL and Manual English.

The questionnaire was sent to 121 hearing-impaired teachers across the U.S.A. Responses were received from 51, or 42%. Two chose not to respond to the attitude survey as part of the questionnaire. The attitude survey is reproduced at the end of this article, including the definitions of ASL and Manual English that were used. For analysis, the respondents were grouped into several groups based on the amount of hearing loss: profound (91 + dB ISO), severe (71–90 dB), moderately severe (56–70 dB), moderate (41–55) and mild (27–40). The profound group was also subdivided into those deafened before two or at an unknown age, and those deafened after the age of two. Tables 2 and 3 summarise the results of the study.

In terms of their own personal background, the majority of the profoundly deaf teachers deafened before the age of two (P—2) attended a residential school for ten or more years while the severely, moderately, and mildly hearing impaired (SMM) had attended integrated schools for 10 or more years. Those profoundly deafened after the age of two (P+2) tended to be about equally divided between the two types of schooling.

The experience in teaching placement of these groups likewise differs somewhat. In all groups, the largest number is at the secondary level: 50% of the P—2 group, 31% of the P+2 group, and 29% of the SMM group. The remainder are spread relatively evenly among other levels, although none of the P—2 and only one each of the P+2 and SMM have taught at the preschool level. Most in all groups have taught at residential programs, and some from all groups have taught at day schools. The P—2 group has done the less day class teaching, and a sizeable number in each group has taught at the college level.

With this experienced background in mind, given the fact that many residential schools have a longer history of contact with American Sign Language than day programs, it is interesting to note the differences shown in Table 2 among the groups in terms of their own stated usage of ASL, Sign English, and Manual English. Those profoundly deaf after the age of two report the greatest use of both ASL and Sign English, while the SMM group reports the greatest use of Manual English. The P+2 group reports the greatest use of the more common suffixes (-ing, -s, -ed, -ly), but it is the P—2 group that shows most use of the less common suffixes (-ive, -ous), although the number and percentage is small (3, or 18%). The P—2 group reports the greatest use of English as a second language (53%), in comparison with 46% for P+2 and 21% for SMM. Conversely, the use of invented signs increases across groups from 35% for P—2 to 39% for P+2 and 42% for SMM. Likewise, a decreasing number across groups felt that ASL was the native language of all deaf children (53%, 46% and 37% respectively). The P—2 group was somewhat more sanguine about the ability of hearing parents to learn ASL, with 59% of that group responding that it was easier for such parents to learn Manual English as contrasted with 69% of the P+2 and 68% of the SMM.

Table 3. Questionnaire items with greatest agreement for each group

			Profound (Before two/After two)	Profound Plus Severe	All
8.	ASL should be discouraged.	F	90% (88/92)	92%	94%
22.	Societal acceptance of ASL is important for the development of self-esteem among deaf people.	F	87% (88/85)	87%	86%
2.	A deaf child's use of ASL hurts his ability to learn.	F	83% (77/92)	87%	84%
9.	Manual English should be discouraged.	F	93% (77/92)	87%	88%
16.	ASL is an inferior language system.	F	83% (82/85)	87%	90%
3.	A deaf child's use of Manual English hurts his ability to learn.	F	80% (82/77)	85%	86%
31.	Widespread acceptance of ASL is important.	T	80% (82/77)	82%	82%
5.	The encouragement of Manual English would be good for deaf students.	T	77% (77/77)	80%	78%
14.	It is ridiculous to encourage children to sign ASL.	F	77% (77/77)	82%	84%
15.	It is ridiculous to encourage children to sign Manual English.	F	77% (77/77)	82%	82%
18.	Teachers have a duty to ensure that students do not sign non-English in the classroom.	F	77% (65/92)	80%	80
20.	The continued use of a non-English Sign Language accomplishes nothing worthwhile for the individual.	F	77% (71/85)	77%	76%
26.	There is much danger involved in accepting ASL.	F	77% (77/77)	82%	86%

Table 3 indicates some interesting differences in attitude among the different groups. All agree on the primary importance of the falseness of the statement that ASL should be discouraged (item 8). The profoundly deaf prior to age two were least sure of this, but the proportion increased as the groups with more hearing were added. There is also an interesting split between those deafened before and after two, in that those deafened prior to two seem less certain about the advisability of using ASL (items 8, 2, 16, 18 and 20). Yet the P—2 group was the most decided that societal acceptance of ASL is important for the development of self-esteem among deaf people (item 22). It could be theorised that this results from the comparative recency of the acceptance of ASL and the possibility that negative views of ASL are still lurking in the psychological backgrounds of this group. On the other hand, the P+2 group tends to be less sure of the falseness of the statement that a deaf child's use of Manual English hurts his ability to learn (item 3), while also not being as sure that widespread acceptance of ASL is important (item 31).

In general, the entire group of hearing impaired teachers is positive towards both ASL and Manual English, while being somewhat more decided on ASL. The questionnaire results showed a reluctance to say all parents should start with *one* of these. While no one came down *against* the use of both ASL and Manual English by schools and teachers, the total group was uncertain about whether schools and teachers could and should use both. Many individuals wrote additional comments on the questionnaire. Only one of these comments was strongly in support of ASL and against Manual English; the tone of the rest was that there is no right or wrong way – it may depend on the child; we should use what is needed from both, and above all we should stop fighting over which signs to use and get on with the business of getting across to the child and teaching him what we think he needs to know.

If these two small scale studies are any indication, what is happening is that as exposure continues teachers are beginning to utilise what works and what they are comfortable with from both ASL and Manual English, with positive attitudes towards both, and children in such an atmosphere are beginning to improve their English skills. How representative such attitudes are of teachers in general (both the deaf and hearing) and of parents and administrators is not clear nor is the question of the attitudes of deaf adults who are not teachers. If, however, deaf teachers represent the middle man between hearing teachers and deaf adults, we are on a positive track.

QUESTIONNAIRE

In recent years many developments have taken place related to manual communication. In answering the following questions, use these definitions:

American Sign Language, ASL: has vocabulary and structure different from English; e.g., 'touch finish California?'

Sign English: uses the vocabulary of ASL, but in English word order; may use an ending such as -ing or -ness sometimes, but not often.

Manual English: includes using initialised signs (such as 'parent' using P hand to touch temple and jaw), endings (-ing, -ed, -ness, -s, etc.), invented signs.

Please check all that apply, below,

Do you

_____ use ASL in the classroom?

_____ use Sign English in the classroom?

_____ use Manual English in the classroom?

_____ use any suffixes or endings sometimes? _____ use them constantly – which?

_____ -ing _____ -s _____ -ed _____ -ly _____ -ment

_____ -ness _____ -ive _____ -ous

_____ use English as a second language teaching methods?

_____ correct your students' speech?

_____ encourage your students to use their speech?

_____ encourage your students to use their hearing aids?

_____ correct your students' production of signs?

_____ use any invented signs to represent English words?

_____ feel that ASL is the native language of all deaf children?

_____ feel that all deaf children and their parents should begin with ASL?

_____ feel that hearing parents find it easier to use a manual form of English than ASL?

_____ feel that schools and teachers cannot use both ASL and Manual English?

We are interested in your opinions about ASL and Manual English. Please answer the following as True (T), False (F), or Not Sure (NS).

_____ 1. ASL looks as good as Manual English.

_____ 2. A deaf child's use of ASL hurts his ability to learn.

_____ 3. A deaf child's use of Manual English hurts his ability to learn.

_____ 4. The encouragement of ASL would be good for deaf students.

_____ 5. The encouragement of Manual English would be good for deaf students

_____ 6. It would hurt deaf peopl's welfare if use of ASL became educationally acceptable.

_____ 7. It would hurt deaf people's welfare if use of Manual English became educationally acceptable.

_____ 8. ASL should be discouraged.

_____ 9. Manual English should be discouraged.

_____10. ASL is the 'in' thing.

_____11. Manual English is the 'in' thing.

_____12. Allowing and accepting the use of any signs that are not English in the classroom will retard the academic progress of the class.

_____13. A child should *not* be corrected by teachers for any kind of signing.

_____14. It is ridiculous to encourage children to sign ASL.

_____15. It is ridiculous to encourage children to sign Manual English.

_____16. ASL is an inferior language system.

_____17. Manual English is an inferior way to communicate

_____18. Teachers have a duty to ensure that students do not sign non-English in the classroom.

_____19. When teachers reject the signs of the student, they do him great harm.

_____20. The continued use of a non-English Sign Language accomplishes nothing worthwhile for the individual.

_____21. We should encourage continued use of non-English Sign Language.

_____22. Societal acceptance of ASL is important for development of self-esteem among deaf people.

_____23. Societal acceptance of Manual English is important for development of self-esteem among deaf people.

_____24. ASL is too imprecise to be of an effective means of communication.

_____25. Manual English is too imprecise to be of an effective means of communication.

_____26. There is much danger involved in accepting ASL.

_____27. There is much danger involved in accepting Manual English.

_____28. If use of ASL were encouraged, signers of ASL would be more motivated to achieve academically.

_____29. If use of Manual English were encouraged, signers of Manual English would be more motivated to achieve academically.

_____30. A decline in the use of non-English signs would have a positive influence on social unit.

_____31. Widespread acceptance of ASL is important.

_____32. Widespread acceptance of Manual English is important.

_____33. All deaf children and their parents should begin with ASL.

_____34. All deaf children and their parents should begin with Manual English.

_____35. Schools and teachers can, and should, use both ASL and Manual English.

Comments:

SOCIOLECTAL JUDGEMENTS BY DEAF CHILDREN

Harley Hamilton

Introduction

American Sign Language (ASL) and Manually Coded English (MCE) are the two 'ideal' or 'standard' forms present in the Hearing/Deaf diglossic community. For discussion purposes hearing and deaf will refer to the speaker's audiological status and Hearing and Deaf will refer to the signer's cultural characteristics. Pidgin Sign English (PSE) is a mixture of the two languages. Schlesinger and Meadow, 1972; Stokoe, 1970; Woodward, 1973c). Figure 1 illustrates this diglossic situation.

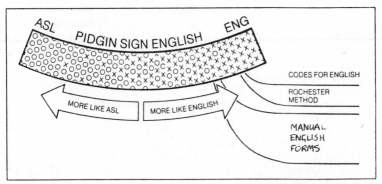

from Baker and Cokely (1980)

Figure 1. Pidgin Sign English – a diglossic situation

It will be noted that hearing loss is not the factor that determines inclusion in one group or another. Rather, the determining factor is the choice of linguistic code (Woodward, 1973a,c,d); Padden, 1980). ASL is considered the language of Deaf people and more English-like signing is generally used by Hearing people.

It has been well documented that young children, some as young as 18 months, are capable of code-switching in bilingual situations similar to the one described above (Meadow, 1972; Giles and Powesland, 1975). However, little is known about how children judge the social group membership of the speaker based on his code. Williams (1970) working with adults and Labov (1972) working with adolescents and adults found listeners highly sensitive to the social function of linguistic codes. In both studies the subjects were quite consistent in labelling the social group membership of the speakers when given a sample of their speech. These studies present no evidence that subjects younger than 13 years of age can consistently label a speaker as a member of a social group based on the speaker's linguistic code (Halliday, 1978). The present study investigates the ability of deaf subjects

(±13 years of age) to label the social group of hearing and deaf signers when presented with a sample of the signer's linguistic code. Also, an attempt is made to uncover the salient features of the signer's code which function as 'cultural markers' for the subject.

Some possible 'cultural markers'

Interlanguage differences

The phonological, morphological, and syntactic differences between ASL and MCE may alert the subjects to the social group membership of the signer. In the area of phonology, a Deaf signer tends to use fewer initialised sign variants. The Hearing signer, may use signs whose handshapes are the first letter of the English word (gloss) for that sign. For example, a Deaf signer may sign PARENTS using a 5 hand to articulate the sign while a Hearing signer may use a P hand (*PARENTS*) and also mark the plural by signing S as the final element of the sign.

In the area of morphology, the use of an S handshape to mark plural would be characteristic of MCE. A Deaf signer may mark the plural of nouns by the use of cardinal numbers, incorporation of number into the noun sign, or repetition (Hamilton, 1979). This is basically a difference in the way the two languages inflect for plural.

The concept of 'a blue ball' may be expressed in ASL as BLUE BALL or BALL BLUE (Hamilton, 1979) while in MCE it would be A BLUE BALL. This example illustrates syntactic differences between the two languages. ASL allows N-Adj. or Adj.-N order for noun phrases and generally does not utilise the determiner A while MCE prefers an Adj.-N order and makes use of the determiner A much as spoken English does. There are many more phonemic, morphemic, and syntactic differences between the two languages but these will suffice for illustrative purposes.

Intralanguage differences.

Hudson (1980) states 'There are, perhaps, linguistic items in every language that reflect social characteristics of the speaker, of the addressee, or of the relationship between them.' Use of similar salient linguistic features by several speakers is indicative of how much experience and how many social characteristics (religion, sex, age, race, region of origin, occupation, interests, etc.) they share. Halliday (1978) suggests that different cultural groups have different accents or dialects (i.e., differential use of phonemic, morphemic, and syntactic items) within the same language. Trudgill (1974) has discussed salient language differences between males and females within the same speech community and Flannery (1946) and Woodward (1979) have found several sex specific linguistic items in Gros Ventre sign language and American Sign Language, respectively. Doughty, *et al.* (1972) state that the language learned by a person is unique to him because of his unique place and experience in the environment. Hearing and deaf people have unique experiences learning MCE and ASL.

The two groups will encounter different experiences in the environment based on the fact that the deaf person may rely more on visual aspects of the world than the hearing person who may, but need not, rely as heavily on visual input. It is likely, therefore, that hearing and deaf signers using the same language, MCE or ASL, may have different 'accents' or 'dialects' in those languages. Such variation in language may serve as stimuli capable of eliciting a response of identifying and then naming the speaker's social group membership (Williams, 1970).

Based on the above, the author hypothesises that there may be two sources for variation in the subject's responses. One may be the inherent difference in the two linguistic codes investigated (interlanguage differences). The other may be the signers Hearing or Deaf 'accent' in the language he is using (intralanguage differences).

Method

Selection of signers
In this study signers were selected to represent the following characteristics: deaf and hearing, male and female, users of ASL and MCE.

In all, stories from 11 signers were selected. All were told to an audience before a videotape camera. The texts were either copied from a stock of videotape at the author's disposal or recorded specifically for this study. ASL texts were selected from a group of tapes made by Joyce media, The Registry of Interpreters for the Deaf, or Hoemann (1976) as examples of the language. The MCE tapes were viewed by the author and judged on the principles used by Gustason, *et al.* (1980) to describe an MCE system. It will be noted that signers in the MCE tapes did not always manually mark past tense, first and second person pronouns, and determiners. Although each signer may have been using consistent rules for these variations, or marking them non-manually, such rules were not found by the author. Marmor and Pettito (1979) have found such deletions to be typical of users of MCE. Therefore, the author concludes that the MCE samples are representative of the MCE the subjects have been exposed to in everyday conversation.

Selection of subjects
The subjects were between the ages of 11 and 16 and were enrolled in a day school program for the deaf. Table 1 specifies the number of subjects in each group.

Table 1. Subjects in each age group

Age	n
11	13
12	10
13	12
14	10
15	15
16	14

74 = total n

Procedure

The subjects were asked to judge if the signers on a videotape were HEARING or DEAF. They were informed that they would respond NOT SURE if they couldn't decide whether the signer was HEARING or DEAF. They were also asked to explain their decision if they could. They were then shown the videotape of the signers. After each speaker, they responded by checking one of the boxes on the response sheet and optionally explaining their decision.

Results

Table 2 shows the signers grouped by hearing loss and code. The numbers listed in the columns Hearing, Deaf and Not Sure are percentages.

Table 2. Total group ratings for signers

		Hearing	*Deaf*	*Not Sure*
Hearing using MCE	1	85.1	5.4	9.5
	5	60.8	17.5	21.6
	11	86.4	4.0	9.5
Hearing using ASL	3	16.2	45.9	37.8
	4	45.9	37.8	16.2
	10	9.4	82.4	9.4
Deaf using ASL	2	2.7	90.5	6.8
	7	9.4	86.4	4.0
	9	32.4	43.2	24.3
Deaf using MCE	6	32.4	33.7	33.7
	8	20.2	64.8	14.8

For hearing people using MCE and deaf people using ASL subjects were generally consistent in their judgements of Hearing and Deaf respectively. For hearing signers using ASL and for deaf signers using MCE there was much greater variability.

Many of the subjects' explanations of the basis of their decisions fell into the following categories:

Salient characteristics of a Hearing signer:

(a) uses speech lip movement,
(b) signs slowly,
(c) signs/stiffly/unskilled,
(d) 'looks', 'acts', 'signs' like a hearing person.

Salient characteristics of a Deaf signer:

(a) uses no speech lip movement,

(b) 'looks', 'acts', or 'signs' like a deaf person,
(c) signs smoothly/skilled,
(d) signs fact.

When subjects were unsure of the signer's status they generally justified their decision simply by stating they were unsure.

The subjects' judgements and accompanying explanations will now be discussed together and relationships suggested.

Signer 11 (hearing using MCE) was judged as Hearing by the largest number of subjects (86.4%) who reported that she possessed all of the salient characteristics of a Hearing signer. Signer 1 possessed three of the four characteristics (speech lip movement, slow signing and 'looked' hearing) and was judged as Hearing by a large percentage, 85.1%. Although Signer 5 also possessed three of the four characteristics of a Hearing person (slow signing, stiff/unskilled signing, and 'looking' hearing) he was judged as Hearing by only 60.8% of the subjects. It appears then that speech lip movement may be a very strong indicator of a Hearing person for the subjects. A review of the tape showed that the speech lip movements of signer 5 were very small and vague. This may account for the lower percentage of Hearing responses. In fact, one 16 year old stated that signer 5 was Deaf because he did not have speech lip movements.

For deaf signers using ASL, lip movement is again important. This time the lack of speech lip movement is considered the salient characteristic. Also accompanying lack of speech movement is the very vague characteristic of 'looking', 'signing' or 'acting' like a deaf person. Signer 2 possessed both these characteristics and was overwhelmingly considered Deaf (90.5%). Signer 7 also possessed these two characteristics, although speech lip movement was not mentioned as often for this signer as it was for signer 2. Signer 7 also was considered to sign fast and smoothly. She was judged to be Deaf by 86.4% of the subjects. Signer 9 was also judged with much variability. He was said to exhibit not only all four Deaf characteristics but also the Hearing characteristics of signing stiffly/unskilled. The mixture of characteristics may have caused this signer to be judged so variably.

The characteristics of Hearing and Deaf listed above may also aid in explaining the varied responses to hearing signers using ASL and deaf signers using MCE. In each of these cases the signer is using a code which does not nominally match his hearing loss. Signer 3 (hearing using ASL) was considered Deaf by almost half (45.9%) of the subjects, but 37.8% of the subjects were unsure. This signer possessed many Deaf characteristics. He was reported to have no speech lip movement, sign smoothly/skillfully, and 'look' deaf. On reviewing the tape of this signer the author paid close attention to his lip movement. In actuality, he was using lip movements similar to those of speech. It seems that while he signed smoothly, appeared to have no lip movement to some of the subjects, and 'looked' deaf to some of them, his lip movement may have been 'Hearing' enough to cause confusion and the responses (37.8%) of unsure. His lip movements did not match his code (ASL) and thus provided a contradictory stimulus similar to signer 5. Perhaps one of the subjects summed it up best when he/she stated the following as the reason for being not sure: 'Because he looks like he's deaf but hearing.'

Signer 4 also presented a confusing image. Almost half (45.9%) labelled her as Hearing while 37.8% considered her Deaf. The most salient characteristics she was reported as having were much more speech lip movement (Hearing), 'looking' hearing, 'looking' deaf, fast signing (Deaf) and smooth signing (Deaf). A review of the tape confirmed that she did use a good deal of lip movement which resembled speech. This further suggests that the presence or absence of speech lip movement is a very important characteristic for determining a person's Hearing or Deaf status. Although he utilised the Deaf linguistic code and some of the signing characteristics of a Deaf person, lip movement functioned to 'give her away' as a Hearing person.

Signer 10 was reported to have no speech lip movement at all. A review of the tape confirmed this. Although he is hearing, his code (ASL) and the accompanying speech lip movements (none) are typical characteristics of a Deaf signer. The great majority labelled this signer as Deaf. These responses are comparable to responses to signers 2 and 7 (deaf) who signed using the same code without accompanying speech lip movement. This very strongly suggests that ASL without speech lip movement is a salient characteristic of Deaf signers. Signer 10 was also reported to be fast and smooth/skilled while signing, which adds to his credibility as a Deaf signer.

Deaf people using MCE were also variably labelled. One-third (33.7%) of the subjects were unsure of the status of signer 6. As with signers 3 and 4, signer 6 was reported to possess characteristics of both Hearing people (speech lip movement, 'looked' hearing) and Deaf people (smooth/skilled signing). He apparently was a very confusing stimulus for the subjects to judge because of these mixed characteristics. Signer 8 also presented a mixture of Hearing and Deaf characteristics according to the subjects' justification. She was considered Deaf because of her fast signing and Hearing because of her speech lip movement. Again, a person exhibiting mixed characteristics is judged with more variability than a person who exhibits only Hearing or only Deaf characteristics.

In order to determine how consistently each age group of subjects judged the signers in comparison to the other age groups of subjects, the following correlation matrix was calculated using the percentage scores of each age group for each signer.

Table 3. Correlation matrix for judgements by different age groups

Age	11	12	13	14	15	16
11		.816647	.777601	.890552	.881903	.858416
12			.763959	.847569	.885766	.867804
13				.809644	.872220	.862640
14					.950350	.959923
15						.956760
16						

While the correlations between each age group are fairly high the highest correlations exist between the 14, 15 and 16 year olds. These correlations are nearly perfect (i.e., 1.00). The responses are such that a trend towards more consistency amongst these older subjects appears. The older subjects were particularly accurate in labelling signers who exhibited only characteristics from one group. Ninety-five percent of the 14–16 year olds labelled signers with only Deaf characteristics as Deaf and signers with only Hearing characteristics as Hearing. This is compared to seventy-six percent of the younger subjects making this same judgement.

Discussion and Conclusions

It appears that a signer using the code which is nominally identical to his hearing loss is consistently judged by the total sample as a member of the group that uses that code. These signers exhibit characteristics which are typical of the code they are using. When a signer uses a code which is not nominally identical to his hearing loss there is much more variability in the subjects' judgement of that signer. These signers tend to exhibit both Hearing and Deaf characteristics. The signer may be exhibiting a mixture of features from both codes. For hearing signers using ASL and deaf signers using MCE the more their 'accent' (consistent use of features from one code) agrees with that used by signers whose hearing loss and code match, the more likely they are to be considered a member of that social group. For example, the consistent judgements were that signer 10 (hearing using ASL) and signer 8 (deaf using MCE) were deaf.

This suggests that intralanguage differences are important for determining a signer's social group as Deaf or Hearing.

Experimental and intuitive corroboration of these findings with those from older subjects is desirable. This becomes more evident when considering the responses of the children by age groups. It appears that as a group, children aged 13 and below are less consistent in judging a signer's social group membership than children older than 13. Perhaps a heightened social awareness is a factor in this difference. Future studies should measure this and other variables and group subjects accordingly so that comparisons can be made. This type of experimentation along with the experimental manipulation of the accent variables, may serve to define features of the Deaf and Hearing codes more precisely.

PART FOUR: PSYCHOLOGY

PSYCHOLOGY AND COMMUNICATION

Introduction

The use of the words 'psychology of' and 'communication' in relation to deafness have often been used as long-distance measuring instruments of the failures of deaf people. Psychology has often seemed to be concerned with discovering difference without acknowledging competence. In this sense social pressures have pushed it more towards a medical view of the world, where it is the difference from 'normality' which has to be attended to. A growing awareness that we cannot adequately describe normality has meant a greater acceptance of the variation in societies and in individuals.

Psychologists have come to examine difference as a natural variant and as a valuable source of information on the nature of processes in language use and thinking. From a psychological point of view it is necessary to understand the processes needed for sign language, in order to communicate effectively and from a deaf person's point of view it is necessary to communicate effectively in order to begin to study the processes involved in sign language use. All of the papers in this section have these two themes underlying their approach and all highlight issues of variation in communication and processing which are claimed to be important for our understanding of sign language.

Kyle suggests a need to consider larger units in sign sentences, at the proposition level, such that we can interpret meaning directly rather than looking for individual signs or components of signs as building blocks. A strong imaginal element in sign language story-telling is highlighted which allows different techniques for deaf people to represent events. The propositions used by hearing people in spoken English in similar story-telling suggests a different type of representation in memory though a similar capacity.

Dawson considers the evidence for the existence of a sign code in memory and suggests that we should also examine the recognition process. In recognising English written words it is possible to demonstrate the effects of a speech code even though there may be in the task no obvious reason for articulating the words perceived. This suggests that all of our English processing involves the use of an appropriate internal code. She addresses the question of how deaf young people approach the same word recognition task and concludes that although sign mediation can be used it may not be used by all deaf people.

Mayberry introduces the task of shadowing (simultaneous repetition of signed messages) as a way of investigating sign fluency in adult signers. Her study compared shadowing with recall of sentences and scrambled sentences in ASL, and highlights important effects of sign experience on ASL use. The technique may prove to be a very valuable tool in the study of internal processing of sign language.

Tartter's concern is with the 'code' in the sense of how information is transmitted in sign. Her starting point is a very important practical consideration of how sign information can be compressed sufficiently for it to be carried in a telephone line. The bandwidth of a video picture is much too great for transmission on current telephone lines and therefore information must be extracted from a video signal which will still allow the deaf receiver to understand the message. The solution to the problem is to use a point-light display generated by attaching retroflective tape to critical parts of the body in signing space. In this paper she is concerned with the parameters of sign and how effectively these are represented in the displays generated. As well as demonstrating how effective communication can be under these reduced information conditions her work casts light on the relative importance of parameters of location, orientation, handshape and movement.

Both Edmondson and Jordan are concerned with communication itself and both consider that there are difficulties in the communication (in sign) of deaf children. Edmondson's technique of the story chain is a fascinating one based on a children's game. A story is told from a pictorial stimulus and then passed independently from one signer or speaker to another. The changes in the story occur naturally, often as an 'effort after meaning' but also as a result of lack of redundancy in the message. According to Edmondson the comparison of final versions (at the end of each story chain) between signed and spoken versions, allows us to compare the effectiveness of communication. The fact that deaf children appear to have more problems in Sign than do the hearing controls in speech, is taken to indicate the need for better models of sign language, i.e., greater involvement of deaf adults in education.

Jordan using a referential task takes a rather similar line although he ascribes the problems in deaf children's Sign to the early stages of introduction of signing in Scottish schools. He does make the important point that deaf children using Sign are better at the referential task than deaf children using oral methods. However, the major thrust of his explanation concerns the nature of the code used and shared by the deaf pairs in his task. In this we return to the major issue of how the the internal code influences the communication.

Montgomery adopts a more radical stance in dealing with communication. His paper develops a number of themes central to a receptive view of sign language interaction. The use of polar coordinates as a way of demonstrating different patterning in sign language production is certainly novel and is worthy of further examination. It is used here to highlight differences in three languages ASL, BSL and British Signed English. His view of the dynamic nature of language use and language interchange informs the second part of the paper where he shows how our attitudes and communicative purpose determine the locus of linguistic control. Greater openness should lead to better understanding of the different forms of communication available to deaf and hearing people. Returning to the practical aspects of communication, he describes a test format for communicative competence which allows comparison of communication in different language media: speech, reading, sign and so on. One can begin to see how to estimate relative competence in communication and can by this method estimate change in competence.

The section therefore begins to attack this inter-related problem of describing communication *and* the processes which underlie it. It is undoubtedly a large area of study and there are different priorities according to the researcher's perspective. The development of this area is of course, crucial to our understanding of the educational process for deaf children and it is to be hoped that these papers will provide useful information in this context.

LOOKING FOR MEANING IN SIGN LANGUAGE SENTENCES

Jim Kyle

'The trouble with deaf people is that they don't use signs.'

This may seem like a rather strange idea to express in a conference on sign language, but it highlights an issue about which I have become increasingly anxious, and as a result of different research projects, about which deaf people have expressed their fears.

If the statement is true, then it is not surprising that we find that hearing people have difficulty in understanding deaf people. The difficulty according to Kyle, Woll and Llewellyn-Jones (1981) is easy to identify though not so easy to explain. Although hearing people can learn to address deaf people in Sign, they very often cannot follow conversations among groups of deaf people. You might then suggest I modify the opening sentence to read that 'Deaf people don't use signs that we hearing people know,', but I think that the problem is more than just a secret vocabulary among deaf people; it is a little more complex. Yet it is not as complex as the serial-parallel process difference discussed at the Dahlem Workshop, nor is it as simple as the difference between manual English and sign language. It is something as vague as the way the language is used, but as explicit as the processes internally which control the way the language is constructed before it is articulated. The issue is of course how basic signs are modulated, modified, ordered and used to make grammatically acceptable sequences in sign language, and in these situations deaf people rarely use citation forms.

Researchers, who are linguists or psychologists, generally speaking attempt to isolate basic units in a problem area. They look for the building blocks or units which will allow us to generate the rules of construction. So psychologists have looked at short term memory for signs as a way of identifying a sign language code, and linguists have picked out signs, found ways of describing them in terms of components, and postulated some of the rules for their combination and modulation. However, having dismantled sign language, when we put it back together again, according to our psychological or linguistic principles, we can often find that it is no longer sign language, i.e., deaf people do not use signs in that way. Many people may feel that of course this will be true in such a young study, and that in the future we will have a better idea from the same approach. But I believe that unless we develop a clearer insight into sign language at a higher level, then we will be unable to work at the level of construction of rules in sign.

This brings us to a second question:

'What sort of language is sign language, anyway?'

Of course, sign language is manual and visual while speech is articulatory and acoustic. Speech has only one articulator, though a large frequency range is commanded by that articulator (increasingly we have become aware of other non-verbal articulators) while sign may use both hands, body position, lips and so on. This allows sign to use simultaneity where different articulators contribute different elements to the overall measage, and allows

Studdert-Kennedy and Lane (1980) to suggest:

'. . . sign language draws on a degree of sequential organisation to implement a parallel linguistic structure while speech does precisely the reverse.' p. 38.

But these are comments about what the language looks like or sounds like, not how the language is constructed. Unfortunately, it is probably the latter principles for construction that we need to know most about if we are to work with deaf people, use their language and understand why we have problems in education.

Bellugi (1980) maintains that the differences between speech and sign are at the surface level:

'We suggest that the abstract grammatical principles and constructs shared by natural sign language and spoken language, arise from the shared central processing mechanisms, and that the more superficial surface differences ar accommodations to differences in the modalities.' p. 137.

But these differences seem very large even at the sentence level as Stokoe (1980) has pointed out. The sentence 'He saw me' in English, is syntactically easy, to specify – (subject-verb-object) – but in Sign these principles do not work. Stokoe explains that the sign is transformed with the elements occurring simultaneously (as in Figure 1).

```
oblique
v hand      He saw me
toward
```

HE-SAW-ME

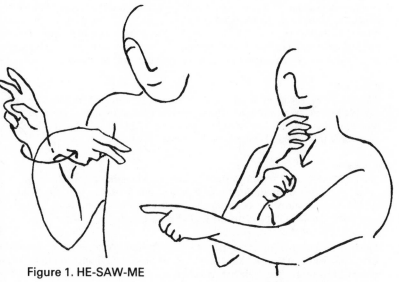

Figure 1. HE-SAW-ME

Figure 2. MAN-THERE

The observer sees *one* sign but not a sign that occurs in any manual. It is therefore a one-sign sentence with the meaning embedded in the simultaneous features of that sign. In other cases the actual meaning can be influenced by the context of signing, and created by making two signs simultaneously (Figure 2).

MAN   There's a man in there
THERE

His examples are valid in BSL and ASL, but neither example can be easily predicted from grammatical theories. Stokoe's conclusion, understandably, is that sign language:

'. . . has such interesting structure and so unusual a system that it challenges all theories of grammar'. p. 138.

No one would disagree with this view, but by and large we have considered the problem only from a 'bottom-up' perspective; find the sign units, then consider how they are combined. However, from a psychological point of view at least, grammar is subject to higher control processes (though not necessarily completely explained by them) and Kintsch (1977) for example, suggests that syntax and propositional structure are determined by higher level semantic processing. In essence some sort of schema or plan of linguistic action determines our speech, and our understanding of language.

In recent tradition, a way of studying this has been to consider stories and, particularly, the recall of stories. I want to describe an experiment whose outcomes I can only partly explain, but which throws some light on the question of what sort of language Sign is, and how we might describe the sentences it produces. The need for such a study arises because when deaf people retell an event from their experience, it seems incredibly rich in imagery, and leads me to the prediction that a deaf viewer of a signed story is generally better able to replicate the story than a hearing person who has heard the same story retold in speech. There is a complex qualitative difference in language used. Deaf people appear to be very accurate in their story, while hearing people tend to infer the outcomes of the story.

The study
This study or recall in speech and in sign is an attempt to examine the complexity of sign grammar when viewed from above, that is from the meaning of the story. The stimulus used was a 1920's silent movie. The film lasts three minutes and consists of three main episodes.

Episode 1
Husband, wife and mother-in-law at home, when the doorbell rings. A postman brings an 'Invitation for One' to a notorious dance-hall. The wife is shocked and returns the ticket to the postman. But, the husband secretly obtains the ticket and pays the postman for his trouble.

Episode 2
Husband leaves the house supposedly to go to the boxing, but goes to the dance hall where he enjoys himself with another woman. Unfortunately they win a Charleston contest which is being broadcast live to his wife and mother-in-law at home. His name is announced over the air.

Episode 3

He returns home and tries to creep into the house, sporting an unexplained black eye. He is accepted back into the family.

The story is inconsequential in a way which allows modification of its meaning and makes it necessary for organisational processes to work on the retailing of it.

The story was shown individually to deaf and hearing people, and they were asked to retell the story immediately, and again after one hour. The deaf people signed to a deaf researcher and the hearing people spoke to a hearing researcher.

Rumelhart (1975) suggests some simple principles for writing down the schema of a story which allow it to be divided into *episodes* and *events*. Using an approach derived from Kintsh (1977) these events may then contain a number of propositions each of which contribute a unit of meaning which can stand alone – they consist of a relational term and one or more arguments. In this interpretation, for English they consist of units with at least a verb and implied subject – 'the bell rang' or 'he gave her a ticket'; while for sign they consist of units containing an action or attribution which constitute an identifiable advancement of meaning (from a deaf transcriber's point of view) and would tend to be translated as a proposition in English – 'MAN-GO' (the man is going) and 'MAN-GONE' (the man has gone) (Figures 3 and 4).

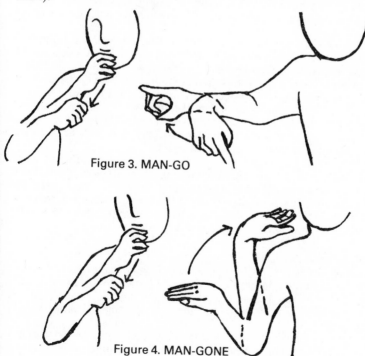

Figure 3. MAN-GO

Figure 4. MAN-GONE

The comparisons are therefore of spoken and signed versions of the same silent film, considered as the communication of a story from one language user to another.

Participants

There were six hearing and six deaf people in this initial examination of recall. The hearing people were secretarial staff in the University aged 30–58. The deaf people were filmed in different locations around the U.K. Their ages ranged from 31–63. They all had been deaf from a early age and had hearing parents. All had severe to profound hearing losses. A seventh deaf and seventh hearing person provided a commentary of the film.

Procedure

For the deaf people the task was introduced at the beginning of a session involving a series of sign language tasks. Each person was shown the silent film, and then introduced to a deaf researcher (the same one each time) who supposedly had not seen this film. They were asked to describe what they had seen in as much detail as they could. Their narrative was video-recorded. Approximately one hour later, they were asked to retell the story (without warning), and again this was video-recorded.

In exactly the same way, the hearing people were individually shown the film then asked for an immediate recall and a recall approximately one hour later. The stories were told to a hearing researcher. Audio recording was made.

Recordings of commentaries of the film, i.e., simultaneous descriptions of the film's content, were made one in Sign by a deaf viewer, and one in speech by a hearing viewer. These, when transcribed, were used to estimate the propositional content of the story, in speech and Sign. It is possible to divide these commentaries into 85 propositions for speech, and 111 propositions in Sign. The reason for the larger amount of grammatical construction in Sign I think relates to the main issue of how information is structured in the language. There is no doubt that the level of accuracy of these accounts and the propositional content is determined by the individuals involved. Qualitatively, there appears to be a difference in the type of propositions used, and it is this which is most interesting. However, it is accepted that there are serious problems in analysis of this data which make the determination of propositions in the surface structure of speech as well as of Sign, extremely difficult. The study claims only to be an initial examination of what is a highly complex, but possibly extremely rich area.

Examination of the Data

Inevitably, the data is very complex and we are only in the initial stages of finding a description for it. The purpose is to examine to what extent the schema or the overall plan used for description differs between deaf and hearing people, and whether this affects or explains the differences in language structure.

There are three major divisions in the story descriptions; episodes, events and propositions. Our examination of deaf and hearing recall therefore revolves around these divisions. By taking a number of hypotheses for analysis we can begin to attempt some answers.

Hypothesis 1
Deaf people and hearing people differ in their descriptions of the story because of different perceptions of world.

There is no support for this hypothesis. All deaf and hearing people reported the main episodes in the story accurately, also the 18 main events in both recalls to the same extent. Comparing hearing peoples' propositional recall to that of the hearing commentary, we find an average of 28% propositions recalled accurately after one hour, for deaf people's signed recall the figure is 29% in comparison to a deaf commentary. These findings reflect a similarity in the process of recall at least at the schema level, and a similarity in the capacity for recall.

Hypothesis 2
Deaf and hearing people differ markedly in the structure of the language production, due to the capacities of the language itself.

Certainly, there are differences between the two commentaries: 111 propositions in sign compared to 85 in speech. These indicate individual differences to some extent, and I do not wish to belabour these actual figures; nevertheless, they provide a yardstick for estimation. However, it is the content of the commentaries which is more interesting. There were 25 one-sign sentences as Stokoe (1980) has defined them (23% of the total). These include examples such as:

MAN SAY NO – *RIVALRY* – WOMAN SAY STAY
Where 'rivalry' consists of alternative upward and downward movement of two G-hands, meaning they disputed who was to go to the door (Figure 5).
and
MAN PANIC – *HOLD* – NO SEND US
Where 'hold' consists of two O hands held in neutral space, meaning 'he held the ticket' (Figure 6).

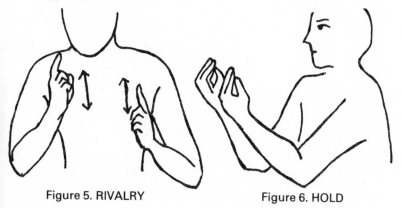

Figure 5. RIVALRY   Figure 6. HOLD

There were four propositions (5%) in the spoken version which were incompletely specified in a way similar to the one-sign sentences. These examples include:

Who is it? – *Ah, the postman* – So now he . . .

and

. . . sending the postman away – *pretending* – that he is as . . .

So there are features in each of these commentaries where there are these different mechanisms at work.

Ten percent of the propositions in sign contained reduplication, while there were no such instances in speech. In addition, there were instances of non-grammatical listings which should not occur in a language such as BSL (Bellugi, 1980).

e.g., WALK – CREEP – APPROACH (Figure 7)

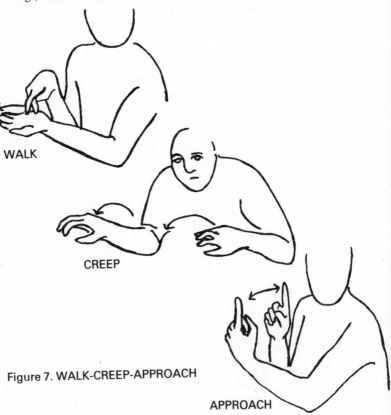

WALK

CREEP

APPROACH

Figure 7. WALK-CREEP-APPROACH

However, it might be expected that these features are highlighted in a commentary where there is little time to organise the meaning and the temporal element has to be specified by reduplication. If these differences between speech and sign exist in recall after an hour, then perhaps we have to consider the existence of a different language structure. Tables 1 and 2 contain transcripts and glosses of a short extract of the participants' recall after one hour.

Table 1. Transcripts of spoken recall of one event after one hour

1. So you next see him on a dance floor and he is dancing a Charleston with some much larger woman than he is.
2. Then the scene switches to the very glamorous Cafe Royale where all the ladies in their beautiful flapper dresses and the men are having a wonderful time and in fact our friend Walter McNab is engaged in a Charleston contest with a young lady of perhaps dubious repute.
3. And actually he goes to this night club that he's got tickets for: there he does the Charleston with some young lady.
4. . . . because he has been at the Cafe Royale all this time – dancing and having a good time.
5. He goes to the Cafe Royale and involves himself in a dance competition, the object of which is to dance the best Charleston. His partner, one Tessa McNab and he have a high old time.
6. . . . and off he goes – but he goes to the Cafe Royale. He gets there and is dancing on the floor with the large tall woman doing the Charleston and everyone around at the sides clapping their hands and cheering them on. . . .

Clearly the spoken versions represent a re-organised view of the event with only Transcript 6 capturing the actual occurrences in the event.

Table 2. Sign glosses of recall of one event after one hour

1. WENT TO DANCE ENJOYED HIMSELF WITH WOMAN ENJOYED.
2. HUSBAND DANCE OTHER WOMAN DANCE MUSIC . . . CLAPPED GOOD.
3. REALLY HE WENT TO c.a.f.e. r.o.y.a.l.e. ENJOYED HIMSELF DANCING WITH GIRL DANCE c.h.a.r.l.e.s.t.o.n. *MIME.*
4. NEXT in c.a.f.e. r.o.y.a.l.e. (STANDING) PEOPLE PEOPLE CLAPPED (STANDING) PEOPLE WEARS SAME BOW (ties) DRESS DRESS UP COUPLE MAN WITH ANOTHER WOMAN DANCE *MIME* DANCE c.h.a.r.l.e.s.t.o.n. d.a.n.c.e. *MIME* DANCE *MIME* GOOD CLAPPED GOOD.
5. NO – DANCE MAN DANCED MAN DANCED WITH c.h.a.r.l.e.s.t.o.n. DANCE WITH WOMAN.
6. i.t. i.s. DANCE h.a.l.l. DANCE HUSBAND ENJOYED HIMSELF WITH OTHER WOMAN ENJOYED.

Even without transcription of body movement, I think it is easy to see the difference in the signed version which support the points in the commentary. These deaf versions capture the richness of the event in a way which is not presented in English.

The question is how this qualitative difference in production can be used to give any insight into sentence construction in Sign. One might describe the signed versions as the reporting of events rather than a rephrasing of the story, and the signers appear to use an event structure rather than a 're-organisation', which normally occurs in spoken English versions.

If sign language tends to report events rather than inferences, we should find an event structure within the recall which most closely reflects the event structure of the original story.

Hypothesis 3
Deaf people in Sign reflect the original events more closely than do hearing people in English.

Examining the actual order of retelling of the story events, we find that in the spoken version, 17% of all propositions recalled were in a different position from the chronological order as reflected in the commentary; only 5% of sign propositions were in different chronological position.

This supports the idea of the re-ordering apparent in the spoken version which is an outcome of the processes fitting the recall to an overall pre-determined schema. The signed version seems more related to the actual events themselves.

Table 3. Simultaneous commentaries on one event from the story

Speech
Oh, now he's on the dance floor with a rather tall dolly bird
very busy doing the Charleston
There were a lot of people
watching them
just the two of them on the floor
doing the Charleston
really quite agile

Sign
MAN AND WOMAN DANCE IN h.a.l.l.
ALL PEOPLE WATCH THEM
CHARLESTON DANCE
DANCE
ALL CLAP CLAP CLAP
DANCE DISCO-DANCE
SHOW DANCE DANCE DANCE

Table 3 has the commentary transcripts for both deaf and hearing, and one can see the obvious similarities in the two. If we then compare the transcripts from Tables 1 and 2 with these, we see that speech produces different recall after one hour, while Sign retains much of the original event structure as described in the commentaries.

We expect this to occur in English, as it is a medium which allows subjects to interpret the task so as to produce inference as an outcome of remembering. There is considerable evidence on this, e.g., Bransford and McCarroll, 1975; Clark, 1975. However, we can now make a weak claim at least that Sign is more likely to be event-structured in representation, and that production is likely to reflect the original events. This does not mean it is iconic or purely visual imagery, since the signs are arbitrary and not transparent. However, there is obviously a large *imaginal* element which is particularly apparent in Sign.

Discussion

At least in this pilot study, sign language when used in narrative differs from speech, not in context or meaning, nor capacity for recall, but in the way the events are reported. It tends to be *more literal* of the original happenings, *more imaginal* in presentation and *deviates much less* from the original sequence of events. This leads to an event-based description where there is less need of explicit referents (as subjects and objects of sentences). As a result, there are increased uses of what deaf transcribers call 'mime' and there is a considerable occurrence of one-sign sentences and propositions. At its simplest, one might say *the Sign task is imaginal,* while *the Speech task is referential; Sign uses an event structure,* while *English creates a different propositional network.*

If this proposal concerning the nature of sign language is valid, it suggests that our views on grammar might require some examination. The examples of HE-SEE-ME may not be a concatenating of three sign units, but rather a simple event-based expression using the sign 'SEE' to present the image of what occurred or could have occurred. One might then predict the grammatical construction from the meaning to be expressed and see its presentation in Sign as a reflection of some event-based schema rather than a syntactic process of the type we generally find in speech. A sign like 'SEE' or 'WATCH' may then become more flexible and more expressive than our English grammatical rules would allow. De Matteo (1977) has made similar detailed claims for visual imagery in ASL as a way of characterising Sign syntax. The results here are consistent with his views. The difficulty, of course, is that a suggestion of image-based Sign is particularly value-laden. It is important to see the outcomes of this study, not as a claim for iconic simplicity in Sign, nor that Sign does not use inference or abstraction, but rather that the task of recall produces a different approach by deaf people in Sign. There is no question of Sign being more basic or not involving 'effort after meaning' but rather it produces a structurally different approach to the task. Whether or not hearing people can, if instructed, produce the same features in speech, is not critical to the fact that deaf people tend to do it spontaneously in Sign. The reason for characterising Sign in this situation as event-structured is that it may help us to describe 'grammatical' aspects of Sign use from a 'top-down perspective and that this may be fruitful.

The argument is therefore that much can be learned from the complex data of Sign narrative, which could be used to guide the study of syntax in Sign. My view is that these findings do not negate a linguistic perspective starting from sign components, modulation and modification, but rather complement and provide an alternative explanatory framework.

Often deaf people do not use the signs that appear in our manuals, nor do they use them in the rule-based way which we have proposed. If we can balance our examination of the components of signs with the consideration of the meaning of events in sign, perhaps we shall reach a clearer view of the nature of sign language much more quickly.

It is true that when deaf people tell a story they do something very different from hearing people. We are only beginning to be aware of the methods available to describe such complex issues among languages. I think, however, that some understanding of these processes is essential to our knowledge and use of sign language.

Acknowledgements

I would particularly like to thank Gloria Pullen and Jennifer Ackerman for their considerable work and advice on this study.

This research was supported by D.H.S.S. grant JR/212/8 for the project 'Sign language Learning and Use'.

SIGN MEDIATION IN A WORD RECOGNITION TASK

Elisabeth H. Dawson

Currently, there is an increasing awareness of, and knowledge about, the features that are encoded, and the processes involved when a word is recognised. In this paper I shall be concerned with an investigation of some of the possible forms of representation used by a group of prelingually deaf individuals for word recognition. Since cognitive processes can never be directly observed, they must be inferred from outward behaviour. In the present study an experimental technique was adopted that has been developed and successfully used by other psychologists with hearing individuals (e.g., Meyer and Schvaneveldt, 1971; Meyer, Schvaneveldt and Ruddy, 1973, 1974). This study was carried out in the context of a broader investigation of the word recognition processes of a group of severely and profoundly prelingually deaf adolescents (Dawson, 1979). Throughout this research, interest was focussed on both general mechanisms and individual differences in the information processing abilities of the deaf individuals.

One must assume that the cognitive representations of verbal material are related to, or constrained by (initially at least), the method of presentation and hence mode of perception. Individuals with normal hearing can both hear verbal language (auditory input) and read verbal language (visual input), whilst the profoundly deaf, who lack functional hearing, can read the printed word, and also 'read' lips, signs and fingerspelled words. In order to be accurately perceived all verbal language has initially to be presented visually to the deaf, and it is the subsequent processing of the visual input, in this case written words, that the present study attempts to probe and investigate.

The importance of language for interpersonal communication is obvious, but from a psychological point of view language is also very important because of its use as a form of representation inside our heads – language allows us to represent knowledge and experience in our everyday lives. Sign language is clearly very important for communication within the deaf community, but the question of its usage as a form of linguistic representation is of crucial concern to a cognitive psychologist. It is therefore of particular interest to investigate the extent to which deaf adolescents, who have acquired sign language and use it fluently with their deaf peers, employ this system as a means of processing verbal information. If manual representation is employed by the prelingually deaf, and we already have some evidence from short-term memory (e.g., Bellugi, Klima and Siple, 1975; Kyle, 1980), then this may have important implications for how verbal information is processed, organised and stored by deaf people. In this paper the major concern is with the possible use of signs as cognitive mediators. Although an investigation of word recognition might not appear to be a very crucial aspect of learning, there is much information to be derived that may subsequently be applied to the process of learning to read.

Previous research into the word recognition abilities of hearing individuals has suggested that words are either converted from their graphemic form into a phonological code which is then used to access word-meaning in the lexicon, or that both visual and phonological representations of the printed word can be used to retrieve meaning in the lexicon (e.g., La Berge and Samuels, 1974; Rubenstein, Lewis and Rubenstein, 1971). Meyer, Schvaneveldt and Ruddy (1974) in summing up a study of word processing in hearing subjects, describe the extent of our present understanding of the factors that influence word recognition:

'Of course, our results do not prove that it is impossible to recognise printed words directly from their visual representations. Visual information is certainly sufficient for recognising some non-verbal objects in the real world. Under various circumstances, people may also comprehend words directly from their visual representations. For example, this could be true of individuals who read non-alphabetic writing such as Chinese' (p. 318).

Their statement referring to the possibility that 'people may also comprehend words directly from their visual representations' may also have some important bearing on word-recognition processes of many prelingually deaf people. In an earlier study (Dawson, 1979) the present author employed the identical experimental method and the same deaf subjects as were used in the present investigation, to see whether the prelingually deaf adolescents would use phonemic and/or graphemic coding. It was also an attempt to discover whether the reliance of deaf people on visual coding in simple memory tasks (e.g., Rozanova, 1970; Frumkin and Anisfeld, 1977) also applied to word-recognition. A significant facilitatory effect of graphemic similarity was found to occur in 25 of the 26 deaf adolescents. A smaller and comparatively insignificant facilitation effect of phonemic similarity (compared to the control word pairs) was observed in 17 of the 26 deaf subjects. The hearing control subjects, on the other hand, showed interference from the graphemically similar words and facilitation for the phonemically related word-pairs. These results have subsequently been supported by Dodd (1980) in her recent investigation of the spelling abilities of a group of profoundly prelingually deaf children. She concluded that her deaf subjects used both phonological and graphemic codes, with the latter probably being the preferred form of representation for many tasks.

In addition to deaf people's use of visual and, to a lesser extent, phonological representation (there are important individual differences here within the deaf population which should not be overlooked), Sign may also mediate the word-recognition processes of certain deaf individuals. The 'signability' of English words has previously been investigated. Putnam, Iscoe and Young (1962), for example, manipulated sign similarity and found that their deaf subjects were capable of discriminating between the members of a pair of words with similar signs, and learned these words faster than those with dissimilar sign equivalents. In another memory experiment, Odom, Blanton and McIntyre (1970) investigated the recall of 16 English words (eight words with sign equivalents and eight without). They reported that their deaf subjects recalled more words than the hearing control group, and attributed this superior word recall of the deaf subjects to their better ability to recall the signable words in the word list. More recently, Conlin and Paivio

(1975) varied the signability (which they defined as 'a measure of the ease with which a word can be represented as a gestural sign') of the words learned in paired-associate word lists. They found that signability facilitated recall for the deaf group but did not effect the recall of the hearing control subjects. Also using a paired-associate verbal learning task, Moulton and Beasley (1975) reported that deaf subjects could code verbal material on the basis of signs.

Bellugi and Siple (1974) investigated the ability of a group of deaf individuals to remember signs taken from ASL, and commented on the relationship existing between an English word and its manual sign equivalent. They postulated that 'the relation between a sign in ASL and an English word is a good deal more remote than the relation between the spoken and written versions of English words' (p. 229). It is this ability to transform information between written words and signs that is investigated here. In another more recent memory experiment, Siple, Fischer and Bellugi (1977) presented a list of signs and English words to a group of deaf college students. Subsequently they tested recognition of the list by presenting a new list of items (in which half were new items and the other half had previously been seen, and of those previously presented, half were in the same form (sign or word) as before, and the others were in the opposite modality). They concluded that the deaf subjects treated the signs and words as lexical elements from two separate language systems, and suggested that signs were better encoded by the deaf, and that the words were possibly sometimes translated into their sign equivalents.

To sum up, the experimental studies reviewed suggest that deaf people often employ a visual form of representation and that some are also able to use phonological coding. It would also seem that sign encoding of English words can be an important factor in the verbal learning of deaf people. The question that now needs to be asked is: do signs mediate at the earlier cognitive stage of word-recognition?

In the lexical-decision task that was used in the present investigation the subjects were required to decide as quickly as possible whether or not a written letter-string was an English word. The cognitive processes involved in the identification of English words were studied as a function of the manipulated relations between pairs of words using reaction time data as a clue to the underlying cognitive operations involved in word-recognition.

Earlier research has shown that signs may be fractionated into smaller, sub-lexical elements. Signs are made up of three major parameters; hand configuration, place of articulation and movement (see early work on ASL by Stokoe, 1960; 1978; and on BSL by Brennan, Colville and Lawson, 1980). Support for the psychological reality of these parameters comes from the study of 'slips of the hand' which suggests the independence of these co-occurring parameters (see chapter 5 in Klima and Bellugi, 1979). In addition to this, studies of the recall of signs from short-term memory suggest that they are processed and rehearsed in terms of the three formational components listed above (e.g., Bellugi, Klima and Siple, 1975).

The effect of similarity of sign equivalents was investigated using pairs of words whose sign equivalents differed on one of the formational parameters, compared with pairs of words which have no sign equivalents and could, therefore, only be represented manually using fingerspelling, and with control words (words with non-similar sign equivalents). The accepted signs of the residential deaf school community were used. The relatively limited vocabulary of the deaf adolescents, together with the experimental constraints, complicated word selection. A great deal of attention was paid to the selection of the stimulus words, using two teachers and two ex-pupils from the school in which I worked to generate possible word-pairs. particular care was taken to ensure that every word was within the reading vocabulary of each deaf and hearing individual tested.

The experiment was designed to test the following hypotheses:

(1) that the deaf subjects would recognise the word-pairs with similar sign equivalents faster than either the control words, or those words without sign equivalents;

(2) that the deaf subjects would recognise the control word-pairs faster than those without sign equivalents which could only be represented manually using fingerspelling;

(3) that the hearing control subjects would process all three types of word-pair equally proficiently since sign language was not a relevant dimension for them.

The Experiment

Twenty-six severely or profoundly prelingually deaf adolescents (13 boys and 13 girls) were randomly selected from the senior department of a residential deaf school. Reading ages ranged from 7.7 to 9.11 years (median: 8.4 years) whilst their chronological ages ranged from 12.7 to 15.8 years (median: 13.11 years). Mean hearing loss was 'cd' (Lewis, 1968) with a mean loss of 79dB for the better ear over the lower frequencies, and 90dB over the higher frequencies.

Twelve normally-hearing children (six boys and 6 girls) from a Middle School, aged 12.5 and 13.3 years, acted as control subjects (median age: 12.10 years). All the subjects were of average or above-average non-verbal intelligence; all were right-handed, and all had normal vision, or vision corrected to within normal limits.

A two-field tachistoscope was used to present the 24 practice and the 96 test stimulus cards. On each card was printed two strings of letters. The 96 test stimuli consisted of 48 Word-Word (W-W) pairs:

Type 1: 16 pairs of words with similar sign equivalents but which are not semantically related (e.g., 'who' and 'sweets').

Type 2: 16 pairs of words with sign equivalents which are not similar, i.e., control words (e.g., 'bird' and 'man').

Type 3: 16 pairs of words which have no sign equivalent and which have to be fingerspelled if they are to be represented manually (e.g., 'tiger' and 'fruit').

The remaining 48 pairs of stimuli consisted of 24 Non-word – Non-word (NW-NW) sequences, 12 Non-word – Word (NW-W) and 12 Word – Non-word (W-NW) sequences. The non-words did not follow the rules of English orthography or phonology, and were not to be found in the English language (using *Webster's New Collegiate Dictionary*, 1976). The non-words were anagrams of the original words and were created by randomly re-ordering the letters within each of the words used in the W-W pairs, thus holding letter frequency and letter-sequence length constant for the words and the non-words. Table 1 shows the 48 W-W pairs used in the experiment.

Table 1. The 48 word-pairs presented in the experiment

Type 1: Words sharing very similar sign equivalents but which are not semantically related:
   who – sweets; nurse – red; black – apple; work – green; poor – biscuit; shop – which; pen – shy; sheep – cruel; library – always; school – soldier; friend – football; live – map: dog – fed-up; please – laugh; soft – easy; mad – rough.

Type 2: Words with sign equivalents which are not similar (control words):

   orange – girl; pencil – face; child – car; house – book; light – nice; plate – flower; spoon – kind; hair – stupid; fire – rabbit; ball – hat; king – coat; film – rain; river – good; sun – fish; bird – man; think – brush.

Type 3: Words with no equivalents:

   tiger – fruit; factory – mile; lake – rose; test – window; field – cheese; way – metal; land – jam; shell – week; lid – farm; carrot – danger; hobby – city; island – about; town – tin; exam – wood; country – gold; picnic – part.

Each subject was tested individually in a 40-minute session which included a block of 24 practice trials which enabled the subject to become totally familiar with the experimental procedure. The 96 test trials were divided into four blocks of 24 trials with a short rest interval between each block. On each trial two strings of lower-case letters were presented simultaneously, one above the other, and the subjects were required to decide as quickly and as accurately as possible whether or not *both* strings of letters were English words and press the 'yes' key to indicate a positive lexical-decision, otherwise the 'no' key was pressed to indicate a negative decision (that one or both of the letter-strings were non-words). Response latency was the dependent variable. The stimuli were presented well above threshold with regard to luminance, clarity and duration (.5 second). Half of the subjects used their preferred hand to indicate a positive decision and their non-preferred for the negative decision, and vice versa for the remaining individuals. On half of the 96 test trials a positive response was correct and on the remaining trials a negative response was correct. Reaction time (RT) was measured (to the nearest millisecond) from the onset of presentation of the stimulus card until one or other of the response keys was pressed. The subjects were instructed to respond as quickly and as accurately as possible; accuracy was emphasised. The subjects were told immediately after each trial whether or not their decision had been correct. Each subject was tested on all 96 pairs of stimuli in random order. The RT and correctness of the judgement were recorded for each of the 96 test trials. The number of errors and the RT data were averaged (medians were used) for each subject prior to statistical analysis.

Results
As can be seen in Table 2 and from Figure 1, speed of lexical decision was affected by the different stimulus categories. As was predicted, the deaf subjects responded faster to the W-W pairs with similar sign equivalents than to the control word-pairs although the difference was not significant, and the words without sign equivalents were processed more slowly than either of the other two W-W categories. This finding suggests that the presence/absence of a sign equivalent was an important determinant of lexical-decision speed for the deaf subjects. In fact 17 of the 26 deaf individuals processed the W-W pairs with similar sign equivalents (averaged across the 16 trials) faster than any of the other stimulus categories. The hearing subjects, on the other hand, recognised the control W-W pairs faster than the word-pairs with similar signs which in their turn were recognised faster than the word-pairs with no sign equivalents. The average differences between the response latencies were smaller than those of the deaf subjects, and none of the differences were significant when compared against the control word-pairs. As might be expected for word-pairs manipulated along a dimension that was irrelevant for the hearing subjects, namely manual representation, the pattern of response latencies was less consistent for the hearing group compared with the deaf group.

The response latency data (using median correct RT) of the 26 deaf and 12 hearing subjects for the three categories of W-W pair were analysed using a 2 × 3 (Hearing status) × (Stimulus-category) factorial analysis of variance with repeated measures on the second factor, and using an unweighted means solution. Of the two main effects only Stimulus-category was significant ($F(2, 72) = 23.84, p < .001$), and the interaction between Hearing status and Stimulus-category was also significant ($F(2, 72) = 5.71, p < .001$).

In addition, planned comparisons were carried out for the deaf and hearing subjects separately, comparing the word-pairs with similar sign equivalents, and also the word-pairs with no sign equivalents with the control word-pairs. The results of the Dunnett Test against Control (Winer, 1971, pp. 89–90) showed that neither of the comparisons were significant for the hearing control group ($t = 0.45$ for the word-pairs with similar sign equivalents compared with the controls; and $t = 0.98$ for the word-pairs with no sign equivalents compared with the controls). These results supported the hypothesis that there would be no significant difference between the average reaction times across the three W-W stimulus categories. For the deaf subjects however, the difference between word-pairs with no sign equivalents and the control word-pairs was significant ($t = 2.04, p < .05$,

Table 2. Median response latencies and percentage error for each stimulus-category

Type of letter-string: Top String	Bottom String	Sign equivalent	Response category	Proportion of trials	Median RT (msecs) Deaf Ss (sd)	Hearing Ss (sd)	Percentage Errors Deaf Ss	Hearing Ss
W	— W	Similar	Yes	.167	722 (151)	720 (151)	3.4	2.7
W	— W	Dissimilar	Yes	.167	731 (179)	690 (135)	3.4	2.8
W	— W	No sign equivalent	Yes	.167	794 (210)	742 (165)	6.0	4.9
W	— NW		No	.125	949 (183)	978 (166)	23.6	28.3
NW	— W		No	.125	815 (212)	812 (193)	12.5	14.8
NW	— NW		No	.125	782 (187)	736 (171)	3.6	1.7

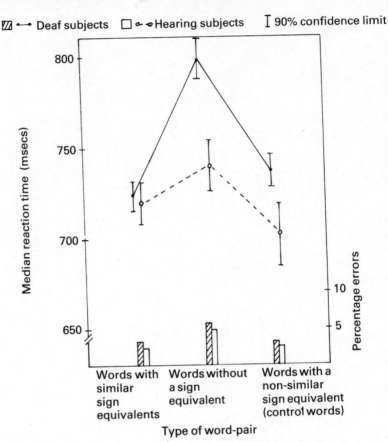

Figure 1. Lexical-decision latency as a function of hearing ability and signability of the word pairs

one-tailed test), whilst the difference between word-pairs with similar sign equivalents and the control words was not not significant ($t = 0.46$). As was hypothesised, deaf subjects did process the control words significantly faster than those without sign equivalents, but the results did not support the hypothesis that words with similar sign equivalents would be processed faster than the control words (with non-similar sign equivalents).

Most of the subjects, both deaf and hearing, responded correctly to the word-pairs faster than they did to the non-word stimuli. They seemed to be carrying out a more exhaustive scanning process for the non-words than for the words, and hence were able to recognise the words faster than they were able to accurately reject the non-words. Overall, the correct negative responses to the three non-word stimulus categories were very similar for both the deaf and the hearing subjects (see Figure 2).

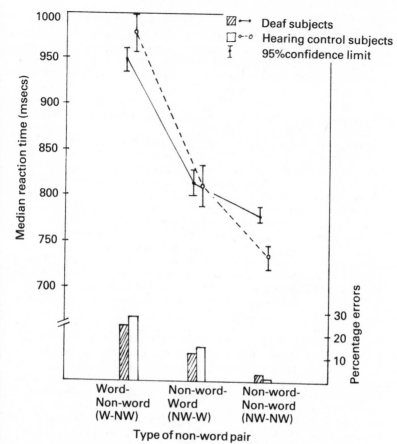

Figure 2. Lexical-decision latency for the non-word pairs as a function of hearing ability

The distribution of errors was very similar to the pattern of median correct response latencies across the stimulus categories, i.e., as the average response latency increased, so did the number of errors. This direct relationship suggests that speed was not being directly traded-off for accuracy.

Discussion

These results do provide indirect evidence of the use of a form of sign representation by the deaf group. When deaf people are given the task of recognising English words from non-words, and given no particular instruction, it seems that the visual information may be translated into a form of representation based on signs, suggesting that sign language is a salient linguistic code for them. Previous studies have shown that sign mediation is an important factor in learning and memory (e.g., Moulton and Beasley, 1975; Odom, Blanton and McIntyre, 1970) whilst the present results suggest that sign mediation is also important for word-recognition, thereby extending the above-mentioned finding to an earlier stage in the processing of printed words, namely visual recognition, rather than storage and rehearsal processes during verbal learning.

The most striking finding was the effect of the presence/absence of a sign equivalent of the English words, irrespective of whether the sign was formationally similar to any other sign. In fact, contrary to expectation, similarity of sign equivalent only produced a small, non-significant facilitation effect relative to the control words. It is assumed that deaf individuals would not discover a sign association between written words unless they were representing the visual image of the printed words into their sign equivalents. Sign language was apparently providing these deaf subjects with a readily available means of processing English vocabulary. The possibility of sign mediation raises the question of covert signing which is possibly similar to covert speech, and may serve the same purpose in cognitive functioning (see Conrad, 1979). Evans (1976) put forward the suggestion that words might be used as 'signals' rather than as symbols by many deaf children. The apparent covert use of a form of sign representation in a lexical-decision task would in fact support Evans' suggestion that words may be used merely as 'signals' whilst signs provide the symbols necessary for thinking.

The present findings also provide experimental evidence to support the idea of Bonvillian, Charrow and Nelson (1973) that English-English word associations are mediated through signs, and would appear to contradict Bellugi and Siple's (1974) postulation that the relation between a sign in ASL and an English word is more remote than between spoken and written versions of English. This sample of deaf individuals at least certainly appeared to be using signs in a close relationship to English words. Conlin and Paivio (1975) were unable to conclude from their study of imagery and signability using a paired-associate learning task, whether the effect of signability which they observed was the result of gestural mediation or rehearsal strategy. It is clear from the results of the present experiment that only sign mediation could possibly account for the speed of word-recognition achieved by the deaf subjects (mean RT 749 msecs. for the 48 W-W trials).

One cannot conclude from the present findings that sign mediation is used for word-recognition by all deaf people, but that it can be used, and was used in a particular experimental situation when isolated pairs of printed English words were presented tachistoscopically, and when semantic variables were not a relevant feature. It is always necessary to remember that there are important individual differences within any deaf population which are related, at least partly, to considerable differences in linguistic skills (speech intelligibility, lip-reading skills, reading skills, sign language skills – see Conrad, 1979). These differences can very easily be overlooked if one assumes a homogeneous sample, or if the researcher fails to investigate what lies behind the average figures usually presented for group data.

Further research using the same technique is needed to replicate the present study and further explore the word-recognition processes of deaf

Figure 3. A preliminary model of the three possible forms of cognitive representation used by the deaf subjects in a word-recognition task

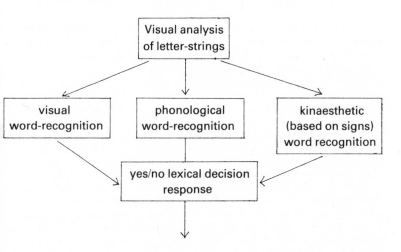

people. At the present time, the findings of this experiment and other research studies would suggest that visual, phonological and sign mediation are independently important in processing words (see Figure 3). We now need to investigate the *relationship*(s) between these possible forms of cognitive representation, and the interaction between them. Also, we need to find out more about the relationship between words and signs, and the properties of a form of kinaesthetic representation based on signs, before we can begin to more fully understand the cognitive operations involved when a child learns to read, and before we can develop more effective education programmes for deaf people.

Acknowledgements
The author would like to acknowledge her gratitude to the headmaster, staff and pupils of the Northern Counties School for the Deaf, Newcastle-upon-Tyne, and of Marden Bridge Middle School, Whitley Bay. This research was supported by the Social Sciences Research Council.

SENTENCE REPETITION IN AMERICAN SIGN LANGUAGE

Rachel Mayberry, Susan Fischer, Nancy Hatfield

In the United States, about 90% of deaf children have parents who hear normally (Schein and Delk, 1974). The figure suggests that most deaf adults who use sign language learned it for the first time from teachers or peers in classrooms and on playgrounds rather than at home around their parent's knees. Thus we are interested in the relationship between how old a person is when she first begins to learn a language and the fluency with which she can produce and understand that language in adulthood. Ideally we would like to describe and measure the relationship between early experience and environment in language learning. In particular, we want to understand better how sign language is learned in childhood and adulthood for both research and educational purposes. How can we distinguish among special patterns of language learning be it signed or spoken, first or second, typical, delayed or disordered? To explore the question, we designed some experiments to examine the relationship between the age at which people first learn to sign and their ability to repeat sentences in American Sign Language, ASL. Before we present and discuss the quantitative data from our first experiment, we will discuss briefly the research that led to our hypotheses. The results demonstrate that signers' ability to repeat ASL sentences depends, in part, upon the length of time they have used sign language and thus help explain the great variation in production and comprehension skills among adult signers.

Variation in Sign Language

Stokoe (1970) originally proposed that signers in the United States and parts of Canada used two dialects of sign language, one a public and the other a private dialect that signers used when they were alone among themselves. He called the situation 'sign language diglossia'. Ferguson (1959) first used the term 'diglossia' to describe two varieties of the same language that speakers use in complementary social situations. Woodward (1973) and Woodward and Markowicz (1975) suggested that the variation in sign language Stokoe described was akin to pidgin and creole languages. They proposed that one dialect of sign language was a pidgin language, a mix of sign language and English which they called 'pidgin-sign English', or PSE. Later, Fischer (1978) also observed multiple linguistic and socioeconomic similarities between pidgin and creole languages and the relationship of pidgin-sign English to American Sign Language. Because pidgin languages are the product of second-language learning and creole languages are the product of first-language learning, there may be an intimate and complex relationship between the age at which a person first learns to sign and the linguistic structure in sign language that he can produce and understand as an adult.

Linguistic Structure

There is a growing list of linguistic structures that linguists have found to occur regularily in ASL, but not in PSE (Wilbur, 1979). The list includes inflections for verb aspect and number that are nested in the movements of signs (Fischer, 1973; Fischer and Gough, 1978: Klima and Bellugi, 1979). ASL uses inflections for nouns and verbs that also are nested in sign movement. In addition, ASL uses a complex set of classifiers (Supalla and Newport, 1978; Newport and Supalla, 1980; McDonald, 1981). Facial expressions and torso movements serve both linguistic and paralinguistic functions in ASL; the nonmanual signals mark phrases, clauses and sentences in ASL, but not in PSE (Baker and Padden, 1978; Liddell, 1978; Reilly and McIntire, 1980).

Age of Acquisition

Several researches have observed that second-generation signers, that is, deaf signers whose parents are also deaf and sign, produce the above ASL morphology in their signing. Their parents usually do not if they are first-generation signers. First-generation signers are deaf people whose parents hear normally and do not sign. Such a signer first learns to sign after infancy outside the home and typically produces a pidgin-sign language, PSE. The deaf children of first-generation signers see their parents use a pidgin-sign language, PSE, but produce a creole-sign language, ASL, instead. Fischer (1978) and Newport and Supalla (1980) have proposed that the differences in the linguistic structure between ASL and PSE reflect the age differences of their learners: Signers who first learn to sign as children produce ASL, but signers who first learn to sign as adults are more likely to produce PSE.

Fluency in Sign language

Native and nonnative signers. Mayberry (1979) found measurable differences in ASL fluency among deaf signers similar to those of native and nonnative speakers. She asked native and nonnative signers to shadow ASL stories (the signer repeats a message while simultaneously watching it). The native signers in Mayberry's study were all congenitally deaf adults who first learned to sign from their deaf parents, second-generation signers. The nonnative, or first generation, signers were all congenitally deaf adults who had normally hearing parents. Their first language was English and they all first learned to sign after 16 years of age.

Both the native and nonnative signers' shadowing accuracy was positively correlated with their ability to answer questions about the stories they shadowed. The native signers shadowed the ASL stories with greater accuracy than the nonnative signers. Much earlier, Treisman (1965) found that speakers who were equally fluent in English and French shadowed prose passages from both languages with equal accuracy. Speakers who were unequally fluent in English and French shadowed their native language with greater accuracy than they shadowed their nonnative or second language. More recently, Ringeling (1979) obtained similar results for speakers of Dutch who shadowed their native Dutch with greater accuracy than they shadowed their nonnative and second language, English.

ASL and PSE. Hatfield (1980) designed a study to determine the degree to which deaf signers show bilingual fluency in ASL and PSE. She presented ASL and PSE translations of sentences such as, 'Birds can't fly' and 'Ice is colder than water' to five groups of deaf signers. She measured the speed and accuracy with which they decided whether the ASL and PSE sentences were true or false. One group of signers had deaf parents from whom they learned to sign. They were native signers who also, as children, attended schools that used some form of manual communication in the classroom. The remaining groups of deaf signers all had normally hearing parents. Hatfield grouped the deaf signers with normally hearing parents according to the age at which they first began to sign (from birth, before 12 years, and after 15 years of age) whether their normally hearing parents signed or not, and whether or not they had attended schools that used manual communication in the classroom.

Hatfield (1980) found that the best single predictor of the signers' ASL skill was the age at which they first began to learn to sign. The best single predicator of the signers' PSE skill was whether they, as children, attended a school that used some form of manual communication in the classroom. The signers who had deaf parents and also attended schools that used manual communication in the classroom showed equal skill on the ASL and PSE sentences. Of the five groups of signers with normally hearing parents, four showed greater skill on the PSE sentences. Only one group showed greater skill on the ASL sentences. Their normally hearing parents did not sign; they first learned to sign before 12 years of age, but did not attend schools that used manual communication in the classroom until they were 15 years of age. Hatfield's results demonstrate that deaf signers possess varying degrees of bilingual fluency in both ASL and PSE. Furthermore, her results demonstrate that signers' fluency in ASL and PSE is related to their childhood experience with each.

We were thus interested in exploring in greater detail a relationship between the age at which a person first learns to sign and her or his ability to repeat ASL sentences. In addition, we also wanted to compare behavioural measures of fluency in ASL.

Hypotheses. We proposed three hypotheses. First, the earlier a person first learns to sign, the more accurately he will be able to repeat ASL sentences. Second, the earlier a person first learns to sign, the more accurately he will be able to repeat grammatical-ASL sentences as compared to scrambled-ASL sentences. Third, the earlier a person first learns to sign, the more accurately he will be able to simultaneously receive and repeat ASL sentences (shadowing) as compared to his ability to consecutively receive and repeat ASL sentences (recall).

Method

To test our hypotheses, we designed an experiment using a $4 \times 2 \times 2$ analysis of variance design with repeated measures on the last two variables. The between-subjects variable was the age at which congenitally deaf, adult signers first began to learn to sign (from birth, from five years of age, between the ages of 13 and 15, and after 18 years of age). The first within-subjects variable was syntactic structure, ASL sentences and scrambled-ASL sentences. The second within-subjects variable was the task of repeating ASL sentences and scrambled sentences either while simultaneously watching them (shadowing), or after watching them (recall). The dependent measure was repetition accuracy.

Stimulus Utterances

Hatfield (1980) originally constructed most of the ASL sentences we used for her sentence verification task. We used 32 ASL sentences which varied in length from 3 to 10 morphemes. The average length of the sentences was 6 morphemes. By morphemes we mean ASL inflections as well as base signs. Next we created 32 scrambled-ASL sentences by randomising the order of the signs within each of the sentences. When we randomised the order of the signs within the sentences, we kept the inflections with their original base signs. Then we mixed the ASL sentences and the scrambled-ASL sentences into two lists of 32 utterances each. Half of each list consisted of ASL sentences and the other half consisted of scrambled-ASL sentences. Within each list we randomised the presentation order of the sentences and scrambled sentences.

We videotaped the experiment's instructions, the practice utterances, and the two stimulus lists. A congenitally deaf, native-ASL signer signed all the stimulus utterances. He signed both the ASL sentences and the scrambled-ASL sentences with normal ASL phrasing patterns.

Subjects

The 44 subjects were all congenitally deaf, young adults who were students and faculty at the National Technical Institute for the Deaf. They ranged in age from 20 to 38 years. We grouped the subjects in terms of the age at which they first began to learn sign language. The first group consisted of 12 subjects, 11 of whom had two deaf parents, and one who had normally hearing parents but who also had two, older deaf siblings. All the subjects in the first group were exposed to sign language from birth in their homes. The second group consisted of 9 subjects, all of whom had two normally hearing parents and first began to learn to sign at school when they were five years old. The third group consisted of 12 subjects, all of whom had two normally hearing parents and first began to learn to sign outside their homes between the ages of 13 and 15 years. The fourth group consisted of 11 subjects, all of whom had two normally hearing parents and first began to learn to sign after 18 years of age.

Procedure

We tested the subjects individually. After explaining the procedure, we showed the subjects the videotaped instructions after which they practised either the shadowing or recall task with two sentences and two scrambled sentences. If the subject had no questions, we proceeded with the first experimental task. When we showed the two lists of videotaped utterances to the subjects, we alternated the two lists with the two tasks so that all the subjects saw all the stimulus sentences and their scrambled counterparts and performed both the shadowing and the recall task. Half of the subjects performed the shadowing task followed by the recall task. The other half of the subjects performed the recall task first. We videotaped each subject's performance.

Data Analysis
Two congenitally deaf, ASL signers transcribed the subjects' videotaped performance. The transcribers noted how many and which signs and inflections in each ASL sentence and scrambled-ASL sentence each subject repeated accurately. They also recorded all the subjects' errors as omissions, substitutions, and additions. We then calculated the percentage of morphemes for each sentence and scrambled sentence that each subject repeated accurately. For the statistical analyses, three-way analysis of variance, we transformed the percentages with Arcsins (Ferguson, 1971). For clarity, however, we will report the data here in mean percentages.

Results
Our hypotheses predicted that the four groups of signers would repeat the utterances with unequal accuracy. We also predicted that the subjects would repeat the ASL sentences with greater accuracy than they would repeat the scrambled-ASL sentences and that they would recall the ASL sentences more accurately than they would shadow the same stimuli. The results support the first two, but not the last, hypotheses. The results demonstrate, first, that the earlier deaf signers have learned sign language, the greater the accuracy with which they can repeat ASL sentences and scrambled-ASL sentences. The results also demonstrate that the order of signs in ASL sentences facilitates signers' ability both to shadow and recall ASL sentences. Last, the results demonstrate that accurate recall of ASL utterances is a more difficult task than accurate shadowing of the same stimuli.

Sentences and Scrambled Sentences

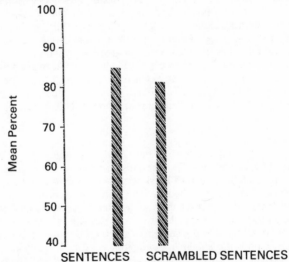

Figure 1. The subjects' mean performance on the ASL sentences and scrambled-ASL sentences

Figure 1 shows the significant main effect of removing sign order from ASL sentences on signers' repetition accuracy ($F = 13.19$; $df = 1, 40$; $p < .001$). The signers accurately repeated a greater percentage of the ASL sentences (85%) as compared to the scrambled-ASL sentences (83%). We originally predicted an interaction between the age at which signers first learned to sign and their ability to repeat ASL sentences and scrambled sentences. We thought that signers who had signed for only a few years would repeat the sentences and scrambled sentences equally well, but that signers who had signed for most of their lives would repeat the sentences more accurately than the scrambled sentences. The data do not support our hypothesis. However, the data suggest that sign order plays a facilitative role in signers' ability to repeat sentences in the tasks of shadowing and recall.

Shadowing and Recall tasks

Figure 2 shows the significant main effect of the repetition tasks, shadowing and recall ($F = 490.21$; $df = 1, 40$; $p < .001$). Overall, the subjects shadowed the sentences and scrambled sentences with greater accuracy (92%) than they recalled the sentences and scrambled sentences (76%). Contrary to our expectations, shadowing single sentences and scrambled sentences was not more difficult than accurate recall of the same stimuli. We hypothesised that doing two things at once, watching and signing a sentence simultaneously, would be more difficult than doing one thing after another, successively watching and then signing a sentence. Although recall may play a role in accurate shadowing, the subject can offset limited recall by faster or closer shadowing, that is, shadowing behind the stimulus at a length of a phrase or single sign.

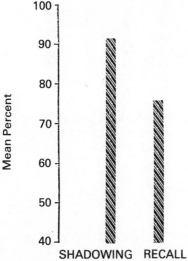

Figure 2. The subjects' mean performance on the shadowing and recall tasks

Groups

Figure 3 shows the significant main effect of grouping the subjects by the age at which they first began to learn to sign ($F = 42.54$; $df = 3, 40$; $p < .00001$). Signers who first learned to sign from birth performed with greater accuracy (94%) than signers who first learned to sign at five years of age when they first attended school (90%). The performance of the first group may be attenuated by ceiling effects. Signers who first began to sign between 13 and 15 years of age and after 18 years of age performed less accurately than the first two groups (80% and 73% respectively). Despite the clear trend for signers to perform with greater accuracy the earlier they first learn to sign, a posteriori analysis showed that the performance differences between adjacent groups was not statistically significant (Tukey's *Honestly Significant Difference;* Kirk, 1968).

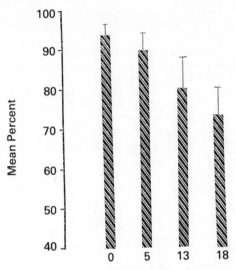

Figure 3. The mean performance and standard deviations of the subjects grouped by the age at which they first began to learn sign language

Groups and Tasks

Figure 4 shows the significant interaction of the groups with the shadowing and recall tasks ($F = 3.49$; $df = 3,40$; $p < .05$). All the groups shadowed the sentences and scrambled sentences more accurately than they recalled the same stimuli. As Figure 4 shows, the disparity between the groups' shadowing and recall accuracy was greater for groups three and four than it was for groups one and two. The effect may be artificially created by a ceiling effect for the shadowing accuracy of groups one and two (98% each).

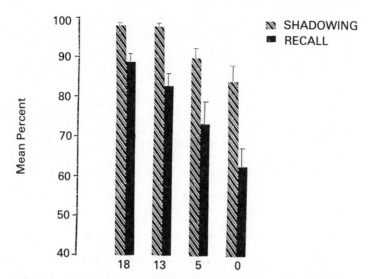

Figure 4. The groups' mean performance and standard deviations on the shadowing and recall tasks

Discussion

The quantitative results of our experiment provide five important findings. First, the results replicate and extend earlier research demonstrating that deaf signers show considerable variability in ASL fluency (Mayberry, 1979). Second, the results demonstrate that ASL fluency is a function, in part, of the number of years a person has signed (Hatfield, 1980). Third, the results show that accurate recall of utterances is a more sensitive measure of ASL fluency than accurate shadowing of utterances. Fourth, the quantitative data replicate earlier research demonstrating that the order of signs in ASL sentences plays a facilitative role in ASL-sentence comprehension (Tweney & Heiman, 1977). However, the data do not support our hypothesis that scrambling sign order in ASL sentences reduces the ability of native-ASL signers to shadow and recall ASL utterances more so than that of nonnative signers. Last, the shadowing performance of the native-ASL signers on the ASL sentences and scrambled sentences is very similar to speech data that Lackner (1980) reported for native-English speakers shadowing English sentences and sentences containing syntactic and semantic errors. In addition to the quantitative data, our experiment yielded great deal of qualitative data in terms of errors. We are analysing the subjects' error patterns in relation to their accuracy scores. The error analysis will give us more descriptive insight into the phenomenon of fluency in sign language.

Our results do not demonstrate that age of acquisition is a critical or determining factor in ASL fluency. Because the 44 subjects in our experiment were all young adults between the ages of 20 to 38, our results show only that the greater the number of years a person has signed, the greater the accuracy with which he can repeat ASL sentences. Clearly, we need to replicate our experiment with signers who are older than 38 years of age.

In terms of the relationship between age of acquisition and second-language learning, McLaughlin (1979) concluded that there is no experimental evidence in support of the hypothesis that children learn a second language more rapidly than adults (Lenneberg, 1967). Adults and children bring very different sets of perceptual, cognitive, and social skill with them to the task of language learning. McLaughlin (1978) concluded that adults learn second-language vocabulary and syntax more rapidly than children, but that children surpass adults in their ability to speak a second language with native-like articulation. We tend to expect greater language proficiency from adults than from children: Burling (1981, p. 12a) succintly summarised the problems he experienced learning Swedish as an adult when he noted that no mother ever took his hand and said, 'Say "excuse me" to the nice man, darling.'

For some time now researchers and educators have known on either an intuitive or observational basis that the sign language skills of deaf adults are quite heterogeneous. The results of much research are beginning to converge. Until we have evidence to the contrary, we must assume that the factors that nurture and guide fluency in spoken language also nurture and guide fluency in sign language. Although there are multiple and fruitful comparisons that researchers can and must make between first- and second-language learning in both spoken and sign language, there are important differences between the two situations. Thus future research must carefully elucidate the similarities and differences among the diverse situations in which deaf children learn language. In particular, future research must examine the similarities and differences among (1) learning sign language as a first or second language in childhood; (2) learning sign language as a second language in adulthood; and (3) delayed first-language learning, be it signed or spoken.

Acknowledgements
The research reported here was supported in part by the National Technical Institute for the Deaf in the course of an agreement with the U.S. Department of Education and by a grant from the National Institute of Neurological and Communicative Disorders and Stroke, 1R23NS17613-01. We thank Frank Woosley for his superb signing skill, the subjects for their gracious and willing participation, Keith Cagel and Sharon Lott for their patient and exacting transcription, and Walter Secada and Pat Siple for their statistical help.

PERCEPTUAL CONFUSIONS IN ASL UNDER NORMAL AND REDUCED (POINT-LIGHT DISPLAY) CONDITIONS

Vivien Tartter, Susan Fischer

Two years ago, we presented results from a preliminary study with Ken Knowlton (Tartter and Knowlton, 1979, 1981) showing the potential feasibility of transmitting American Sign Language (ASL) across telephone lines. The requirements were twofold. First, the ASL signal had to be sufficiently compressed to fit into the telephone bandwidth; this involves approximately a thousand-fold reduction in information from a black and white TV picture. Second, the reduced signal had to be readily comprehended by signers so that little or no training would be necessary for relatively natural conversation.

We demonstrated that two pairs of signers were able to converse naturally when all they viewed of each other were displays of 27 moving spots of light. These will be described in more detail shortly. The results were preliminary in that: (1) we only estimated that these displays could be converted to telephone bandwidth, and (2) we did not have a precise measure of what our subjects were seeing – conversation is redundant with respect to topic, social rules, syntax, semantics and 'cherology', and this redundancy could have allowed our subjects to guess correctly at substantial portions of the signal. The study that we are presenting today was aimed primarily at resolving this second issue, to determine precisely what formational feature values are visible from the point-light displays, in the absence of other redundancy.

The point-light displays were created following the procedures described by Johannson (1973) and Kozlowski and Cutting (1977), among others. Small pieces of retroflective tape (bicycle tape) are affixed to the body and then the individual is videotaped with the only light source being a bright light next to the videocamera. The placement of the light ensures that the tape pieces reflect directly back, at the camera, and the body leaves a relatively dim image. Appropriate adjustment of the playback monitor eliminates all but the brightest spots, the tape pieces.

To convey sign in particular, the trick is to select a good configuration of tape pieces. We placed one on the nose and 13 on each hand: one at each finger and thumb tip, one at the back of the second joints of each finger, and four around each wrist. Our hope was that this was sufficient for conveying information about the four formational parameters of sign, location, handshape, orientation and movement (Stokoe, Casterline and Croneberg, 1965; Battison, 1974, 1978). Relative location could be seen by hand movement in relation to the nose, handshape and orientation by the number of finger dots visible, the distance between them, and their spatial configuration, and movement, by the change in position of these spots over time on the monitor. Note that this particular configuration of spots eliminates facial expression (which, of course, is important in sign; e.g., Fischer and Forman, 1981) but does indicate head movement by movement of the nose spot. And Mayberry (1979) has suggested that some aspects of facial expression may be conveyed redundantly in head movement.

215

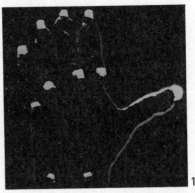

1a   1b

The first figure shows a black and white photograph of the back of one
glove in normal and high-contrast lighting. It is important to note that the
point-light effect is best for moving displays: a static display (as in a freeze-
frame on videotape) looks like a random collection of spots; common motion
of the spots introduces organisation (Johannson, 1973).

As we mentioned, the focus of the present study was to discover whether
(and which) values of the formational parameters were perceptible with
these configurations. This is of general interest with respect to sign
perception, in that only a small number of studies have examined the
perception of Sign under various kinds of distortion, to determine critical
perceptual features in Sign. These previous studies have looked at a single
kind of distortion: video 'snow' (masking) (Lane, Boyes-Braem and Bellugi,
1976); Poizner and Lane, 1978; Stungis, 1981), interruption (Grosjean, in
press) or point-lighting (substantially different from ours – Poizner, Bellugi
and Lutes-Driscoll, 1981; Bellman, Poizner and Bellugi, 1981). Moreover
each has examined only one formational parameter, holding the others
constant, and each has measured perception of single, isolated signs.

Difficulties exist with generalising about sign perception across studies
since the distortion type can affect perceptual strategy (see, for an example,
in speech perception, the reanalysis of the data of Miller and Nicely (1955) by
Wish and Carrol (1974). Moreover, the perceptual strategy can also be
affected by presenting signs in context with the other parameters varying, as
is true in normal use.

Our study was designed in part to correct for these problems and address
the general issue of sign language perception in addition to the specific issue
of sign language compression. To these ends, we compared perceptibility of
all the parameters within one study, under two conditions of distortion,
common to all parameters, and within a more natural language setting.

Method
With the assistance of Keith Cagle, a native deaf signer and trained ASL
informant, we selected nine minimally contrastive pairs of signs for each
formational parameter, embedded the members of each pair in the same

ASL sentence frame, and filmed production of each sentence under normal videotaping conditions, and under the point-light (DOTS) condition already described. One tape was made for each filming condition, containing the sentences randomised so that one member of each pair was in the first half of the tape, and the other in the second half.

For each sentence a cartoon was drawn to capture the meaning of the sentence and make clear the distinction between the members of the minimal pair. Sample sentences and the cartoons for each are:

1. Orientation: That woman serves/walks skillfully.

2. Location: The man has a bad headache/toothache.

3. Movement: My grandmother fell in love with the piano/typewriter.

4. Handshape: The two of them love to dance/paint.

We asked 14 highly fluent ASL users to look at the signed sentences and select the cartoon best suited to what they thought they saw. Note that this avoided subjects' having to respond in English. (Instructions were presented in ASL by an ASL informant.) All subjects were presented with a short introduction to the DOTS condition and four sample sentences – about five minutes practice in all. Eight of the subjects were presented with half of the normal tape followed by both halves of the DOTS tape and then the second half of the normal tape. The remaining six began with the second half of the DOTS tape, then both halves of the control tape, and then the first half of the DOTS tape. The answers were later scored as right or wrong. Note that pure guessing could produce scores of 50 percent correct.

Results

Figure 10 shows the 36 pairs tested, and is marked according to those pairs which were perceived significantly better than chance in either condition. The asterisk implies better than chance performance (as determined by a Z-approximation to the binomial) for the normal condition; the exclamation mark, better than chance performance for the point-light displays.

Several points should be noted: (1) neither condition of distortion produced better than chance performance for *all* pairs, (2) the normal condition was better than the point-light display, (3) some of the formational parameters were easier (had more pairs perceived better than chance) than others, and (4) those pairs easier in normal videotaping conditions were also easier in the DOTS condition and conversely.

These observations were upheld by subsequent analyses, summarised in Figure 11, and each merits discussion. With respect to the first point, we computed t-tests for each condition comparing actual performance both to chance and to perfection, and found that for both conditions, there were

LOCATION	ORIENTATION	MOVEMENT	HANDSHAPE
*'VOLUNTEER - CURIOUS	*'SOCKS - STARS	THREAD - SPAGHETTI	IRISH - PRINCIPAL
*' PRINT - BIRD	*'WANT - FREEZE	PLUG-IN - APPLY	APPROVE - STOP
* APPLE - KEY	* WORK - ROCKS	*'TYPEWRITER - PIANO	WATER - VINEGAR
* FORGET - BETTER	*'EACH OTHER - SCIENCE	PATIENT - SUFFER	* RAIN - DYE
* BUGS - DEVILS	*'BEAR - MONKEY	* DRIVING - CARS	TIME - POTATO
* BORING - UGLY	*'WALK - SERVE	* SOAP - PAINT	* FINISH - DON'T WANT
*'TOOTHACHE - HEADACHE	* ARGUMENT - ALARM	* JOIN - QUIT	AGREE - BET
*'GUILTY ALARM	*'BLUE - MIRROR	* SCHOOLS - PAPERS	* DANCE - PAINT
*'BOOK OPEN DOOR	* FISH - FLAG	DEMAND - DIG	* WORSHIP - WRESTLE

'BETTER THAN CONFIDENCE INTERVAL FOR CHANCE (NORMAL)
'BETTER THAN CONFIDENCE INTERVAL FOR CHANCE (DOTS)

Figure 10

SUMMARY STATISTICS
CONDITION × FEATURE × SUBJECTS ANALYSIS OF VARIANCE

SOURCE	df	MS ERROR	F
CONDITION	1,13	0.004	100.56, p< 0.001
FEATURE	3,39	0.006	53.58, p< 0.001
CONDITION × FEATURE	3,39	0.007	4.52, p< 0.01

t - TESTS COMPARING PERFORMANCE TO CHANCE AND PERFECTION

	CHANCE	PERFECTION
DOTS	t (35) = 6.10, p< 0.001	t (35) = 10.84, p< 0.001
NORMAL	t (35) = 8.33, p< 0.001	t (35) = 5.76, p< 0.001

Figure 11

significant differences. Inasmuch as *both* videotaping conditions produce a signal distortion as compared to real life, the difference from perfection is not surprising: normal videotaping reduces depth information, colour contrasts, update rate, etc. Each of these aspects is present also for the DOTS and, in addition, as should be obvious, the point-light displays also remove facial expression, specificity of location, redundancies in finger and arm positions, etc. Moreover, in both conditions there was no linguistic redundancy, nor pictorial redundancy: e.g., subjects not only had to understand 'serves' from the display, but also understand that that was intended in the cartoon. Thus, some difficulties were likely to exist. Nevertheless, in both conditions performance was still significantly better than chance.

Given that the distortion was greater in the DOTS condition, we expected that performance would be poorer. An important question is: do the point-light displays uniformly degrade performance on each formational parameter? To test this, an analysis of variance was computed averaging across pairs, to compare performance on each parameter in each distortion condition. Figure 12 summarises these results: DOTS was significantly

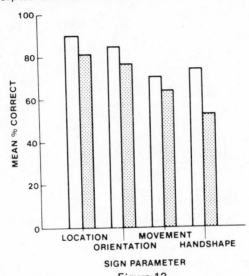

Figure 12

harder than the normal condition, some parameters were easier than others (Figure 11) and the difficulty of the parameters varied significantly with distortion condition. Figure 12 illustrates this interaction more clearly:

1. One can see an almost equal decrease in performance from normal to DOTS for all parameters except handshape.
2. Location and orientation are easiest in both conditions.
3. Movement is the hardest in the normal condition, but since the point-light displays so drastically reduced performance for handshape, this produces the most errors in the DOTS condition.

Discussion

There are several interesting findings here. The first is the general ordering of the parameters – with location distinctions more discriminable than handshape distinctions. Memory studies, e.g., Bellugi and Siple (1974), Klima and Bellugi (1979), have found that compared to unorganised lists of signs short-term recall for organised lists improved if list members shared handshape and deteriorated if they shared location. They explained this by postulating that handshape was difficult to recall, and thus that being able to control it, improved performance; whereas location was salient in storing information about signs, and sharing it produced confusion among list members. Our results suggest that the salience of location applies to perception as well as memory, as does the difficulty with handshape.

The second is the very poor performance in the DOTS condition for handshape – 53% correct, not significantly different from chance. The poor performance was indicated in our earlier demonstration (Tartter and Knowlton, 1981), since the most frequent requests for repetition were in fingerspelling, which in ASL is produced by sequences of handshapes, with shared locations and for the most part movement and orientation as well. It is interesting to note that handshape discriminations are not absolutely necessary, to understand: there is an ASL game which plays on the redundancy of handshape by keeping it constant during conversation; such games do not exist for the other parameters. And, in our earlier study, generally subjects could understand, given the other redundancies available. Nevertheless, an improvement in the point-light configurations, to improve handshape distinctions, is certainly desirable, to facilitate easy understanding.

The third interesting result is the fact that the two conditions ordered the other parameters in roughly the same way. The two conditions produced a similar within-parameter error pattern as well: the same pairs were difficult in both. To elaborate on this: locations on the face generally produced more confusion than those elsewhere on the body perhaps because smaller distances are involved (Siple, 1978): orientations which had as distinctive feature the presence vs. absence of the fingertip (WORK-ROCK, ARGUMENT-ALARM) were most difficult in both, and handshapes which were distinguished by the number of fingers extended (WATER-VINEGAR, TIME-POTATO) or whether the fingers were straight or bent (APPROVE-STOP) were perceived with most difficulty. The fact that the between- and within-parameter error patterns were roughly the same for both conditions suggests that the same perceptual strategies were being used.

Conclusions

This study has provided some important insights into sign perception and the feasibility of using the point light displays described by Tartter and Knowlton (1981) to compress sign. First, it appears that the minimal distinctions in location and orientation are more perceptible than those in handshape and movement. This has not been assessed before, in part because previous studies have examined perception of each parameter separately from the others. Second, perception of minimal distinctions in ASL is highly resistant to distortion. Third, the point-light configurations seem to be processed in the same manner as normally videotaped signs as indicated by the similarities in error patterns. And finally, the great weakness in the point-light configurations is in their ability to convey handshape, and this should be improved. Even without such an improvement, however, the results of the present study suggest that the distortion produced by the point-lighting, still passes information about many features of the sign signal, and thus when coupled with the normal redundancy present at other levels of the language, may be a suitable system for compression of information to a telephone bandwidth.

Acknowledgement

We are especially grateful to Keith Cagle for his invaluable assistance in construction and production of the stimuli and in administering the experiment. We also thank David Banks and Kathy Monsu for their help in scoring the data, Andrew Rothman for the artistic renditions of the sentences, and Osamu Pujimura and Robert Whitehead for their support and suggestions. This research was partially funded by Bell Laboratories. Fischer's research is supported under an agreement between the Department of Education and NTID.

THE STORY CHAIN

William Edmondson

Background

In earlier papers on deaf children's communication I put forward the idea that a communication equilibrium may be reached amongst the children in a classroom (say) which is tolerant of great linguistic idiosyncracy (Edmondson, 1980, 1981). It was suggested that this comes about partly because the deaf child is encouraged to be very interpretative, by the hearing community (where interpretation is an important part of lip-reading) and also, it is conjectured, by other deaf children whose individual linguistic behaviour will foster the belief that a necessary part of communication is interpretation. Acceptance of the need for interpretation, and of its value in communication, is coupled with an acknowledgement (maybe only tacitly) that individuals with whom one is communicating vary considerably amongst themselves. Note that interpretation is a linguistic skill and not just a receptive skill, as it so often appears to be in schools. It seems at least probable that interpretative skills start out as receptive skills – and that this is due partly to the flow of communication in school and at home – but later become transformed so as to include productive behaviour.

It is helpful here to take time to consider the notion of interpretativity in the context of human communication generally. The claim is not that such activity is abnormal or that the sign language of children dependent on such skills is unnatural; all languages require interpretative skills to some degree. Context sensitivity is a topic in linguistics which is clearly relevant here – context sensitivity depends upon interpretation (or otherwise the term would have no meaning) and for obvious reasons is more likely to be observed in spoken languages and signed languages (written languages of necessity must be more formal and context free). Context sensitivity and interpretativity are to be expected wherever a culture has a poor tradition of passing language from generation to generation or where a culture has no written language, or both. This topic could be discussed at greater length – this brief discussion is included here to show that there is nothing unusual about interpretation in a linguistic context.

With regard to the current position of sign language in schools (in Britain), my feeling is that we may be straining the skills of the children and curtailing their linguistic development by requiring, essentially, too much interpretativity, thereby supporting an environment which is tolerant of too much idiosyncracy.

The Need for Experiment

Of interest to both the linguist and the teacher is the implication that in a linguistic environment like that encountered in schools for the deaf in Britain we may expect to find communication failure. Greater tolerance of idiosyncracy carries with it a higher risk of failure. The suggestion that deaf children in classrooms do not always communicate effectively amongst themselves will come as no surprise to teachers.

However, there are at least two issues of interest to teachers and linguists, which invite experimentation. The first is the need to demonstrate the communication difficulties, in a valid and controlled way, outside the classroom. The value of doing this is that the evidence is then available to a wider audience (than is the classroom evidence). The second is of greater theoretical significance and is to do with the notion of idiosyncratic language. Does idiosyncratic communication involve idiosyncratic grammar or must it be limited to semantic/lexical idiosyncracy? My understanding of this issue leads me to suggest that idiosyncratic grammar is to be expected (see also Fischer, 1980).

Experiments need to be designed, or so it seems, around a paradigm with the following characteristics. Communication failure must be expected from time to time and must be acceptable to the people involved. The procedure used must work with hearing or deaf subjects and it must be suitable for children as well as adults. The material used should be linguistic in nature (c.f. Jordan, this volume), so that only the linguistic skills of the subjects are assessed. The nature of the communication failure must not be restricted in any way.

The Paradigm

Bartlett, in his book on remembering (1932), describes an experimental procedure which he calls The Method of Serial Reproduction. I have based my experiments on a very similar technique which exists – probably in many cultures but certainly in the 'English' speaking world – as a children's game. For this the children arrange themselves so that in turn they can have a message whispered into one ear, which they then repeat into the ear of the next child, and so on. At the end the last child tells his version aloud and all is merriment as the various versions are compared with the original. This procedure – the imperfect passing of an unwritten message from one person to the next – I call the Story Chain, and it seems to me to be a very rich experimental paradigm. It offers a very natural way of studying several aspects of the process of communication – memory, perception, variation and some of the differences between the use of language for dialogue and monologue. The game as described does, however, need some modification if the study of memory and perception are not of prime concern.

The Story Chain procedure which was actually employed did not *require* the participants to misperceive or misunderstand, they were merely required to pass on the message as faithfully as possible. With hearing children the success of the game depends upon misperception induced by the whispering. However, with deaf subjects the presumed idiosyncracy and interpretative-ness in communication behaviour is considered likely to induce sufficient error to ensure that procedure resembles the children's game. It was assumed that this prodedure would be sufficiently motivating to ensure a good sense of participation in something 'game-like' – that, in fact, the subjects would find the task interesting and good fun. The procedure does have its drawbacks however, and it is appropriate at this juncture to consider the techniques in a little more detail.

In the communication environment under discussion we have to consider that variation limiting is taking place, that is, that the language models of deaf children are sufficiently different one from another for communication to be just tolerably unsuccessful and critically dependent on interpretative skills. Failure must be expected and unsurprising (that is, in normal communication experience) and it seems likely that this is due in part to grammatical differences as well as semantic and lexical difficulties.

One question, therefore, which we should address is how can the Story Chain be used to detect idiosyncratic grammar? We could proceed to answer that by assuming that the Story Chain data will contain sufficiently complex misunderstandings which leave one with no choice but to assume the idiosyncracy is there. Another possibility which seems to be worth exploring arises from consideration of how a dialogue would proceed if language were indeed such an individual thing. The conjecture is that dialogue in sign language is likely to involve negotiation of grammar as well as lexicon and therefore that communicative success will have to depend on frequent monitoring of the addressee's understanding.

The experimental implication of this is that the ability of a story teller to monitor his addressee's understanding might be open to experimental influence through alteration of the Story Chain procedure. Specifically, if some sort of monologue condition could be contrived (and there are two possibilities for this) then some of the processes of negotiating understanding could be examined. In fact this possibility was explored experimentally, although space limitations prevent more than a passing mention. The focus in this paper is on the straightforward dialogue Story Chain, and the asumption is that idiosyncracy will reveal itself clearly in the transcripts.

The work reported here is preliminary for two reasons at least. First of these is the organisational one of coping with a widely dispersed subject population, the need to discover how long Story Chains take to record, the need to 'get a feel' for the experiment. The second important factor is that the scale and nature of the effects, the frequency of their occurrence, the significance of the many different variables, all of these were unknown. Before planning any 'full scale' experiment these factors must be explored, and the purpose of reporting such work, as here, is to make possible a shared exploration leading, it is to be hoped, to a worthwhile full scale experiment.

Method

The *materials* used for starting the Story Chain were obtained in the following way. Individuals (see below) were shown pictures which they were required to describe – 'for the benefit of another person' – 'telling someone what you saw'. The descriptions were elicited picture by picture and each person could take as long as they wished to look at each picture which was then described from memory. This was done in an attempt to induce communication behaviour rather than a mere recitation of a list of items. The descriptions were video taped and the tapes edited to provide sequences of brief passages, each passage being used to start a Story Chain. Descriptions were obtained in speech and sign language.

The *subjects* used to produce the starting material for the speech condition were several members of staff in the Psychology Department at Bedford

College. The final edited tape contains descriptions from four individuals.

The people employed to produce descriptions in sign languages were (1) the author's principal informant, who comes from a deaf family – British Sign Language is her first language; (2) the informant's younger hearing brother; (3) a prelingually deaf man from a hearing family; (4) a man deafened at nearly nine years by meningitis, also with hearing parents.

The *subjects* used for the Story Chains were, for the speech condition, two groups of offspring of members of staff (three brothers, aged 13 years, 12 years, and 10 years, and a brother and sister pair, 11 and 7 years respectively). The ordering of the subjects in the chain documented below preserved the family relationships, i.e., the two groups were not broken up.

The five deaf boys who participated were classmates in a school for the deaf which had participated in the earlier observational work. The school is nominally oralist although it is becoming increasingly interested in the use of sign language. The boys, aged between 14 years and 16 years, had taken part in the earlier work and thus were well-known to the experimenter. They all come from hearing families where they are the only deaf child.

The five deaf adults taking part were recruited from the informant's deaf club (as were two of the subjects used to produce the starting materials) and thus were familiar with each other's signing and with some of the signing which they were to see on tape. These subjects, four women and one man, all come from deaf families and thus are 'native' users of sign language. Two related individuals were not placed in succession in any chain order.

None of the groups of subjects were matched for age, IQ, socio-economic-status or hearing loss. For the deaf children data are known for IQ and for hearing loss.

The *tapes* were made on SONY ½″ open reel machines, using cameras adapted for low light level work (fitted with silicon tubes), and SONY microphones.

The *conditions* used were as follows. With the hearing children only face to face dialogue was tried. The first child in the chain watched and heard the description which was thereafter passed down the chain by face to face retelling. Questions and interruptions were discouraged.

For the deaf children both monologue and dialogue conditions were employed. The monologue condition (which was employed first) was one of two possibilities. After watching the tape of the description the first child in the chain signed his version – to camera – and the first addressee watched the performance on a monitor. The procedure was then repeated, addressee became addresser and signed to camera for the next addressee. (Recordings were made of both participants.) The identity of the addressee was always known to the addresser. The Story Chains in the dialogue condition began the same way, but the exchanges were face to face (both participants were recorded). Questions and interruptions were kept to a minimum. The experiments took place in a spare room in the children's school, on one day. (Both deaf and hearing children were taped in practice sessions. The author was the final addressee in all the children's chains.)

The experiments involving the deaf adults were organised slightly differently. The monologue condition used was not that used with the children. Instead each version of the story was delivered to the same addressee (the deaf informant). The addressee next in the Story Chain watched the taped performance of the story prior to performing for the informant. There seemed to be no need for practice and so this was omitted. One week later the same adults returned to college for the dialogue experiments. However, to combat boredom noted on the first occasion the order of people in the chain was reversed; the order was otherwise kept constant throughout each condition. (For the deaf children the same order was maintained throughout.) As with the deaf children four stories were used for monologues and four for dialogues. The order of the stories was kept constant for all subjects.

Results

Although we shall return again later to consideration of the paradigm a few comments are in order here. The task did not seem interesting enough for the participants and this may have had some influence on recall; attentiveness too may have been influenced. This is difficult to detect with the hearing children, although they were bored by the end of the experimental session. The deaf participants seemed to be very attentive (dialogue between deaf people requires of the adressee total visual attention – communication halts if the addresser suspects that the addressee is not attending). The deaf children did not appear to be performing for the experimenter (there were no glances to camera, for example). Thus at this pilot stage of the work I am inclined to accept the children's communication at face value. If the deaf children appear uncertain of why they are doing the experimenter's bidding, as occasionally seems to be the case, I remain of the opinion that they are not 'signing English' (or anything of this sort) for my sake.

The complete set of transcripts comprises 20 Story Chains which, with their starter passages, constitutes too much material for inclusion here. I have therefore selected for discussion just one Story Chain theme – PETSHOP – which is given in appendix I in the form of the starter passages, spoken and signed, along with direct transcripts and translated transcripts. This particular corpus of data is representative of the dialogue condition and furnishes illustrations of many points. It is sometimes necessary to refer to the larger corpus of transcripts but this is done as infrequently as possible.

Comparison between the deaf children and the deaf adults and between the deaf children and the hearing children reveals a distinct qualitative difference. As expected the deaf children appear more error prone and willing to elaborate. More detailed examination of the transcripts reveals something about the errors. Here we see that the deaf children appear to make errors indicative of failure to understand, not just vocabulary but also the way the language is put together, thus supporting the original contention (as well as demonstrating the utility of the paradigm). In contrast, the adults make errors of a less exaggerated nature.

The Story Chains reveal that the deaf children are not understanding one another fully, and that this is not entirely due to deficits in vocabulary – errors reveal misunderstanding of the grammar of the language. The monitoring behaviour, or addressee sensitivity, which was predicted is also found. Furthermore, two unexpected and related indications of idiosyncracy with linguistic implications are revealed in the Story Chains: ego-centrism and unusual role-play.

The translated transcripts show clearly that the deaf children are doing less well than either the deaf adults or the hearing children. Comparison of the first and last versions of the story in each of the three chains makes this obvious, and it is not the case that any single individual is the major source of misunderstanding, in any of the chains.

An example of the sort of misunderstanding for which we are looking appears in the interaction between M.KI and L.TI where, in the direct transcript (see Appendix 1) we find:

lady (talk with another)

is reproduced as:

lady says.

Addressee sensitivity and monitoring of the interaction is shown by some of the children, in two ways. The first is easily detected in the translated transcripts – see for example M.KI who appears concerned that L.TI has understood what the story is about (before getting on with it). This behaviour is seen (with variations) in the adult's chains as well. The second form (also seen with the adults) is not obvious from the translated transcripts. It is the use of synonyms for signs in repetition – for example, M.KI, in the utterance translated as the sentence:

The lady is buying a lot of things.

uses two different signs for 'buying', one after the other. That this behaviour gives emphasis is not disputed; emphasis can be considered to be the marking of items not adequately given prominence in the structure of an utterance. It is also the case that emphasis is given by simple repetition – as is done by L.TI for the same phrase ('buy a lot'). The use of synonyms, it is suggested, is emphasis for the benefit of the addressee.

Ego-centrism is revealed in the performance of M.KI, and D.BA reveals in his performance unusually rapid alterations in role-play (from boy to lady to boy to shopkeeper to boy – this does not emerge in the translation). Ego-centrism and role-play obviously have grammatical significance. In fact role-play can be thought of as a significant grammatical device. It is also noticeable in the adults' performances in the PETSHOP chain (and elsewhere), and Gaby makes what seems to be an error when she shifts roles apparently inappropriately (this is only clear from the tape). (See also Bellugi and Fischer, 1972.)

Other general errors are of interest. For example, the lack of gender and number continuity in the sign chains contrasts with the hearing children's grip on the number of birds in the cage and the number and gender of the people involved. Once again, the errors are grammatically significant. In this case, however, we find that the performance of the adults is not error free (in a general sence it was not expected to be – sign language is an interpretative activity for adults too).

The deaf adults and children made a few perceptual errors, not enough to be worth reporting here – extension of the work with monologue chains will pursue this topic.

Discussion

The small sample of data given here is typical of the full corpus obtained. The conclusion seems inescapable, sign language is a very interpretative means of communication and in the school context it is likely to be not entirely successful. The reasons for this are readily understood in terms which are purely linguistic (Edmondson, 1981) as well as sociolinguistic (Edmondson, 1980, 1981).

The implications are many and diverse. For the development of the experimental work the implications are (a) that the paradigm is promising and should be developed, (b) that specific sources of error can now be predicted and the procedure needs to be altered accordingly (for example, by careful construction of Story Chain starter passages), (c) that more realistic dialogue should be attempted and contrasted with monologue conditions (not discussed here but clearly of interest in connection with perceptual errors).

The work has been criticised because not enough training was given to the children and because only one informant was involved in the translations. It is not accepted that these points have any major significance for the outcome of the study. In an important way the transcripts and translations speak for themselves – both the training of subjects and the use of a plurality of informants/translators will not necessarily make the results more clear cut or more acceptable. Similarly, analysis of the chains produced (one interesting suggestion was to use a story grammar of some sort, see, e.g., Mandler and Johnson, 1977) does not necessarily make the results more believable or even more quantifiable. (Nonetheless, the development of the experimental work will be influenced by the helpful comments and discussion which I encountered at Bristol).

Implications for theory, and for further research work, are (a) that communication behaviour which is idiosyncratic and interpretative can be subjected to experimental enquiry, (b) that the theoretical approach advocated appears valid in an interesting way, (c) (more remotely) that individualism in communication should be studied in relation to skills related to communication, such as memory for letters of the alphabet (where there is much heterogeneity in some deaf children who have been studied; see, for example, Edmondson, 1978), and also in relation to the general heterogeneity of the deaf population (Dawson, 1979).

Conclusions

Two practical conclusions can be drawn. The first of which is that language achievement in the deaf probably continues through late adolescence into the third decade. This is important for those who work with the 'adult' deaf community, and there are implications for post-school or 'further' education opportunities for the deaf.

The second conclusion is one which I think will be of particular interest to teachers. It is often assumed, by those who consider oralism to be wrong-headed, which it is, that the children's use of sign language in school is a clear demonstration of the medium which should be used, which it is not. Accepting my conclusions (and the suspicions of some teachers) the latter is only a demonstration of the *type* of medium which should be used. If my arguments are accepted then it is obviously important for both linguists and educationalists to acknowledge that school Sign is inadequate and needs adult linguistic influence from the deaf community. We risk otherwise doing our work and our cause (for so it still is) a disservice by being seen to be dishonest).

I conclude with the argument that what the children are actually revealing is a preference for an apparently unsatisfactory means of communication in place of the supposedly effective methods offered by oralism. For how much longer must they express in this way their vote of no confidence in oralism?

Acknowledgements
I am very grateful to all who took part in the experiments, and to the staff of the school for the deaf where some of the work was done.

I am indebted to my informant Melinda Napier for her invaluable and good humoured assistance. Without her help this study would not have been possible. I am very grateful to the Leverhulme Trust for their financial support. My thanks also go to all those people at the Symposium who offered comments and criticism. Responsibility for the contents of the paper is, however, entirely mine.

APPENDIX 1

Transcripts of the Story Chains
The starter passage for the hearing children was re-recorded, transcribed by audio-typist, checked and retyped. The chain was transcribed by the author.

The sign language transcriptions were made by the author's informant, in conjunction with the author. Capital letters are employed in the conventional way for 'I' and sentence initially. Elsewhere they indicate fingerspelling (and this occurred quite frequently, sentence initially – presumably reflecting the influence of orthography on sign language). The main feature of the transcripts is the use of () brackets. Any word, words or phrase enclosed in () is either a comment or description, or it is a sign which is *not* accompanied by a lipreadable mouth movement. That is to say, most of the signs transcribed (as glosses) are accompanied by identifiable lip patterns. This is apparently a characteristic of Southern English Sign Language. Words in italics indicate a lipreadable mouth movement which is *not* accompanied by a sign. Superscripts indicate signs with a different form, and other devices used are [idiom] and |pause|. Punctuation is inserted where it seems clear from the tapes, not where it would seem appropriate from the translation. The purpose of the "direct transcripts" is to record, as closely as possible, what is found in the sign language on tape.

The translations are to be considered a secondary, or even tertiary, form of the data. They are included in response to comments and criticism received at the Symposium. They make clear the manner in which the Story Chains develop and thus facilitate comparisons which the reader may wish to make. They were done by the author's informant (in conjunction with the author) direct from the tapes and with only occasional reference to the transcripts.

Transcript
Starter for Speech Story Chain (dialogue condition)
PETSHOP
Kath.
The second picture is a scene of a petshop um |p|. A cage with three birds at the top left of the picture, a lady behind the counter, on the shelves some packets of fishmeal in the under the counter a tank containing a couple of fish, in front of the counter a boy |p| apparently conversing with the lady behind the counter, |p| a woman with a dog under her arm is being shown dog collars by a man, above her head is a rack with dog leads.

Transcript
Starter for Sign Story Chain (dialogue condition)
PETSHOP
Melinda.
Boy (little) in PET shop want buy powder food for fish went in wait wait long time because (there) lady (there) in the way ask man (I) want dog collar (carry). Difficult want don't want man (shows different collars). Boy wait wait [at last] lady what do you want boy ask for fish food. Give buy. Out. Lady still there arguing over dog collar.

Translation
Starter for Sign Story Chain (dialogue condition)
Melinda.
A boy wants to go into a petshop. He wants to buy powder, food for fish. He goes in and has to wait a long time because that lady is in the way, asking a man for a dog collar. She is being difficult, and keeps on changing her mind – wanting this, wanting that. The man keeps on handing over the collars for her to see. The boy waits and waits, then at last a lady comes up and asks what does he want. The boy asks for fish food. The lady gives it to him and he buys it, then he goes out. The lady is still there arguing over the dog collars.

Transcript
Hearing Children's Spoken Story Chain (dialogue condition)
PETSHOP
D.WI.
The picture showed er a petshop and there was a cage with three birds in the window |p| and er the second picture |p| showed a lady standing at a counter |sh and em| there was some fishmeat in the shelves |p| coz there was also another lady with a dog under her arm |p| er there was something above the first lady's head |p| and there was a lady behind the behind the counter |p|.

M.WI.
In the in the first picture em there was a petshop and there were three birds in the cage in the window-sill in it. And then the second picture there was er a lady in front of the counter a counter and there was some fishmeat somewhere and there was erthe woman behind the counter and another lady somewhere else and there was something above the first lady's head.

J.WI.

In the first picture there were two birds no two or three birds in a cage on a window-sill. In the second picture there was a woman standing in front of a shop counter or a counter and there was a woman behind it and there was another woman in the shop and she had something over her head.

D.WE.

In the first picture there were some birds in a cage two or three birds. And in the second picture there was this lady at a counter and she we— and there was a lady behind the counter and there were several other ladies and one lady had something over her head. And that's it.

E.WE.

There was this umm la lady. There was this birdcage with several birds in three I think and umm and there was this lady at a counter and em and a lady behind the counter and then there were several other others and umm one of them had something something on her head and that's all.

Translation
Deaf Adult's Signed Story Chain (dialogue condition)
PETSHOP
Lily.

A boy wants to go to a petshop. He wants to buy food for his fish. He arrives at the shop and finds he cannot be served because a lady there is arguing with a man in the shop. They argue for a long time as the lady is not satisfied with her dog's collar. Whenever the shopkeeper offers her another collar she changes her mind. The boy waits until at last the man asks him what he wants. The boy asks for fish food. The shopkeeper wraps it up and gives it to the boy. The lady is still arguing over the collars. A lot of trouble and bother over the collars.

Diana.

A boy went to the shops. He wants to buy food for the fish, but in the shop he finds a man arguing with another man, complaining about a dog collar. They kept him waiting. Then at last the man served him, asking him what he wanted. He asked for some fish food, which the shopkeeper gave him. But the two men went on arguing over the collar.

Gaby.

A boy went to a shop to buy some fish food. Inside he saw a man, the shopkeeper, arguing with one of the customers, another man. They argue and he waits, until at last the shopkeeper comes up and asks what he wants. He asks for food for his fish, and he gets this from the shopkeeper. He goes out, and sees the two men still arguing over the dog collar.

Patsy.

A boy wanted to go, to go to the shop to buy something. When he got there he saw a man arguing with a customer, yes a customer. They were rowing, so he waited. Then the man asked what he wanted and he asked for fish. But the boy found the two boys, the man and woman still arguing – no, two men – arguing on and on over the dog's collar.

Jack.

A boy went shopping and saw a man arguing with a customer. The boy waited but the argument carried on, so the man came up and asked what he wanted. The boy said he wanted to buy fish but he was interrupted by the continuation of the argument.

Transcript
Deaf Adult's Signed Story Chain (dialogue condition)
PETSHOP

Lily.

Boy (little) want in shop PET shop want to buy for fish food (points). Arrive shop [surprise] can't serve because lady (there) argue with man (there) in the shop. Long time (dispute) not satisfied with her dog collar (unreliable) what *do* you want change change. Boy wait wait wait [at last] man said what *do* you want (I) want for fish food (ah) man (open) give finish. Lady still argue argue argue still over collar trouble bother over collar.

Diana.

A boy want to the shop. HE wants to buy food for fish. But he find the man have arguing with (there) man in *the* shop. Complain something *about* the dog collar. KEEP him waiting [at last] (the) man (serve) ask what *do* you want I want food for fish. Give him some (that's that). But still they arguing over (points) collar.

Gaby.

A boy went to shop want to buy some fish food. Got in saw man, shopkeeper, (the commas given by pointing to one side) arguing arguing one of customers, man (points) customer argue argue. Wait wait [at last] (he came) what *do* you want I want some food for his fish (serve) gave him some. (went out) (saw) still arguing two men over dog collar.

Patsy.

A boy want to go *the* (shop) want to go to shop to buy something AND saw there A man arguing with CUSTOMER CUSTOMER arguing row (points) (watch) (he) (given by pointing) waiting (then) the man (what) *do* want you you? To buy fish found both boy, man two and woman arguing men two arguing for long time. Arguing over dog's collar.

Jack.

Boy went to shopping ans saw man arguing with the CUSTOMER. Boy waited (go on) but still arguing *so* man come and said what *do* you want want buy fish but still interrupt arguing.

Translation
Deaf Children's Signed Story Chain (dialogue condition)
PETSHOP
M.KI.
A boy wants to go to a shop to buy something, food or something, O.K.? I wait in the shop while the lady is busy serving another lady. This lady is buying a lot. I wait and wait, wishing they would hurry, but she's busy. I get fed-up. At last, a man comes. I want fish food. I ask – they have it – he gives it to me – I buy it and that's it. I go out.

L.TI.
A boy wants to go shopping and – uh? what's that? Oh well. The lady – no, boy – went into the shop and . . . what? and lady – no, boy – goes into the shop. Then the lady says – she says – wait until she's finished buying. The boy waits for the lady but she says she is too busy buying. Some other lady comes in, queue barges, and buys a lot. The boy is still waiting. She finished and left. The boy asks the lady – he wants to buy fish food. The lady says alright and gives it to him. That's it, he goes, finish.

D.BA.
A boy went to a shop. He wanted to buy sweets. A lady queue barged and said she was first. The boy was surprised. A lady said "you are pushing in – the boy was here first". The boy paid. The lady was annoyed and left. The boy, I think, wandered about and asked "I want food, fish food, packet". That's all.

B.SU.
A boy is walking to go shopping for sweets. In the shop a lady jumps the queue and elbows him aside. he looks up, annoyed. The man says, crossly, "I was serving the boy first". Then he pays for the sweets. Then he wanders again and walks into another shop, a fish and chip shop. That's all.

K.TI.
Two boys go to a shop. "I want to buy sweets." Alright. Some lady bumps into one – he looks puzzled. The man says "don't interrupt". The two boys say "alright" and go shopping again for fish and chips.

Transcript
Deaf Children's Signed Story Chain (dialogue condition)
PETSHOP
M.KI.
Boy want to go shop buy something (thumb up = O.K. understand?) |p| me wait in shop lady (talk with another) busy lady buy buy wait wait come on (no) busy (pointing in reference to another customer) fed up wait [at last] man came food fish fish food ask alright give me buy out finish off that's all.

L.TI.
Boy want |p – short and left hand still active| buy to shop (then) |p| (go in) what? (in response to D.BA. request for repeat) (shrugs). The lady (shakes

head) boy boy went to shop |p – was distracted by D.BA. (who looked at W.Ed.) and looks at W.Ed.| lady (or) boy (go) shop. Then lady said lady said bought finish boy wait for the lady but lady said too busy lady buy some (other) lady come in (= jumps the queue) buy buy buy boy wait (repeated action) finish (went off) boy ask lady want food buy (food) fish lady alright give finish go finish.

D.BA.

Boy went to shop want buy sweet (but) lady (jumps the queue) me (i.e. lady first buy. (me) boy (surprised). Lady (i.e. shopkeeper) push in (= you pushed in) go (= wait your turn) boy (= this boy) first. Pay. Lady (frustrated) off. Boy |p – signs (think)| boy [go up to counter] I want food want the f food want fish food (packet) fish finish.

B.SU.

(someone walking) go to shopping sweet (jumps the queue) (repeated) lady (jumps the queue) (elbows him aside) (boy looks up annoyed) man serving (push in) go away first only (that) boy (looks smug) buy sweet (then) (went out walked around) to again (walks) again |p| (headshaking = I'm wrong) to chips fish. That's all.

K.TI.

Two boy go to shop want to buy sweet right somebody lady (bumps into boy) mand said (don't interrupt) |p|. Two boys (said) alright went out to another shop fish chips finish.

REFERENTIAL COMMUNICATION AMONG SCOTTISH DEAF SCHOOL PUPILS

I. K. Jordan

One aspect of sign language that has been given little attention by both linguists and educators is the efficacy of the system. How well do the users of sign language understand each other? The reflexive response to that question is that signers understand one another quite well, thank you. In fact, it has sometimes been suggested that sign language is universal, or nearly so, and that deaf signers from all over the world understand each other easily (Battison and Jordan, 1976). However, research shows that when deaf signers view a foreign sign language, they, in fact, cannot understand it (Jordan and Battison, 1976). Other research, with eight and eleven year old children, found deaf children to be less able to communicate accurately than their hearing peers (Hoemann, 1972). These studies suggest that the reflexive response given earlier might not be entirely correct. At the very least, these studies point out the need for additional research.

Researchers of communication among hearing children have suggested that there is a specific communication ability, different from linguistic ability, which develops separately from and *following* linguistic ability (Krauss and Glucksberg, 1970) This suggestion seems to have profound implications for deaf children. There is no question that deaf children are generally quite deficient in English linguistic ability. At the same time, it is common knowledge that more than 90% of deaf children have two hearing parents. The large majority of deaf children are therefore not exposed to sign language until they begin school and socialise with older deaf children. Compared to their hearing peers, then, young deaf children, even deaf children who attend schools which support the use of sign langauge, are probably deficient in the linguistic ability of *any* language. What effect does this linguistic deficiency have on their communication ability? More specifically what effect does it have on their ability to communicate in sign language?

We all know that the linguistic deficiency in sign language seems to disappear quickly. Without ever having any formal instruction in sign language, deaf children become fluent users. Deaf children have also been shown to prefer sign language to other language systems and to better understand information when it is presented to them in sign language (Johnson, 1948; Klopping, 1972). It should be interesting, then, to study the ability of deaf children to communicate with each other in sign language. By examining the sign language communications of a large number of deaf children from the time they begin school until they are ready to leave, we should be able to learn much more about how and when fluency is achieved.

One experimental technique which has been used successfully in investigating the communications of deaf people is the referential communication technique (e.g., Jordan, 1975). This technique provides a measure of "communication accuracy", an objective measure of the ability to communicate which does not require any subjective evaluation of the "quality" of a communication (Mehrabian and Reed, 1968). The technique also allows for careful control over the stimuli or subject matter to be communicated.

In this study, the stimuli to be communicated were designed and constructed to require descriptions of increasing linguistic complexity. Thus, while beginning signers may be able to succeed at the early trials, it is assumed that only fluent signers will be able to communicate all of the material. For that reason, these stimuli should lead to results which will show developmental trends in achieving communication competence. In addition, by comparing the communications of oral deaf and signing deaf children and of deaf and hearing children across age groups, we should get an objective measure of how much and what kinds of communication is taking place among these children. Information such as this is of crucial import to teachers and other professionals working with deaf children.

Method

Subjects: Participants in this study were deaf children from four Scottish schools for the deaf, three of which used total communication and one which used the oral method. Also included were a number of hearing teachers of the deaf and a small group of hearing children from the Lothian Regional school district. The entire student populations from all four schools for the deaf were tested.

There were 12 3½–5 year olds, 38 6–7 year olds, 54 8–10 year olds, 66 11–12 year olds, and 86 13–15 year olds.

Stimulus Materials: The referents that the subjects were to describe were five inch square drawings, presented in sets of six on a circular disc of 20 inches in diameter. There were 25 discs, and the descriptions required were of increasing complexity. The early stimulus pictures required only a noun. For example, from a set of six animals, any one could be described with a single word or sign. Subsequent picture sets required nouns and modifiers, the correct use of prepositions, subject-verb-object constructions, comparatives and perspective.

Experimental Setting and Procedure: Subjects were selected from the same classes and run in pairs. This method of selection insured that the subjects were well acquainted with one another and were age-matched to within six months. The sender of the description looked at the entire set, then described the referent picture to the receiver. During the description the receiver could not see the stimulus set. After the description, a hood was reversed so that the receiver and not the sender could see the picture set. Subjects took turns describing pictures while the experimenter recorded the descriptions and noted the receivers' responses. The original intention was to have all subject pairs do all 25 picture sets, but in practice, several of the sets, notably those requiring perspective, were too difficult. Therefore, the number of sets varied with different subject pairs, but all subjects did at least ten.

Results

Results will be presented in two parts. First, I will present some data and discuss the quantitative results. Next, I will talk about some of the interesting qualitative results, that is, about the content of some of the descriptions.

Quantitative Results
Because all of the subjects described at least ten referents, the number correct of those ten will be used as the measure of communication accuracy. An individual with a communication accuracy score of ten would have successfully described all ten of the pictures. A person with a communication accuracy score of five, would have successfully described half.

The first analysis concerned age differences. Figure 1 shows the mean communication accuracy scores for all the deaf subjects, separated into four age groups, 6–7, 8–10, 11–12 and 13–15. An interesting developmental trend appears.

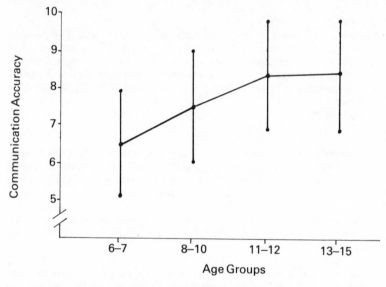

Figure 1. Mean communication accuracy scores with plus and minus one standard deviation for all deaf subjects

There are very clear increases in communication accuracy with increasing age until the children reach age 12. There is nearly no increase between the 11–12 group and the 13–15 group.

Taking into acount the standard deviations, it can be seen that statistically there are differences between groups 6–7, 8–10 and 11–12, but the 11–12 group and the 13–15 group are virtually the same.

It is interesting to speculate as to what might cause this plateau. In looking more closely at the development of communication skills, the oral deaf children (i.e., the children from that school which used the oral method) were separated from the signing deaf children. These data are shown in Figure 2.

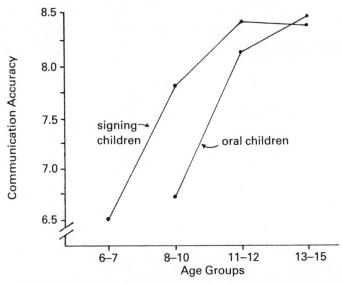

Figure 2. Mean communication accuracy scores presented separately for oral deaf and signing deaf subjects

Several things are notable about this graph. First of all, when the data are plotted separately, it can be seen that for the oral children, communication accuracy continues to increase slightly through age 15. Next, there is no data presented for a 6–7 year old oral deaf children. The task was attempted with several six and seven year olds, but even with the help of their classroom teachers no consistent responses could be obtained. For the six and seven year old oral children, interpersonal communication was virtually nil. In fact, the performance of oral 8–10 year olds compares with the performance of the signing 6–7 year olds. The signing deaf children performed better at all age groups except the oldest, and this difference was very small. For the oral deaf children communication accuracy was 8.48 and for the signing deaf children communication accuracy was 8.36. The most interesting differences between the oral deaf children and the signing deaf children are at the younger ages, 6–7 and 8–10.

The next results are comparisons between deaf and hearing children. The performance of the hearing children was quite different from that of the deaf. The youngest hearing children (aged 6–7) communicated well. Their mean communication accuracy score was 7.67. Eight to ten year old hearing children had a mean communication accuracy of 8.5. This is better than even the oldest deaf children. Hearing children who were in the 11–12 age group scored right at the ceiling for the ten pictures; their mean communication accuracy score was 10.0. These data appear with the data for the deaf subjects, in Figure 3.

Some final quantitative data concerns teacher-pupil communication. Eighteen classroom teachers of children aged 6–12 and three teachers of

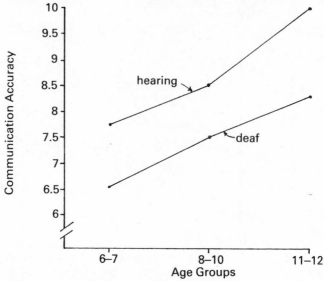

Figure 3. Mean communication accuracy scores for deaf and hearing
subjects

children aged 3½–5 years participated. Teacher-pupil communication
accuracy for the communication pairs of teachers and 6–12 year old pupils
was 9.29. Analysed by age, these data are very interesting. Figure 4 shows
the mean communication accuracy scores for the deaf signing children in the
first three age groups and the teacher-pupil communication data for the same
age groups. The children were able to communicate much more accurately
with their teachers than among themselves.

The teachers of the infant children, aged 3½–5 were asked to
communicate only five of the pictures. Even five pictures seemed to be at the
limits of the attention spans of these youngest children. Nevertheless, there
was real communication between teacher and pupil even at age 3½. These
three teachers communicated with a total of 12 children, and the mean
number of correct picture identifications out of a possible five was 4.33.

Qualitative Data

Much more interesting from the point of view of sign language research is a
look at some of the qualitative data. The most striking thing during this
research was the way in which deaf children structured their communications, the way they put together their signs. The term "proposition
ordering" will be used when talking about the order of signs in an utterance
to avoid talking about English word order.

Nouns and Modifiers: Some of the early pictures required a noun and one
or two modifiers. For these, the order of propositions did not seem to make
any difference. The utterance "CUP, ORANGE AND WHITE" was

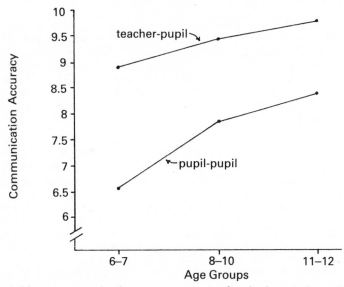

Figure 4. Mean communication accuracy scores for signing pupil-pupil
dyads and teacher-pupil dyads

understood just as easily as "ORANGE AND WHITE CUP". However, in later picture sets, there were often two nouns to be modified. In one picture set, the referent pictures showed a black cat on a pillow under a bed. One description was signed "BED, UNDER, CAT, BLACK, PILLOW". Is the cat or the pillow black? The description does not answer that question. As interesting as the ambiguity possible in a communication such as this is the fact that there seemed to be no favoured proposition order for nouns and modifiers. "DOG, BLACK COLLAR" and "DOG, COLLAR BLACK" both occurred with equal frequency.

Prepositions: The positioning of prepositions had a profound effect on communication accuracy in this task. One picture set included a table and a book. One picture showed the book on the table, and another showed the table on the book. The most frequently signed utterance when describing the picture of the table on the book was "BOOK ON TABLE". When this description was related to deaf adults and to teachers of the deaf, they were not surprised. They all said that this is a common sign language structuring which means "book . . . there is a book", "table . . . on which there is a table". This is a very logical and sensible explanation, and on the surface it looks quite correct. However, when a subject saw "book, on table", he invariably chose a picture of a book on a table, not a picture of a table on a book. What is more, often two prepositions were placed differently in one description. A common description for a picture of a cat on a pillow under a bed was "BED, UNDER CAT ON PILLOW". Here "UNDER" seems to follow one rule and "ON" a different rule. It would indeed be interesting to learn what these rules are. It just doesn't seem logical that one can place the preposition either before or after the word it modifies. There must be contexts where only one or the other order is correct. It often seemed that in a given pair of subjects the two were following different rule systems. For example, in one subject pair, a boy saw the signed utterance "BOOK, ON TABLE" and chose the (incorrect) picture of the book on the table. He was then told to describe the picture of the book on the table to his partner. He signed "BOOK ON TABLE"·

Subject-Verb-Object: The same preposition ordering difficulties arose in picture sets requiring subject-verb-object constructions. In a picture which showed a cat biting a dog's tail, a common signed utterance was "CAT, DOG, TAIL, BITE". Subjects who saw such a description were equally likely to be right or wrong. The same thing was true for the other subject-verb-object picture sets. A picture of a girl pushing a boy in a wagon was often described as "BOY, GIRL, PUSH". This utterance was ambiguous. However, occasionally the object was repeated, that is, "BOY GIRL PUSH BOY". This utterance was much more clear. Adding the object at the end was much more likely to lead to a correct identification, that is, a successful communication.

Perspective: Another quite interesting finding from this research was the difficulty the subjects had with perspective. Because sign language is a visual/spatial language, it would seem that describing spatial aspects of a stimulus picture should be easy. It was not easy at all. In fact, with very few exceptions, not even the oldest deaf children could describe them successfully. The problem arose in that the perspective of the sender and the perspective of the receiver of the sender and the perspective of the receiver were not the same. When the sender described from *his* perspective, but the receiver looked for a picture which matched his own perspective, the receiver did not choose the correct picture. Suppose a sender saw a picture of a girl standing on the right and a boy on the left, both of whom were facing to the right. Now when the sender positioned them (as nearly all senders did) on his right and left, then the receiver saw them standing on *his* left and right. Also, when the sender indicated that both were looking toward the right, the receiver saw the "look" sign going off towards his left. Nearly none of the deaf subjects came to an agreement that their perspectives were different.

Summary: In brief, then, these are the results of the study. For this communication task, hearing children performed better than did deaf children. Signing children out-performed oral deaf children at all age groups except the oldest, 13–15. Young deaf children performed better in teacher-pupil dyads than they did in pupil-pupil dyads. The communication ability of deaf children increased with age until age 12, after which it seemed to reach a plateau. The ordering of prepositions in the signed constructions of these deaf subjects varied. Finally, perspective, which seems to lend itself well to a visual communication system, was very difficult in this task.

Discussion

Deaf children took to the task of referential communication of drawn pictures quite easily, and the stimulus materials kept their level of interest high. The results suggest several areas that deserve attention.

In looking at the quantitative communication accuracy scores, several questions present themselves. Why was it impossible to obtain communication accuracy measures for 6–7 year old oral deaf children when signing deaf children as young as 3½ years could complete at least part of the task? This question becomes even more important when we note that virtually all of the young, signing children come from homes with two hearing parents and are taught by hearing teachers. Teachers who were questioned about this explained the results by talking about the years of "input" necessary in an oral program. Only after the input phase is complete can one expect any output from the child. What is important here is not *why* there is such a difference, but simply the fact that the difference exists. It is evident from these data that for young deaf children, signing is a better communication mode than speaking and lipreading.

Why did young deaf children from hearing homes communicate better with their hearing teachers than they did among themselves? One thing to note is that the teacher-pupil pairs did better at ages 6–7 and 8–10 than the hearing pupil-pupil pairs. This suggests that the difference is in part a lag in the development of a specific communication ability, and not something having to do only with sign language or deafness. But the difference is more than that. Eleven and twelve year old children who have often been in class together for up to six years still communicate better with their teachers than they do with each other. One possible reason is that they perceived the communication task as a school-work type task.

Virtually all of the teachers communicated in signed English (SE). When the deaf pupil was paired with his teacher and saw her signing in SE, then he, too, signed all of his descriptions in SE. Now this is not to suggest the SE would be more efficient in this task than British Sign Language (BSL).

What it does suggest, however, is that right away, at the very beginning of the task, the teacher and pupil reached an implicit agreement that they would use a specific language code, namely SE. This type of code agreement is necessary for accurate communication, and too often it was obvious that agreement was never reached in pupil-pupil pairs.

Deaf pupils in Scottish schools which use total communication theoretically have a number of language codes at their disposal. In the main, they can use either something close to SE or something close to BSL Perhaps it would be better to talk in terms of SE and non-SE. In the course of the research a trend appeared that was very evident and very regular. The children in the junior classes (up to age 12) tended to use something close to SE, while the senior children (13 and older) tended to use non-SE more often. This was true in three cities in Scotland, and conversations with others in the field suggest that it is true for deaf schools in general, both in the United Kingdom and abroad. It was clear in this task that sometimes the two children were not sharing a code. Also, as said earlier, sometimes in one utterance a child used one English word order and one non-English word order.

Part of any communication is an agreement about which language or code the communicators will use. To do this, of course, they must know that they are able to switch from one code to another. They must also be able to judge which codes their communication partner can use. This is one aspect of sign language communication that has received very little attention, but it is evident that it needs much more study.

The plateau that appears in the data after age 12 can perhaps be explained by the code sharing. The younger children were more likely to use SE, They were also more likely to speak while signing, which leads to a more English-like signing. When the desscriptions were obviously English, perhaps this led to an implicit code agreement. In describing the picture showing a table on a book, an eight year old boy signed and spoke simultaneously, "It is a white book. It has a white table on it." An eleven year old boy from the same school described the picture of the table *in* a book by signing and saying, "A book with a table was on the first page." Not only are these descriptions quite precise, but because they are obviously encoded in English, they also encouraged code sharing. That is, these descriptions fit *only* in the grammatical structure of English. They do not fit the grammatical structure of BSL. The receivers would likely interpret them as being English. The two communicators would thus use the same code. With older children, constructions such as "BOOK ON TABLE" were more probable. This construction has two very different possible interpretations. It fits into the structure of English *or* BSL. If the receiver is using an English code, it means "there is a book on a table". If the receiver is using a BSL code, it means "there is a table on a book". Because the one sign utterance can be seen as following either code, code sharing is less likely. In fact, the use of a BSL code by one child and the use of an English code by the other child will actually interfere with communication when code agreement is not reached.

There are other possible reasons for the plateau. Simple attrition is one. The best pupils in the junior schools will sometimes transfer to another school for their secondary courses. Another, and perhaps more important, factor is the communication history at the schools. The education of deaf children in Scotland is a very dynamic field, and many educational methodology changes have taken place in recent years. In one of the schools, the senior children had been taught by the oral method, two-handed fingerspelling, American one-handed fingerspelling and total communication. In the two other schools which used sign language, their recent communication history was also quite mixed. Virtually all of the 15 year old pupils had been taught with more than one communication method during their school years. Is there any wonder why children like that might find code agreement difficult?

Very closely related to code agreement is the agreement necessary for the successful communication of pictures requiring perspective. The few subject pairs who were successful with the perspective pictures made an explicit, verbalised agreement. One pair was especially interesting. One of the subjects had caught on quite quickly to the change in perspective and tried to explain it to her partner. She never did succeed in teaching her partner, so instead she told her to forget everything she had tried to explain and just go ahead and sign. Then, when acting as a sender, this girl would describe in the perspective of her partner. When acting as receiver, she would again assume her partner's perspective. This led to accurate communication for every perspective picture even though one of the communicators completed the whole task and left the room never having a clue that her partner was doing something special.

It seems that the ability to assume another's perspective is a fairly sophisticated communication ability that apparently develops naturally out of other communication and cognitive skills. Why does the communicaion of deaf children appear to lack this ability? This is another area that needs additional study.

Finally, are there acceptable and non-acceptable sign constructions for nouns and modifiers, prepositional phrases and subject-verb-object sentences? As an example, the stimulus picture showing a dog biting a cat's tail led to at least four different descriptions: "DOG, CAT, TAIL, BITE", "DOG, BITE, CAT, TAIL", "CAT TAIL, DOG, BITE", and "CAT, DOG, BITE, TAIL". Are these all equally acceptable in BSL? A description of BSL can tell us whether they are equally acceptable or which is more acceptable, but this research suggests that only one, that one which follows the English word order, i.e., "DOG, BITE, CAT, TAIL" consistently leads to a successful communication. It seems, therefore, that another area that needs additional study is the relationship between proposition ordering in sign language and English word order. This is especially important for sign language use in education.

Summary

This research was begun by asking one basic question: How well can deaf children communicate with one another? For a referential task, the answer to that question is that they do not communicate very well. However, deaf children who use sign language communicate better with one another than deaf children who use oral methods, especially at younger ages. Also, deaf children who use signs and share a language code have an advantage over deaf children who do not share a code.

It is always dangerous to make a longitudinal generalisation from a cross-sectional study, but tempting here to do so. Would the plateau that appears in the data at age 12 be there if the study was to be done five years in the future? Total communication programs in Scotland are learning as they go. Just a few years ago, it was still considered taboo to sign and parents were virtually never encouraged to do so. Sign language classes for parents are common and quite popular today. The recognition and acceptance of sign language will almost surely lead to earlier linguistic competence among deaf children. This earlier linguistic ability should, in turn, lead to earlier communication ability.

OPEN COMMUNICATION OR CASTROPHE?
A MODEL FOR EDUCATIONAL COMMUNICATION

Section 1 by George Montgomery and Gordon Mitchell
Section 2 by John Miller and George Montgomery
Section 3 by George and Joan Montgomery

Introduction

To gain understanding of a complex part of our very complex universe the typical scientific approach is to reduce that complexity to a simplified model, manipulate the model, gain insights, and then – the difficult bit – return to complexity and apply the insights acquired to untidy reality.

For example, an elephant sliding down a ski-slope is reduced to a mass, a velocity and an angle. A precise prediction of its ultimate position may then be calculated but much is lost in the process, including the whole of elephant personality and identity, all of elephant pride and culture including the rare art of skiing for elephants. If however the elephant skis over a cliff this constitutes a catastrophe in which little of the inner core of essential elephantness survives.

Figure 1 shows such a reductionist simplification using the catastrophe model of Réné Thom, applied to the communication problems of deaf children. This clearly indicates how a divergence into linguistic isolation may occur by the operation of two dimensions on the control surfaces namely a dimension of dominant *focus* of visual attention and a dimension of dominant *locus* of linguistic control.

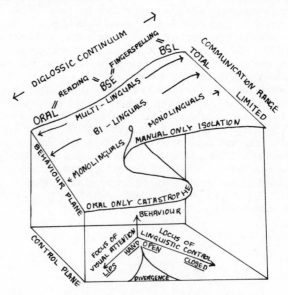

Figure 1. Open Communication or Catastrophe

The following paper investigates some aspects of the actuality represented by the model. The first section takes a narrow reductionist look at a variety of space-time measures which are found to differ between three visual languages, American Sign Language (ASL), British Sign Language (BSL) and British Signed English (BSE). The second concerns the importance of an open, accepting locus of control in language and the third the theme of open communication in the classroom and clinical practice. Finally, the related paper by King Jordan (this volume) restores life to the reductionist elephant by describing the complex reality of visual social interaction centred on a referential task.

Section 1: A Comparative Analysis of Video records of ASL, BSL and BSE Transmissions of Varying English Texts

Space Time Measures in Sign Languages

The origins of this investigation derive from a RNID international seminar of total communicators and oralist practitioners at Garnett College, London (Henderson, 1976). Here, Michael Reed brought up the question of the span of visual acuity between hand and mouth. Whether or not lip and manual patterns could always be perceived at the same time was seen as a crucial factor in the feasibility of simultaneous, if not total communication. In the course of discussion McCay Vernon mentioned the desirability of hand movements to be styled so that the view of the mouth was not occluded.

These questions seemed not unrelated and both susceptible to objective laboratory investigation. Accordingly a series of transmissions of varying English texts under systematically manipulated experimental conditions was consequently recorded on video tape in English spoken in conjunction with signing in ASL, BSL and BSE.

It seemed reasonable to expect that some light might be shed on these crucial questions and that the technique employed could be more generally applicable. At the least it was worth finding out if a few basic parameters could identify sign languages, dialects and individual styles.

This takes parsimony close to incredibility: all grammars leak but this is almost all sieve letting away, amongst much else, the whole of intelligibility and meaning. Yet common mathematical and natural principals underlie the dynamics of movement and the structure of language. Neither movement nor language develops in vacuo and language variables are as isomorphic to motoric performance variables as are the virtually infinite multivariate rhythmic and accoustical combinations of the flamenco guitarist dependent in exact one-to-one relationship on the elegant manual configurations which produce them in real time. Whilst it is difficult intuitively to visualise with Turvey (in Bellugi and Studdert-Kennedy, 1981) how a formal theory of language and a formal theory of motor coordination and control would be *qualitatively* indistinguishable, his suggestion that complex biological systems execute in two modes, the linguistic-informational and the dynamic and that these are complementary and irreducible one to the other, at once questions the autonomy of language (or flamenco) and gives hope that the present analysis of space-time motor movement will eventually prove not too remote from features of sign languages.

To initiate this analysis then, let us look at video taped protocols in three sign languages and see what a computer digest of basic dimensions of motor performance can show.

Four women and four men drawn from right-handed signing deaf persons, teachers, social workers and those with deaf members of the family provided the material to be sampled. They were asked to put into "total communication" four types of English texts: 1. Classroom English, 2. Colloquial English, 3. Scientific English, and 4. "Romantic" Novelist's English. Subjects used whatever sign language came most readily to them without direction and three groups emerged:

1. The *ASL Group* used a variety of ASL influenced by "simultaneous" English tending to the H end of the Stokoe (1969) diglossia.
2. The *BSL Group* because of the nature of the task were necessarily fluent in written English as well as BSL.
3. The *BSE Group* consisted of ex-oral teachers with just over a year's experience of signed English. They used BSL signs in English word order with a few additional signs for articles and few grammatical markers.

During recording all subjects used signs with fingerspelling and attempted synchronous speech. Examination of recordings suggested basic measurements as in Figure 2 would map out features of signing and fingerspelling space. In accord with the observation that the moves in between sign or finger alphabet segments, which may not even be perceived from the receptive view, are as important as meaningful elements in expressive performance and cannot be discounted in examining the use of space; sampling of movement was representative of all subjects under all conditions by taking ten second freezes throughout the whole recording.

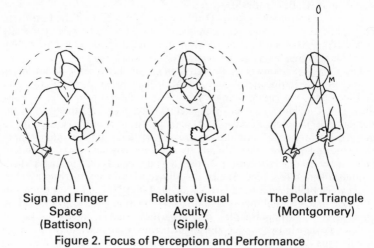

Sign and Finger Relative Visual The Polar Triangle
Space   Acuity   (Montgomery)
(Battison)   (Siple)

Figure 2. Focus of Perception and Performance

This approach gives a different, more valid, measure of the use of space than those derived from citation-form stills.

Measurement of hand position was made by polar coordinates relative to the mouth as absolute cartesian coordinates are more affected by gross body inclination and movement. The mouth position can move as an integral part of a few signs, e.g., IGNORE turns away from the emphasised negative right A-hand pivot. LUCKY may be made by a slight turn of the head to the left to facilitate the light nip of the right ear lobe between the right thumb and forefinger. TEMPT moves towards the right hand pulling outwards of lapel, collar or dress. But usually the gaze is maintained to the recipient and the mouth M is stable point of reference. The other two points were taken at the centre of each palm R and L as in Figure 2. This gives the MLR triangle which enables precise measurement of the hand-mouth relationships to be made for values such as ML, LR, RM and angles OML and OMR. As these values are related by trigonometric functions they may be used inferentially not simply descriptively.

Analysis of data yielded many significant relationships between the values of the polar triangle and language features. From the outset, however, this study was less concerned with what emerged from the laboratory than with how this could be related to clinic and classroom. Much of the learning of deaf students in school as well as in further education programmes is via the printed word in English especially in courses aiming at formal qualifications by examinations. Thus a crucial question in the acceptance of Sign in education of deaf children is how far is it compatible with the examination, qualification and employment target language – English? Because of this 'applied' design, generalisation to sign languages as they arise in spontaneous conversation and conclusions about the relative faithfulness of translation could only be made very tentatively if at all. For this was not a comparison of social communication in indigenous sign but an exercise in mapping into speech and sign from written English texts – a task which above all other should favour the transliterative tendency in BSE.

Results

Text Differences: It was suspected that differences between English styles may favour different languages. For instances, "social" BSL was predicted to be better with colloquial English and BSE with formal English. Perhaps the formal/informal register would be apparent in motor style. Perhaps the emotional English of the "romantic script" would centre on the torsal area reserved for BSL signs such as FEELING, JEALOUSY, LIKE, LOVE, HATE, EXCITEMENT, KIND. Perhaps evidence of the paucity of orectic vocabulary in deaf children alleged by M. M. Lewis would be found. In the event few useful correlates with the type of text emerged.

Tests of significance of difference (t-tests) between the means of BSL and BSE for each text separately were calculated. All texts except the "classroom" sentences took significantly longer to deliver in BSE than in BSL. In the "scientific" text 3 the dimensions RL was longer in BSL and RM longer in BSE. Overall the relationship of English "register" to sign language used was not significant.

Sign Language Differences were many and detailed. Table 1a shows highly significant Analysis of Variance differences between Languages on control variates ML, RL and Rate of Transmission and a measure of symmetry.

The proportions of both fingerspelling and alphabetisation were greatly different between languages with the one hand alphabet influence on BSE an unexpected finding (Table 1b).

Table 1. Differences in Language Features

1a. *Mean Values (ANOVA) Scientific Script*

	ASL	BSL	BSE	df	F	P
ML	105.39	86.68	80.66	2,169	7.24	.0010
MR	70.39	72.14	81.56	2,169	2.32	.1019 NS
RL	67.42	55.73	41.74	2,169	5.73	.0039
Symmetry	1.15	1.52	1.78	2,169	20.43	.0000
Time in Secs.	158.26	191.26	209.16	2,169	45.20	.0000
N	28	84	50			

1b. *Percentages (Chisquare) All Scripts*

	ASL	BSL	BSE
% Fingerspelling	30.0	34.5	44.0
% Alphabetisation	4.5	1.0	8.6
% Numerification	1.0	0.0	0.0
% Pure Sign	64.5	64.5	47.4
N	90	197	116

$$x^2 = 21.25, df 6, p = .0017$$

The polar triangles of Figure 3 summarise the differences in use of space in the three languages. More detailed diagrams of the mean polar coordinates of each of the three languages giving ipsilateral and contralateral placings for both hands and the actual spread of all positions, were generated by computer. The three circles of Figure 3 show the strikingly different proportions of cross-lateral placings. The proportion of the active (right) hand in the contralateral hemisphere and the total percentage of cross-overs of both hands, each correlate highly with rate of transmission suggesting that it is quicker to use ipsilateral signs.

Actual use of sign space is more ellipsoid than circular in proportion to the frequency of close-together two-hand signs used. For these signs the polar angles are negatively related. OMR = 360° – OML. As the contralateral arm has a much smaller reach than the ipsilateral arm, close-handed signs draw the ipsilateral arm towards the body at a distance which correlates significantly with the size of the polar angle. This foreshortens sign space at the horizontal axis:

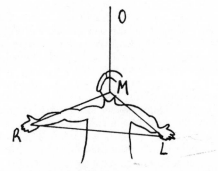

Polar coordinates OML/ML pinpoint Left Hand
Polar coordinates OMR/MR pinpoint Right Head

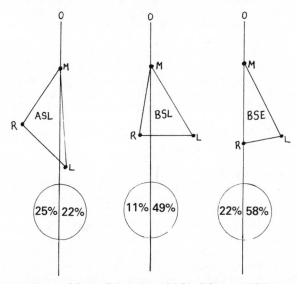

Mean Dimensions of Polar Triangles of ASL, BSL and BSE to scale and
(in circles) proportional frequency of lateral crossover

Figure 3. Sign Mean Dimensions

Arm	Angle	r	n	p
MR	OMR	.17	403	.000
ML	OML	.23	403	.000

In the BSL and BSE transmissions, crossovers are mainly of the right hand
to the left side. This is due to the strong influence of fingerspelling when
starting with written material. With American one-hand fingerspelling the
recipient must perceive a right hand transmission in the left visual field with
relatively few crossovers to the right visual field. Diagram 3 shows that in the

incidence of crossovers British languages with two-hand fingerspelling are paradoxically less symmetrical than one-handed performance. By using the left hand as tab and crossing the active right hand to the opposite side BSL and BSE present fingerspelt material in the right visual field of the receiver, giving direct access to the left-hemisphere of the brain which is usually the one dealing with language. With normally functioning inter-hemisphere commisures, information may be transmitted from hemisphere to hemisphere virtually instantaneously so that it is possible to learn to cope with stimuli habitually presented in either visual field. Hebrew readers, for example, habitually reading from right to left, identify words briefly shown in the left visual field slightly better than words similarly shown in the right visual field. With readers of English – a language written from left to right – there exists an advantage for words seen in the right visual field, i.e., a left hemisphere advantage (Mishkin and Forgays, 1952). But this learned advantage is much greater for English than for Hebrew and when the influence of horizontal scanning habits (irrelevant to the reception of fingerspelling) are removed, a right visual field advantage for both English and Hebrew obtains (Barton, Goodglass and Shai, 1965). This evidence suggests that there is an advantage in the hemisphere "pre-wired" to receive information directly although this advantage is slightly obscured by the effects of later learning. Despite speedy cross-hemisphere transmission, the first hemisphere to acquire information exerts priority of function, as information to the second hemisphere may be inhibited, modified or selectively delayed. By right hand performance in the right visual field of the receiver, BSL and BSE optimise expressive and receptive conditions for right hemisphere.

Focus of Visual Attention
Siple (in Stokoe, 1980) has described the operation of relatively confined areas of relative visual acuity in a way which suggests that Reed had noted a parameter of importance.

Figure 2 shows an area of about 5″ radius around the face as yielding full acuity with decline in relative acuity to .5 and .25 at each concentric circular line. Saccadic jumps to different sign or hand areas could occur to attend to signs and mouth in rapid succession which is for practical purposes simultaneously. But this apparently imposes a demanding vigilance task and the focus of visual acuity is held relatively constant. The approach from perception concerns receptive communication whilst Vernon's question concerns expressive visual communication. The two are obviously complementary and a language evolves by the interaction of each on the other.

Thus physical performance constraints become perpetual constraints and vice versa, a close mapping of performance to perception being necessary to convey meaning from the expressive to the receptive communicator.

Figure 2 also reflects the physical limits of sign space as described by Stokoe and Battison (1978). It is worth asking if it is the physical performance which tends to stabilise the focus of visual acuity rather than the perceptual. This seems more likely as the rapidity with which weightless light beams can move, vastly outpaces the human arm which, by leverage becomes much more of a weight to bear in proportion to its extension from the centre of Stokoe's "neutral space". (Pointers on instruments of measurement used in physics are more sensitive the longer they are but their increasing weight over leverage introduces error. This is solved by using light rays as pointers giving a weightless lever as long as required.) Thus it is not so easy for the arm to make rapid leaps from the opposite extremes of sign space. Nor do hands make instant quantum jumps from meaningful sign to meaningful sign as derivation of generalisations about sign space from still citation forms in dictionaries ignoring transitional positions could suggest. Point light studies or the present computerised video images show the kinetics more faithfully.

To quantify motor performance complements of focus of visual acuity, the present study used left and right hand measures of the discrepancy between distance of hand from mouth and distance to the other hand. It seemed not unlikely that proximity would be a good guide to focus of visual acuity. As the two hands form integral meaningful gestalts it is unlikely that one of them would be associated more with the mouth than with the other hand. Yet this happens in the "circular finger" WHO in BSL and ASL and joint mouth-hand signs appear to be even more frequent in Scandinavian sign languages (Vogt-Svendson, this volume).

Quantitative estimates of the relative proportions of focus of visual acuity are thus attempted for both hands via the dimensions set out in Figure 3. As the problem seemed universal, frequencies for all three languages were first inspected.

	Mouth nearer than other hand	Other hand nearer than mouth	Total
Right hand	142	261	403
Left Hand	71	332	403

Further breakdown of right hand and left hand, mouth to hand proximity discrepancy showed that the right hand values were highly significantly related to sign languages used whereas left hand values were not significantly related.

The active hand is thus more likely to be nearer to the mouth than the passive hand. This brings it closer to the main area of maximal visual acuity according to Siple but with increasing risk of that occlusion of the lips which Vernon would have us avoid.

Occlusion of the lips would occur with greater frequency in visual languages which did not attach meaning to lip configurations: Vernon's warning is not simply about a cosmetic improvement in style. In fact, the incidence of occlusion is so rare (four right hand occlusions only out of 403 positions overall) as to be well below significance – for most persons in the group occlusion did not occur. This low chance of occlusions is no more a hindrance to communication than the momentary distraction of intervening smoke, shine in glasses, glare or passers-by, no more dislocating than is extraneous noise and conversion of others in spoken communication. Most "occlusions" in sign do not effectively obscure the configuration of the lips, e.g., SECRET, HOT, RED, FRIDAY. Fully occlusive signs are hard to find, e.g., BOOK would be if styled unusually highly. Fingerspelling is conducted in ASL, BSL and BSE clearly separate from the lip area. Factor analysis showing a lip-sign factor separate from a fingerspelling factor may relect this difference (Henderson, 1976).

As Vernon indicated, occlusive signs are often changeable into non-occlusive signs by style rather than a change of sign. Again, what looks in still photos like a considerable list of potentially occlusive signs, all TALK derivatives from the mouth, all SEE derivatives from the eyes, all THINK derivatives from the brow are less evident using time sampling as many occlusive signs consist of a momentary tap in the face area as if deliberately designed to be less evident using time sampling as many occlusive signs consist of a momentary tap in the face area as if deliberately designed to be obliterative for as little time as possible. The thread of communication recovers in a robust way from such brief interventions.

Low occurrence of occlusion implies use of lip configurations in total communication otherwise its avoidance would be pointless. Another clue comes from proximity discrepancies. If lipreading has an equal role then it would seem reasonable to expect that the proportions of MR to LR would be equal The focus of visual acuity is not so constant, however, and a focus quotient $\frac{ML \times 100}{LR}$ may give one estimate of its likely value. It seems evident that occlusion and mouth proximity are contrary tendencies but the thin chance of occlusion makes it worth exploiting the concentration of landmarks in the small area that constitutes the human face.

The balance of attention to oral or manual components of total communication - the dominant focus of visual acuity – is beyond question a major determinant of linguistic behaviour and is accorded this status in the control surface of our topological model of language in Figure 1.

Section 2: Locus of Linguistic Control

It was suggested in our first section that the locus of linguistic control is a major determinant of the status of a language on the behaviour surface of the catstrophe model of Figure 1. This locus is the siting of the natural or formal authority which decides which elements belong to a language and which do not. A locus may be a formally constituted committee, like the Academies which guard the purity of the French and Afrikaans languages, or a single inventor like Sir Richard Paget or Orin Cornett. Control may rest with the interplay of evolutionary forces within a community or depend upon a "written constitution" of general selective principles like American Signing Exact English (Gustason and Zawolkow, 1980).

A locus of linguistic control tends usually to exercise a selective rather than a creative function and hence the main way in which it can vary is along the open-closed dimension. Open control is as fluid, flexible, cosmopolitan, understanding and tolerant as closed control is crystallised, rigid, linguocentric, parochial, solopsistic and intolerant. A relapse into the oral-only catastrophe and its complementary segregation of the manual-only group, if closed control is exercised, follows according to our model. Those of us concerned with the application of total communication in schools cannot view this relapse with complacency as a remote contingency. The rebirth of extreme auralism in England entrenched in the leadership of the association of teachers of deaf children threatens not only total communication but all visual language, even the oral channel of lipreading. Nor must we overlook the unwelcome fact that administrators of deaf clubs, interpreters, and even sign language researchers may have a conservationist interest in the maintenance of the status quo in language which could incline some deaf people to monolingualism. Like anthropologists who guard their tribesmen from contamination by even the introduction of a steel axe lest it destroy the pristine purity of their stone-age heritage, we may define a sign language so pure that it runs through father to son in three generations, thereby ensuring that it is typical of one-hundreth of the ordinary deaf populace, 90 per cent of whom have hearing parents who do not know indigenous sign. A steel axe may destroy kinship dominance in 'stone-age" societies – but it is also very useful for felling trees. Similarly BSE may be slow, Paget clumsy and unaesthetic, but the pragmatic results of these Sign systems reflected in the vocabulary test norms of 267 children in eight Scottish schools (Montgomery, 1981) clearly indicate their usefulness for children with hearing parents and hearing teachers. In Aberdeen School, Paget is used explicitly to preserve the adult sign language from interference. In most other Scottish schools for the profoundly deaf a Signed English is used as a compromise. In Donaldson's the school language is British Signed English which keeps signs as close as possible to the BSL which deaf staff and visiting social workers use and which senior pupils have always acquired themselves.

The attitude to linguistic imports (often called loan words or borrowings which is misleading because loans are by definition returned by the borrower) is an obvious clue to tolerance in the locus of linguistic control. Less obviously the use of compounds is a complementary clue. For where a language has been declared "pure", new ideas are not represented by imports but by compounds of existing forms.

English is the international import-export language par excellence. Alien imports are rapidly assimilated and treated as native: a glance at the K section of any English Dictionary shows imports from the most remote parts of the earth: Kamikaze (Japanese), Kebab (Turkish), Ketch (Dutch), Kraal (Afrikaans), Kris (Malay), Ku Klux Klan (American).

The ensuing richness of vocabulary has helped to make English the most widely established language in general use and British Sign Language follows English in its open approach to "good" imports. In fingerspelt form any word from any language is usable, a degree of tolerance which makes even English appear to be a conservative importer. Yet some of the most characteristic BSL logos are the compounds which express a new idea, e.g., "hotdog" by the two familiar signs HOT and DOG. These semantic compounds are usually structural compounds, crossing main tab boundaries in the way described by Battison (1978) for ASL and following the "gravity" high tab and to low tab tendency noted in Swedish Sign Language by Wallin (this volume).

Believe	is signed	THINK-TRUE
Decide	„ „	THINK-LAW
Experience	„ .„	THINK-LIST
Explain	„ „	SAY-MEANING
Forgive	„ „	SAY-ERASE
Knowledge	„ „	KNOW-LIST
Promise	„ „	SAY-TRUE

As with elements in chemical compounds (e.g., H_2O), language elements are compounds if together they are quite different than when separated. Sign compounds seem also to be shown by this structural leap. Thus FACE-BAD for "ugly" and LADY-KING for "queen" seem not to be true compounds semantically and this is reflected in their structure. The equivalent in spoken language would be to differentiate by intonation "That redskin has a red skin".

The duality of attitude to the import/compound issue in BSL seems to be related to the extreme variance between the H and L forms of its diglossic continuum. Like the theologically impossible comprehensiveness of the Church of England, BSL embraces all believers in paternal acceptance without too close scrutiny of actual practice. The high proportion of fingerspelling in the H variety of BSL makes for an open exchange with English and the low incidence of fingerspelling in the L variety coincides with a more parochial purist outlook which prefers compounds of native roots. Examples of the latter have already been listed and examples of imports from English are equally plentiful. For example, the sign for SEEM (a downward facing flat hand pulled in a salute-like movement from the eye) is identical with the sign for BEEN except that it is pulled away from the mouth. There is no semantic similarity between these two logos in BSL and the only link is via English phonology.

The fluidity of cross-cultural exchanges of Sign Languages logos suggests that those who would freeze history and constrict natural evolutionary developments are doomed to fail. Certainly in education, fluidity is an essential prerequisite to development: any closed, wrapped-up package of learning is dead before it leaves the drawing board. In society, too, closed languages lead to closed communities – it was no accident that the developing state of Israel rejected ghetto Yiddish as the language of their new country. Conversely, it would seem that an open, tolerant locus of linguistic control would improve relationships between deaf and hearing people.

Section 3: Open Communication in Clinic and Classroom

Standardised tests of lipreading, fingerspelling, auditory vocabulary, speech, reading and writing produced by item analysis have been used for over a decade in Scotland for the Educational and Vocational Guidance of deaf children. Tables of norms for the expressive and receptive forms of these tests are regularly updated.

The tests have been validated against later vocational criteria and against concurrent Teachers' ratings which themselves suitably calibrated by computer, constitute another source of evaluation of the communication skills open to deaf children.

Yet because ratings, although having overall validity, may generalise (halo) an individual's abilities, and because standardised tests produce mode specific vocabularies and sentence forms, no direct comparison of modes is possible. One solution to the problem of intermodal comparisons we call the Open Communication Tests. This technique employs a random item deck of 99 cards each with a numbered sentence printed on one side (the verbal side) which describes a non-verbal picture match of this sentence on the reverse (the picture side). The cards are hand sized and may be shuffled to randomise in the manner of playing cards. The pictures printed on each card show a variety of objects, animals and everyday scenes originally selected by a clerical assistant unacquainted with educational methodology or current classroom standards thus maintaining a "man-in-the-street" vocabulary rather than a teacher's vocabulary of particularly teachable words. This was important when comparing different communication modes as each mode has a slightly different order of difficulty resulting in differentially "readable", "audible" or "lipreadable" vocabulary items being selected.

Conventional standardised tests of communication skills characteristically present modes singly not conjointly and have employed specially appropriate separate vocabularies derived from item analysis. Such tests give optimal validity for testing individuals but because each has a biased vocabulary they are not so useful for strict comparison of the efficiency of the various communication modes. The present technique makes modes comparable by testing them singly or in combination by reference to the common item deck, presenting a randomised selection of the 99 items six at a time as a multiple choice test.

Although usually comprising 99 items, in fact it can be regarded as a virtual infinity of items as each card becomes quite different in difficulty and discriminative power according to the context of the other five distractor cards and to the less immediate context of the sequence of foregoing cards. This presents an open context more akin to the varying context of ordinary functional social communication than the fixed context of standardised tests of comprehension and vocabulary: hence the name "open communication".

Although the sentences chosen are dependent upon the associated pictures this does not always lead to a "picturable" vocabulary as it is possible for the sentence to refer to a picture as a whole without using words of objects directly pictured. For example, there are many pictorial representations of "sea" but "It walks under the sea" (a crab) or "It is a sea-shell" do not directly portray a sea-scape.

The random item deck may be used for many purposes such as teaching literacy skills through teacher-directed teaching and testing routines or by guessing-games played by students themselves. Another use to which the random format lends itself is the educational or psychological experiment whereby new communication hard-ware or other techniques may be formally evaluated. Perhaps the most obvious use would be for standardised assessment by educational psychologists and teachers. As the tests are not restricted "closed" tests it would be obviously invalid to use them to test children who have had access to them for language and speech training sessions or other classroom routines. Assessment tests may be of the conventional fixed-context standardised attainment type or employ the randomising facility of the carded item deck. Tests may compare expressive or receptive communication efficiency between single or combined modes or compare these same channels with a time delay thus testing memory. In all tests comparison may be made to a reference sample giving a normative evaluation. It is sometimes more fruitful to examine the individual's strengths and weaknesses by comparing his performances on different modes with each other by the ipsative approach. In all these comparisons whether within individuals, between groups or against a reference group, the randomised scores are directly comparable and readily lend themselves to graphic comparisons. Figures 4 and 5 show profiles of communication. Such histograms often show extreme discrepancy in individual use of channels of communication. They present results in a form which is easily understood by clients and other lay men. The need for such an understandable path to realistic lay appreciation of communication ability is not small, the benefits of enlightenment not trivial.

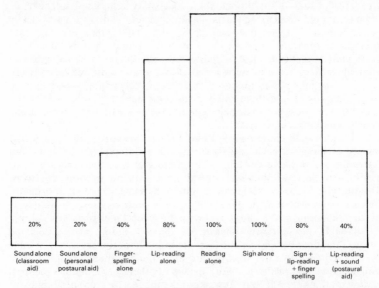

Figure 4(a). Communication Profile of a 12 year old deaf girl with previous history of reading difficulties, now on PGSS

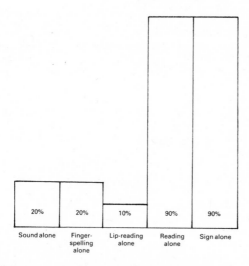

Figure 4(b). Communication Profile of a 15 year old partially deaf boy taught in an oral class

Conclusions

The model presented in the initial stages serves as a framework for analysis of communication. It has been shown that the focus of visual attention towards oral or manual components of communication is a major determinant of linguistic behaviour; second that the form of communication is shaped by the locus of linguistic control; third, that communication modes may be meaningfully compared to give understanding of the various strands of total communication. Early application of this model to individual and group guidance suggests that realistic awareness of communication abilities and potentialities is essential to healthy language development.

Love conquers all – linguistic, racial, religious, class, economic and educational barriers are all regularly crossed by marriage (Montgomery, 1981). It is a measure of the immensity of the problem of profound deafness that the deaf-hearing barrier is not more commonly crossed. With a more tolerant locus of linguistic control in sign languages, a more open attitude to alien and pidgin variants of indigenous languages, with more native signers in schools and more teaching of indigenous sign to hearing people, both hearing and deaf languages cannot but flourish in mutual respect. Then the integration of deaf people with general society and the acceptance of more hearing people into deaf society will go a long way to ending the loneliness and isolation so many deaf people endure today.

Acknowledgement is due to Mrs. Barbara Crawford, Secretary of Donaldson's Research Unit, for aid in data collection, the collation of test norms and preparation of scripts, and to Mr. Martin Colville, for giving many months of patient tuition in BSL, without which this project would still be on the drawing board.

PART 5: OVERVIEW

In this section, Professor Stokoe sums up the papers presented. He suggests a context and framework for integrating the work of sign language researchers. There is no doubt that this is of particular value in setting the work reported here within a much wider perspective of developing science in the area of deafness. He re-affirms the views that language research may be able to learn a great deal from the studies of sign language.

His emphasis on the importance of non-manual aspects of signing is useful in suggesting what is becoming a widespread view of the scope of the signed message. Deaf people use more than their hands in giving information and the acceptance of the totality of the message is almost certainly indicative of community membership. The general interest in the deaf community is clearly another theme which has emerged and it is in this sense that Professor Stokoe claims to be an anthropologist. His contribution to the conference was significant indeed and this final overview here allows the reader an important insight into the organisation of current studies in sign language.

SIGN LANGUAGES, LINGUISTICS AND RELATED ARTS AND SCIENCES

Professor William Stokoe

I have been asked to sum up or reflect and react to all other papers here. For those of you who like short papers, I can give you my reaction in just one multi-channel sign – "WOW".

This has been a wonderful conference for three reasons: the accommodation, food and service here have been outstanding, and Bristol, Bath and the Wine Fair we will leave with deep regret and return to whenever possible. Second, this has been a richly satisfying intellectual experience. What I have gained from the papers and the discussions in this room and all over the campus is especially gratifying to me – my own personal involvement I will explain as we go on. But third, and topping the physical and mental delight of this conference, I have enjoyed the pleasure of your company. I have enjoyed meeting, interacting, debating and experiencing with you a week to remember.

I should tell you that I am not a linguist – at least not as that label is now used. My doctoral study, commenced 38 years ago, was in English and Classical Languages and Literature. I could claim to be a philologist, but I won't. I did have a summer course in 1957 which was called "Linguistics for Teachers of English", but that course treated linguistics as an interesting sub-area of the real subject – cultural anthropology. So I call myself an anthropologist, but I won't use that label much either. What I would like to become if I live long enough is a philosopher, and this conference and those of the last few years really make me feel like one of the philosophers in Plato's Academy. You know, it must have been really much like our conference, back there in Athens – a group of friends seriously discussing the issues that interest them most and enjoying both the discussions and the feeling of being together in an important task.

Sign language is too large a subject to be captured and tied up in one science, or in half a dozen. Sign language may be too vast to be caught by science at all, and we are reminded that no matter how carefully we investigate sign languages, the true stuff of poetry, all that matter we cannot make a science out of, will escape our most rigorous analysis.

This conference demonstrates how hard it is to get sign language research into neat disciplinary pigeonholes. The papers presented might be divided along traditional lines. That classification, however, would leave remainders, and would also put together papers that are quite different in method and scope. Besides, as I said before, I am not a linguist, and I want to classify this rich intellectual feast without again using the word linguistics.

The classification I have come up with is in Figure 1. This classification is no more than my own attempt to reduce fine presentations to the "magic number seven, plus or minus two". I think I can find a strong theoretical linkage within the lists, but just as good a case could be made for connections from list to list.

With all of them laid out like this, I note with satisfaction that exactly one-

Figure 1

fourth are by deaf members of our group. (In the final collection, only one-fifth of the papers were by deaf presenters.) I say "with satisfaction" because it was just ten years ago when I wrote that our field would not come of age until deaf researchers were involved in their own right. One-fourth is not enough perhaps – we could use an equal number of deaf and hearing investigators easily – but it is an excellent gain over the few or none who could be found only five years ago.

With even greater satisfaction, I note something else – after all anyone could have said what I said in 1972: it should be obvious that sign languages cannot really be studied without the insight of their native users. But I really stuck my neck out in that same book, when I used a whole chapter to argue that we must have much more information about the facial and other non-manual components of signing. Remember, at that time, two or three research centres were just setting out to define the major and minor parameters of a sign as handshapes, hand movements, hand location, hand orientations, etc., etc. – as if sign language was a matter only of what the hands were doing.

If I were not so intellectually stimulated by the work of deaf researchers and the work on non-manual parts of signing. I would probably be shedding tears of overfilled emotion at this vindication of my double prophecy. Six of our papers are on non-manual or multi-channel signs, and half of them are studies by deaf researchers. We now have a new fund of knowledge about what may be the larger part of signing. All this is such good news that it seems to inspire me to attempt another prophecy.

This new information about sign language away from the hands comes at just the right moment. Earlier this summer there was a conference in California on the Facial Action Coding System (the system of analysis and notation of facial changes developed in the last several years by Paul Ekman and Wallace Friesen). The F.A.C.S. is possibly the most complete and accurate and workable system yet invented for research on facial signals. It is the system that my colleague Charlotte Baker has been using in her investigation of non-manual actions in ASL discourse.

Back to the F.A.C.S., I was overjoyed to find that while I was watching and listening to the presenters, watching the articulation of British, Norwegian and Swedish facial and multi-channel signs, I had no difficulty at all in assigning to each, one or more of the numbers of the F.A.C.S. This is really a breakthrough in sign language research, but it is more: research in non-verbal communication (NVC) has lagged, because facial changes are so complex and so difficult to analyse. Now, or very soon I predict, the new research in sign languages will lead to better understanding of NVC. We will generally know much more about how all people use their faces and bodies to communicate. Once again sign language researchers will lead the way.

I wish I had the space to comment on each paper – or even on each of these groupings because all of them are food for thought. They give us something to build on.

The state of the art in sign language research is nothing to be ashamed of, and the state of the art in European research will surely put American researchers on their mettle so as not to be left behind.

One section I will have time to give special mention, is the one I have labelled "Biology". But it might have been called "the roots of language". I am very glad that we have had this paper to remind us that all language begins as expression in physical action, and begins as reception and understanding in the perceptual systems. These systems have not been fully enough studied. This is also an area of much interest to me.

We do believe with George Montgomery that the direction and angular displacement at shoulder, elbow and wrist are crucial in sign language description – perhaps as important as tongue displacement is in spoken language phonetics. Also, the really basic nature of human perceptual systems means that our receptive or visual phonetics of sign language is just as much in need of radical re-examination as is our productive or articulatory sign language phonetics.

Already I think we can see a general trend. Information from each of the areas is needed in all the others. Moreoever, artistic use of sign language may be even more illuminating than prosaic, routine, everyday or laboratory use of sign language. But the most exciting prospect for the future I see is the more complete unification of language studies and human science that the conference is foreshadowing.

Most would agree that language is well worth research time and effort and the money it costs – if it *is* science of the whole language complex and not ever and ever smaller reduction into tiny segments. But now it is clearer than ever that any language research has to consider signed languages along with spoken languages. It is just as important that language study takes language in its double context. One context is the human organism that sends and receives the language signals. Much study has been done on the physiology of hearing and of speech, but the physiology of vision and of higher brain centre control of the face and arms and hands has not really begun, except as we hear rumours of it in this conference. The other context of course is more familiar. This context in its widest aspect is called culture. It is what people who use language use it for. What are the users doing? How do the language messages relate to the users and to their other behaviour and to their relationships to one another? An anthropologist studying cognitive maps that members of the culture have in their heads, needs to know how the mothers pass on the culture to their babies (Carolyn Scroggs gives a good glimpse into that process – it is multi-channel linguistic and visual, and above all tactile). But we must also study how children communicating with other children pass on reliable and sometimes flawed cultural knowledge from child to child.

The deaf community is different from all other cultural groups with a shared minority language and identity. Part of that difference comes from the fact that 90–95% of deaf children are born into hearing families. This means that in the deaf community the culture passes from child to child much more than from parent or adult to child. I must agree with both William Edmondson and Martin Colville: deaf children communicate beautifully and fluently – but much of what they communicate is simply not reliable information, is false or confused. Culture passed from child to child is bound to be like that.

When you think carefully and introspectively about that truth, you may be in for a shock. For example, I recall quite clearly over almost 60 years that all my early sex education – the biology of sex and the social and cultural overtones – was learned from other children, my age or a litle older. But I also recall even more clearly (because the discovery was sometimes traumatic) that most of that cultural knowledge was either a little mixed up or out and out wrong.

So we need knowledge not just about the systems of sign languages, but also about the messages in the sign languages actually used by children and adults in real life situations for real life purposes. We may not need to close all our laboratories yet, but let's make sure that the problems and data we take into our laboratories are real problems and real data and come from the natural productions of real people.

Because sign languages are better than spoken languages at reminding us how fully the whole organism is involved in language, I think we will find more and more studies using our sign language research to get at the real sources of language. Making word-signs and sentence-signs involves the whole person. All the senses work; all the perceptual systems combine to take information in. Otherwise the human brain, the central processor is operating with "less than a full deck" (behaves as if feeble minded). With its information and with a human brain, the human organism constructs a sign, and then with much more of the whole organism than we usually realise, the sign – either spoken or signed – is transmitted.

Forgive me if I repeat the thing I have been saying and writing for twenty years; language is not what voices do – language is not what hands do (and language is not what linguists think it is) – but language is what people associating with people do.

Now and in the next few years, we will see the study of language becoming more integrated – not just tiny fractions of the system, not just tiny constructs whose psychological reality is debated to the third decimal point – but studies of the organism, the communication and interaction systems, and the culture that these systems have evolved to signify. The study of language in the future (if it behaves as I say it should) will integrate the biological organism with the culture shared by natural groups of the same kind of organism. The research reported here gives me confidence that language study of any real worth will have to behave that way. The language sciences cannot ignore sign language research any longer – indeed the leading linguists I know are already fully aware of sign language research, and are intensely interested.

Again, I wish I had time to comment on each presentation, because I have something favourable to say about each of them – though of course some more than others. And again, I would like to look especially at one study, because like the work on non-manual components in BSL, Swedish and Norwegian signs, it actually marks a breakthrough.

Virginia Volterra has discovered a very fundamental principle in the gestures of proto-language of hearing and deaf infants. Both hearing babies and deaf babies make deictic gestures – they point to things and people and action – and so do other animals. Both hearing babies and deaf babies also make referential gestures. They perform bodily actions that stand for cognitive concepts. This is a quantum jump from pointing, but it is also found – traces of it anyway – in the behaviour of other species. But, here is the crux; only human babies put two referential gestures together to make a larger unit of referential meaning.

And here is the breakthrough: only when the people around the deaf baby are using a sign language, does the deaf baby put two such gestures together with language-like syntax.

Human interaction is necessary, and the infant must have the experience of hearing or seeing referential symbols combined in order to try it.

I will not try to list all the implications this has, both for applied and for theoretical studies, but I cannot resist showing you how Virginia's discovery makes parts of one puzzle fall into place. For several years I have been seeing evidence and receiving reports that deaf children in deaf families of the right kind begin putting referential symbols into two-unit sentences months earlier than hearing children begin their own two-word utterance stage. Now the explanation of this is simple. The deaf children with signing parents have a lifetime experience – nine or ten or twelve months – of seeing referential gestures combined into sentences with larger reference, and with this experience naturally they do so themselves. Hearing infants have the same language capabilities, and begin as Virgina finds by making the same kind of gestures, but they have to go through a stage of separating out their vocal gestures from their body gestures, and a stage of shaping their vocal gestures into referential words before they catch on to the fact that their speaking, hearing parents are making sentences out of words.

To sum up now, I want just to tell you the lesson these papers have reinforced for me: that lesson is that reductionist techniques go on splitting reality into smaller bits and the smaller bits into still smaller bits and so on *ad infinitum* – and the other side of that lesson is that language study must never lose sight of the still little-understood human organism, and all its parts and functions while keeping in view also the whole social and cultural context of language. In this way sign language research can lead to a more human science of language, a science that takes people (deaf and hearing) as its field. Only then will it be a science of humanity, full of interest to people.

CONTRIBUTORS

Brita Bergman Institute of Linguistics, University of Stockholm, Stockholm, Sweden

John Bonvillian Department of Psychology, Gilmer Hall, University of Virginia, Charlottesville, Virginia 22901, U.S.A.

Mary Brennan BSL Research Project, Moray House College of Education, Holyrood Road, Edinburgh, EH8 8AQ, Scotland

Elisabeth Dawson Department of Applied and Social Studies, Essex Institute of Higher Education, Victoria Road South, Chelmsford, Essex CM1 1LL, England

Margaret Deuchar School of European Studies, University of Sussex, Falmer, Near Brighton, BN1 9QN, England

William Edmondson Psychology Department, Bedford College, Regents Park, London, NW1 4NS, England

Viv Edwards Department of Linguistics, University of Reading, Whiteknights, Reading, England

Susan Fischer National Technical Institute for the Deaf, Rochester, New York 14623, U.S.A.

Gerilee Gustason Department of Education, Gallaudet College, Washington DC 20002, U.S.A.

Harley Hamilton Atlanta Area School for the Deaf, Charleston, Georgia 30021, U.S.A.

Nancy Hatfield University of Washington, Seattle, Washington 98195, U.S.A.

King Jordan Gallaudet College, Washington DC 20002, U.S.A.

Jim Kyle School of Education Research Unit, University of Bristol, 19 Berkeley Square, Bristol BS8 1HF, England

Paddy Ladd British Deaf Association, 38 Victoria Place, Carlisle, CA1 1HU, England

Lilian Lawson British Deaf Association, 38 Victoria Place, Carlisle, CA1 1HU, England

Filip Loncke Free University of Brussels, Brussels, Belguim

Betsy McDonald CIDI/NTID, Rochester Institute of Technology, Rochester, New York 14623, U.S.A.

Rachel Mayberry Northwestern University, Program in Audiology and Hearing Impairment, 2299 Sheridan Road, Evanston, Illinois 60201, U.S.A.

John Miller University Department of Psychology and Research Unit, Donarldson's School, Edinburgh, Scotland

John Mitchell University Department of Psychology and Research Unit, Donaldson's School, Edinburgh, Scotland

George Montgomery, University Department of Psychology and Research Unit, Donaldson's School, Edinburgh, Scotland

Joan Montgomery University Department of Psychology and Research

Unit, Donaldson's School, Edinburgh, Scotland

Lesley Novak   Department of Psychology, Gilmer Hall, University of Virginia, Charlottesville, Virginia 22901, U.S.A.

Michael Orlansky   Department of Psychology, Gilmer Hall, University of Virginia, Charlottesville, Virginia 22901, U.S.A.

Carolyn Scroggs   Lewis and Clark College, Portland, Oregon, 97219, U.S.A.

William Stokoe   Linguistics Research Laboratory, Gallaudet College, Washington DC 20002, U.S.A.

Vivien Tartter   Rutgers University, Camden, New Jersey 08102, U.S.A.

Bernard Tervoort   Institute for General Linguistics, Spuistraat 210, University of Amsterdam, 1012 VT Amsterdam, The Netherlands

Marit Vogt-Svendsen   The Advanced Teacher Training College of Special   Education, Hosle, Norway

Virginia Volterra   Institute of Psychology, CNR Via dei Monti Tiburtini 509, 00157 Rome, Italy

Lars Wallin   Institute of Linguistics, University of Stockholm, Stockholm,   Sweden

Bencie Woll   School of Education Research Unit, University of Bristol, 19 Berkeley Square, Bristol, BS8 1HF, England

G.L. Zaitseva   Science Research Institute of Defectology, Academy of Pedagogical Sciences of the U.S.S.R., Moscow, U.S.S.R.

REFERENCES

Ahlgren, I and Bergman, B. (eds.) (1980) *Papers from the First International Symposium on Sign Language Research*. Stockholm: Swedish National Association of the Deaf

Ahlgren, I and Ozolins, B. (1980) Översättning till teckenspräk. In Engwall, G. (ed.) *Litterär Oversättning*. Stockholm: University of Stockholm

Altman, E. (1973) *Some Variables in Mother and Child Interaction Related to Linguistic Competence in Severely Hearing Impaired Children*. Unpublished Ph.D. diss., Long Island University, The Brooklyn Centre

Anderson, L.B. (1978) A Comprehensive Typological Analysis of Sign Language Vocabulary. Unpublished paper

Anthony, D. (1971) *Seeing Essential English Manual: Volumes I and II* Anaheim, California: Anaheim Union High School District

Argyle, M. (1975) *Bodily Communication* London: Methuen

Association of Teachers of English to Pupils from Overseas (ATEPO) Birmingham Branch (1970) *Work Group on West Indian Pupils Report*

Babbidge, H.D. (1965) *Education of the Deaf: A Report to the Secretary of Health, Education and Welfare by his Advisory Committee on the Education of the Deaf*. Washington, D.C.: U.S. Department of Health, Education and Welfare

Baker, C. (1976) What's not on the other hand in American Sign Language, in *Papers from the Twelfth Regional Meeting of the Chicago Linguistic Society*. Chicago: University of Chicago Press

Baker, C. (1978) How does 'Sim-Com' fit into a Bilingual Approach to Education, in Caccamise, F. and Hicks, D. (eds.) *Proceedings of the National Symposium on Sign Language Research and Teaching*

Baker, C. (1980) On the terms verbal and non-verbal, in Ahlgren and Bergman (eds.)

Baker, C. and Battison, R. (1980) *Sign Language and the Deaf Community: Essays in Honor of William C. Stokoe*. Silver Springs: National Association of the Deaf

Baker, C. and Cokeley, D. (1980) *American Sign Language: A Teachers' resource text on grammar and culture*. Silver Springs: T.J. Publishers

Baker, C. and Padden, C. (1978) Focusing on the non-manual components of American Sign Language, in Siple, P. (ed.)

Baratz, J. (1970) Educational Considerations in Teaching Standard English to Negro Children, in Fasold, R. and Shuy, R. (eds.) *Teaching Standard English in the Inner City*. Washington, D.C.: Centre for Applied Linguistics

Bartlett, F.C. (1932) *Remembering: A study in Experimental and Social Psychology*. Cambridge: Cambridge University Press

Bates, E. (1976) *Language and Content: The acquisition of pragmatics*. New York: Academic Press

Bates, E., Benigni, L., Bretherton, L., Camaioni, L. and Volterra, V.

271

(1977) From Gesture to the First Word: On Cognitive and Social Prerequisites, in Lewis, M. and Rosenblum, L. (eds.) *Interaction and the Development of Language*. New York: Wiley

Bates, E. Benigni, L., Bretherton, I., Camaioni, L. and Volterra, V. (1979) *The Emergence of Symbols: Cognition and Communication in Infancy*. New York: Academic Press

Bates, E., Camaioni, L. and Volterra, V. (1975) The acquisition of performatives prior to speech. *Merrill Palmer Quarterly, 21,* 205–226

Battison, R. (1974) Phonological deletion in American Sign Language. *Sign Language Studies, 5,* 1–14

Battison, R. (1978) *Lexical Borrowing in American Sign language*. Silver Springs: Linstok Press

Battison, R. and Jordan, I.K. (1976) Cross Cultural Communication with Foreign Signers: Fact and Fancy. *Sign Language Studies, 10,* 53–68

Bellman, K., Poizner, H. and Bellugi, U. (1981) Invariant characteristics of some American Sign Language morphological processes. San Diego: Salk Institute Working Paper.

Bellugi, U. (1976) Attitudes towards sign language: Is there a need for a change? *British Deaf News Supplement*. October

Bellugi, U. (1980) Clues from the similarities between signed and spoken language, in Bellugi, U. and Studdert-Kennedy, M. (eds.)

Bellugi, U. and Fischer, S. (1972) A comparison of sign language and spoken language. *Cognition, 1,* 173–200

Bellugi, U. and Klima, E.S. (1972) The roots of language in the sign talk of the deaf. *Psychology Today, 6,* 61–76

Bellugi, U., Klima, E.S. and Siple, P. (1975) Remembering in signs. *Cognition, 3,* 93–125

Bellugi, U. and Siple, P. (1974) Remembering with and without signs in: Bresson, F. (ed.) *Current problems in psycholinguistics*. Paris: Centre Nationale de la Recherche Scientifique

Bellugi, U. and Studdert-Kennedy, M. (eds.) (1980) *Signed and Spoken Language: Biological Constraints on Linguistic Form*. Berlin: Verlag Chemie

Bergman, B. (1979) *Signed Swedish*. Rosenludstrychunit: National Swedish Board of Education

Berke, L. (1978) Attitudes of Deaf High School Students Towards American Sign Language, in Caccamise, F. and Hicks, D. (eds.) *Proceedings of the National Symposium on Sign Language Research and Teaching*

Berko-Gleason, J. (1973) Code Switching in Children's Language, in Moore, T. (ed.) *Cognitive Development and the Acquisition of Language*. New York: Academic Press

Bickerton, D. (1974) Creolization, Linguistic Universals, Natural Semantics and the Brain. Paper presented at the International Conference on Pidgins and Creoles, Honolulu, Hawaii

Blanton, R.L. and Brooks, P.H. (1978) Some Psycholinguistic Aspects of Sign Language, in Schlesinger, I.M. and Namir, L. (eds.)

Bloom, L. (1973) *One Word at a Time*. The Hague: Mouton

Bloomfield, L. (1939) *Language*. London: Allen & Unwin

Bonvillian, J.D., Charrow, V.R. and Nelson, K.E. (1973) Psycholinguistic and educational implications of deafness. *Human Development, 16,* 321–45

Bonvillian, J.D. and Nelson, K.E. (in press) Exceptional Cases of Language Acquisition, in Nelson, K.E. (ed.). *Children's Language,* Vol. 3. New York: Gardner Press

Bornstein, H., et al. (1972–present) *Signed English series.* Washington D.C.: Gallaudet Press

Bornstein, H. (1980) Signed English: A First evaluation (A Research Report), in *Directions: Recent, Current and Projected Research at Gallaudet,* Washington, D.C.: Gallaudet College Press

Bornstein, H., Hamilton, L., Saulnier, K.L. and Roy, H. (1975) *The Signed English Dictionary for Pre-school and Elementary Level.* Washington, D.C.: Gallaudet College Press

Boskis, R.M. and Morozova, N.G. (1959) On the development of mimetic language in deaf and dumb children and its role in the processes of instruction and education, in *Training and Education of the Deaf and Dumb.* Moscow: M. Uchpedgiz

Bowerman, M. (1978) Words and sentences: Uniformity, individual variation, and shifts over time in patterns of acquisition, in Minifie, F.D. and Lloyd, L.L. (eds.)

Boyes, P. (1972) Visual Processing and the Structure of Sign Language. Unpublished paper

Boyes-Braem, P. (1981) *Significant features of the handshape in American sign language.* Unpublished Ph.D. dissertation, University of California at Berkeley

Bransford, J.D. and McCarrell, N.S. (1975) A sketch of a cognitive approach to comprehension, in Weimer, W.B. and Palmero, D.S. *Cognition and the Symbolic Processes.* Hillsdale, N.J.: Lawrence Erlbaum Associates

Brasel, K. and Quigley, S. (1977) The influence of certain language and communication environments on the development of language in deaf individuals. *Journal of Speech and Hearing Research, 20,* 95–107

Brazelton, T.B., Kowslowski, B. and Main, M. (1974) The origins of reciprocity: the early mother-infant interaction, in Lewis, M. and Rosenblum, L.A. (eds.). *The Effect of the infant on its caregiver.* New York: Wiley

Brennan, M. (1976) Can deaf children acquire language? An evaluation of linguistic principles in deaf education. *Supplement to British Deaf News,* February issue

Brennan, M., Colville, M.D. and Lawson, L.K. (1980) *Words in hand: A structural analysis of the signs of British Sign Language.* Edinburgh: Moray House Publications

Brooks, W. and Emmeret, P. (1976) *Interpersonal Communication.* New York: William C. Brown Co.

Brown, R. (1973) *A First Language.* Cambridge, Mass.: Harvard University Press

Brown, R. (1977) Why are signed languages easier to learn than spoken *languages*? Paper presented at the First National Symposium on Sign

Language Research and Teaching, Chicago

Bruce, R.V. (1973) *Alexander Graham Bell and the Conquest of Solitude.* London: Gollancz

Bruner, J.S. (1966) On Cognitive Growth, in Bruner, J.S., Olver, R.R. and Greenfield, P.M. (eds.) *Studies in Cognitive Growth.* New York: Wiley

Bruner, J.S. (1975) From communication to language – a psychological perspective. *Cognition, 3,* 255–87

Bullowa, M. (1979) (ed.) *Before speech: the beginning of Interpersonal Communication.* Cambridge: Cambridge University Press

Burling, R. (1959) Language Development of Garo and English Speaking Children, *Word, 15,* 45–68

Burling, R. (1978) *Man's Many Voices.* New York: Holt, Rinehart & Winston

Burling, R. (1981) Social constraints on adult language learning. Paper presented at the New York Academic of Science Symposium on First- and Second-Language Learning

Camaioni, L., Volterra, V. and Bates, E. (1976) *La Communicazione nel primo anno di vita.* Torino: Boringhieri

Carmichael, L. (1964) The early growth of language capacity in the individual, in Lenneberg, E.H. (ed.) *New Directions in the Study of Language.* Cambridge, Mass.: M.I.T. Press

Cokely, D. and Baker, C. (1980) Problems with rate and deletion in simultaneous communication: (A Research Report), in *Directions, Recent, Current, and Projected Research at Gallaudet.* Washington D.C.: Gallaudet College

Cokely, D. and Gawlik, R. (1973) Options: A position paper on the relationship between manual English and sign. *The Deaf American, 25,* No.9, 7-11

Cokely, D. and Gawlik, R. (1980) Childrenese as Pidgin, in Stokoe, W.C. (ed.) *Sign and Culture.* Silver Springs: Linstok Press

Collis, G.M. (1979) Describing the structure of social interaction in infancy, in Bullowa, M. (ed.)

Comrie, B. (1976) *Aspect,* Cambridge: Cambridge University Press

Conlin, D. and Paivio, A. (1975) The associative learning of the deaf: the effects of word imagery and signability. *Memory and Cognition, 3,* (3) 335-40

Conrad, R. (1979) *The Deaf School Child: Language and cognitive function.* London: Harper and Row

Corrigan, R. (1978) Language development as related to stage and object permanence development. *Journal of Child Language, 5,* 173-89

Corrigan, R. (1979) Cognitive correlates of language: differential criteria yield differential results. *Child Development, 50,* 617-31

Covington, V. (1980) Problems of acculturation into the deaf community. *Sign Language Studies, 28,* 257-85

Crandall, K. (1975) A comparison of signs used by mothers and deaf children during early childhood. *Proceedings of the Convention of American Instructors of the Deaf.* Washington, D.C.: C.A.I.D.

Cross, T. (1977) Mothers' speech and adjustment: the centribution of selected listener variables, in Snow, C. and Ferguson, C. (eds.) *Talking to*

Children. London: Cambridge University Press

Cross, T. (1978) Mothers' speech and its association with rate of linguistic development in young children, in Waterson, N. and Snow, C. (eds.) *The Development of Communication*. London: Wiley

Crump, S. (1979) *The Language of West Indian Children and Its Relevance for Schools*. Unpublished M.A. Dissertation, University of London, Institute of Education

Crystal, D. (1980a) Neglected grammatical factors in conversational English, in Greenbaum, S., Leech, G. and Svartvik, J. (eds.) *Studies in English Linguistics: for Randolph Quirk*. London: Longmans

Crystal, D. (1980b) *A First Dictionary of Linguistics and Phonetics*. London: Andre Deutsch

Crystal, D. and Craig, E. (1978) Contrived Sign Language, in Schlesinger, I.M. and Namir, L. (eds.)

Crystal, D. and Quirk, R. (1964) *Systems of Prosodic and Paralinguistic Features in English*. The Hague: Mouton and Co.

Dawson, E.H. (1979) *Cognitive functioning of prelingually deaf children*. Unpublished Ph.D. thesis, University of Durham

Dawson, E.H. (1979) Are the deaf really a homogeneous population? *Teacher of the Deaf, 3,* 188-93

De Camp, D. (1971) Towards a Generative Analysis of a Post-creole Speech continuum, in Hymes, D. (ed.)

de Crinis, M. (1932) Die Entiwicklung der Grosshirnrinde nach der Geburt in Ihren Beziehungen zur intellektuellen Ausreifung des Kindes. *Wien. Klin. Zschr., 45,* 1161-1165. (quoted in Carmichael, 1964)

De Matteo, A. (1978) Visual Imagery and Visual Analogues in American Sign Language, in Friedman, L. (ed.)

de Stefano, J. (1973) (ed.) *Language, Society, and Education: A Profile of Black English*. Belmont, California: Wadsworth Publishing Co.

de Villiers, J. and de Villiers, P. (1978) *Language Acquisition*. Boston: Harvard University Press

Deuchar, M. (1978) *Diglossia in British Sign Language*. Unpublished Ph.D. Dissertation, Stanford University

Deuchar, M. (1980) Language planning and the treatment of BSL: Problems for research, in Ahlgren, I. and Bergman, B. (eds.)

Dodd, B. (1980) The spelling abilities of profoundly prelingually deaf children, in Frith, U. (ed.) *Cognitive processes in spelling*. London: Academic Press

Doughty, P., Pearch, J. and Thornton, G. (1972) *Exploring Language*. London: Arnold

Dunst, C.J. (1980) *A Clinical and Educational Manual for Use with the Uzgiris and Hunt Scales of Infant Psychological Development*. Baltimore: University Park Press

Edmondson, W.H. (1978) The short-term memory of deaf and hearing children for some letters of the alphabet, in Gruneberg, M.M., Morris, P.E. and Sykes, R.N. (eds.) *Practical Aspects of Memory*. New York: Academic Press

Edmondson, W.H. (1980) Aquisition of sign language in an unfavourable setting, in Ahlgren, I. and Bergman, B. (eds.)

Edmondson, W.H. (1981) Sign language in an unfavourable setting: a perspective, in Woll, B., Kyle, J.G. and Deuchar, M. (eds.) *Perspectives on British Sign Language and Deafness*. London: Croom Helm

Edwards, J. (1979) *Language and Disadvantage*. London: Edward Arnold

Edwards, V. (1976) *Language and Comprehension in West Indian Children*. Unpublished Ph.D. Thesis, University of Reading

Edwards. V. (1979) *The West Indian Language Issue in British Schools*. London: Routledge and Kegan Paul

Edwards, V. (1980) Black British English: a bibliographical essay on the language of children of West Indian origin. *Sage Race Relations Abstracts, Vol.5*, Nos.3 and 4, pp. 1-25

Edwards, V. and Ladd, P. (1981) The Linguistic Status of British Sign Language. Manuscript, Bulmershe College of Higher Education, Reading

Ekman, P. (1973) *Darwin and Facial Expression*. New York: Academic Press

Erting, C. (1978) Language Policy and Deaf Ethnicity in the United States. *Sign Language Studies, 19,* 139-152

Erting, C. (1980) Sign Language and Communication between adults and children, in Baker, C. and Battison, R. (eds.)

Evans, L. (1976) Communication in question, in *The Harrogate Papers: Four papers given at the RNID/NCTD Education Meeting at Harrogate in October*. London: RNID

Fagan, J.F. (1976) Infant's recognition of invariant features of faces *Child Development, 47,* 627-638

Fasold, R. (1968) *Isn't English the First Language Too?* NCTE Annual Conference Proceedings, Milwaukee, Wisconsin

Fasold, R. (1971) What can an English Teacher do about non-standard dialect, in Jacobson, R. (ed.) *Studies in Teaching English to Speakers of other Languages and Standard English to Speakers of Non-standard Dialects*. Special Anthology Issue and Monograph 14 of *The English Record*

Fasold, R. (1975) *Languages of Education: How to Decide*. Indiana: Indiana Linguistics Club

Federlin, T. (1979) *A Comprehensive Bibliography on American Sign Language: A Resource Manual*. New York: available from the author, at 106 McDougal Street, New York, New York 10012

Feldman, H., Goldin-Meadow, S. and Gleitman, L. (1978) Beyond Herodotus: The creation of language by linguistically deprived deaf children in Lock, A. (ed.)

Ferguson, C. (1959) Diglossia, *Word, 15,* 325-340

Ferguson, C. (1971) Absence of copula and the notion of simplicity: a study of normal speech, baby-talk, foreigner talk and pidgins, in Hymes, D. (ed.)

Ferguson, C., and de Bose, C. (1977) Simplified registers, broken language and pidginisation, in Valdman, A. (ed.) *Pidgin and Creole Linguistics*. Bloomington: University of Indiana Press

Ferguson, G. (1971) *Statistical Analysis in Psychology and Education*. New York: McGraw-Hill Book Co.

Finnestad, K. (1961) *A Basic Sign Language Vocabulary for Western Canada.* Unpublished B.D. Thesis, Luther Theological Seminary

Firth, G. (1966) *The Plate Glass Prison.* London: Royal National Institute for the Deaf

Fischer, S.D. (1973) Two processes of reduplication in the American Sign Language. *Foundations of Language, 9,* 469-80

Fischer, S.D. (1975) Influences on Word Order Change in American Sign Language, in Li, C.N. (ed.) *Word Order and Word Order Change.* Austin: University of Texas Press

Fischer, S.D. (1978a) Sign language and creoles, in Siple, P. (ed.)

Fischer, S.D. (1980) The issue of variation: some consequences for sign language research methodology, in Ahlgren, I. and Bergman, B. (eds.)

Fischer, S. and Forman, J. (1980) Causative construction in American Sign Language. Paper presented at the Linguistics Society of America Winter meeting

Fischer, S. and Gough, B. (1978) Verbs in American Sign Language. *Sign Language Studies, 18,* 17-48

Fishman, J. and Lovas, J. (1970) Bilingual education in sociological perspective. *TESOL Quarterly, 4,* 215-22

Flannery, R. (1949) Men's and Women's speech in Gros Ventre. *International Journal of American Linguistics, 12:3,* 133-35

Folger, M.K. and Leonard, L.B. (1978) Language and sensorimotor development during the early period of referential speech. *Journal of Speech and Hearing Research, 21,* 519-27

Forman, J. and McDonald, B. (1978) Investigations into the NP and VP in ASL. Paper presented at NSSLRT, Boston

Forman, J. and McDonald, B. (1979) Constructing a Phrase Structure Grammar of ASL. Paper presented at NATO Advanced Studies Institute, Copenhagen

Fridman, R. (1980) Proto-rhythms from non-verbal to language and musical acquisition, in Key, M.R. (ed.) *The relationship or verbal and non-verbal communication.* The Hague: Mouton

Friedman, L.A. (1975) On the semantics of space, time and person reference in ASL. *Language, 51,* 940-61

Friedman, L.A. (1976) The manifestation of subject, object and topic in American Sign Language, in Li, C.N. (ed.)

Friedman, L.A. (1978) (ed.) *On the Other Hand.* New York: Academic Press

Frishberg, N. (1975) Arbitrariness and Iconicity: Historical Change in American Sign Language. *Language, 51,* 696-719

Fromkin, V. and Rodman, R. (1978) *An Introduction to Language.* New York: Holt, Rinehart and Winston

Frumkin, B. and Anisfeld, M. (1977) Semantic and surface codes in memory of deaf children. *Cognitive Psychology, 9,* 475-93

Furth, H. (1973) *Deafness and Learning.* Belmont, California: Wadsworth Publishing Co.

Gannon, J. (1980) *Deaf Heritage: A Narrative History of Deaf America.* Silver Springs, Maryland: National Association of the Deaf

Gesell, A. and Amatruda, C.S. (1947) *Developmental Diagnosis: Normal and Abnormal Child Development. Clinical Methods and Pediatric Applications,* (2nd ed.). New York: Hoeber

Gesell, A. and Thompson, H., assisted by C.S. Amatruda (1934) *Infant Behaviour: Its Genesis and Growth.* New York: McGraw-Hill

Giles, H. and Powesland, P. (1975) *Speech Style and Social Evaluation.* London: Academic Press

Givón, T. (1979a) (ed.). *Syntax and Semantics, Vol. 12,* New York: Academic Press

Givón, T. (1979b) From Discourse to Syntax: Grammar as a Processing Strategy, in Givón, T. (ed.)

Goldin-Meadow, S. (1975) *The Representation of Semantic Relations in a Manual Language Created by Deaf Children of Hearing Parents: A Language You Can't Discuss Out of Hand.* Ph.D. dissertation, University of Pennsylvania

Goldin-Meadow, S. (1977) Structure in a manual communication system developed without a conventional language model: Language without a helping hand, in Whitaker, H. and Whitaker, H.A. (eds.). *Studies in Neurolinguistics, 4,* New York: Academic Press

Goodman, K. (1973) Dialect Barriers to Reading Comprehension, in De Stefano, J. (ed.)

Grosjean, F. (in press) Sign and word recognition: A first comparison. *Sign Language Studies*

Gustason, G. (1979) The Dynamics and Interaction of American Sign Language and New Signs, in Caccamise, F. and Gustason, G. (eds.). *Manual/Simultaneous Communication Instructional Programs in the Educational Setting.* Washington, D.C.: Gallaudet College

Gustason, G. (1981) Does Signing Exact English Work? *Teaching English to the Deaf, Vol. 17,* No. 1

Gustason, G., Pfetzing, D. and Zawolkow, E. (1972, 1975, 1980) *Signing Exact English.* Los Alamitos, California: Modern Signs Press

Gustason, G. and Zawolkow, E. (1980) Using Exact English in Total Communication. Los Alamitos: Modern Signs Press

Haas, M. (1944) Men's and Women's Speech in Kosati, *Language, 20,* 142-49

Halliday, M. (1978) *Language as a Social Semiotic.* London: Arnold

Hamilton, H. (1979) The Noun in American Sign Language, unpublished Working Paper, Georgia State University

Hansen, B. (1975) Varieties in Danish Sign Language and Grammatical Features of the Original Sign Language, *Sign Language Studies, 8,* 249-56

Hatfield, N. (1980) *An investigation of bilingualism in two signed languages: American Sign Language and manually coded English.* Unpublished dissertation, University of Rochester

Henderson, P. (1976) *Communication Methods Used in the Education of Deaf Children.* London: RNID

Herskovitz, J.M. (1941) *The Myth of the Negro Past,* New York: Harper and Brothers

Hess, R. and Shipman, V. (1968) Maternal Influences upon Early Learning: The cognitive environments of urban pre-school children, in Hess, R. and Bear, R. (eds.). *Early Education.* Chicago: Aldine

Hoemann, H.W. (1972) The Development of Communication Skills in Deaf and Hearing Children. *Child Development, 43,* 990-1003

Hoemann, H. (1976 *The American Sign Language: Lexical and Grammatical Notes with Translation Exercises.* Silver Springs, Md.: National Association of the Deaf

Holmes, K.M. and Holmes, D.W. (1980) Signed and Spoken Language Development in a Hearing Child of Hearing Parents, *Sign Language Studies, 28,* 239-54

Hudson, R. (1980) *Sociolinguistics,* New York: Cambridge University Press

Hume, D. (1896) *A Treatise of Human Nature.* Oxford: The Clarendon Press

Huttenlocher, J. (1974) The Origins of Language Comprehension, in Solso, R.L. (ed.) *Theories in Cognitive Psychology: The Loyola Symposium.* Potomac, Maryland: Lawrence Erlbaum

Hymes, D. (1971) (ed.) *Pidginisation and Creolisation.* Cambridge: Cambridge University Press

Ingram, D. (1978) Sensorimotor Intelligence and Language Development, in Lock, A. (ed.)

Ingram, R.M. (1978) Theme, Rheme, Topic, and Comment in the Syntax of American Sign Language, *Sign Language Studies, 20,* 193-218

Ives, L. (1976) *A Screening Survey of 2060 Hearing Impaired Children.* Carlisle: British Deaf Association

Jensema, C. (1977) Three Characteristics of Teachers of the Deaf Who are Hearing Impaired. *American Annals of the Deaf, 122,* No. 3, 307-9

Johnson, E. H. (1948) Ability of Pupils in a School for the Deaf to Understand Various Methods of Communication, *American Annals of the Deaf, 93,* 194-213; 258-314

Johansson, G. (1973) Visual Perception of biological motion and a model for its analysis. *Perception and Psychophysics, 14,* 201-11

Jones, P. (1979) Negative Interference of Sign Language in Written English. *Sign Language Studies, 24,* 273-79

Jordan, I.K. (1975) A Referential Communication Study of Signers and Speakers Using Realistic Referents, *Sign Language Studies, 6,* 65-103

Jordan, I.K. and Battison, R. (1976) A Referential Communication Experiment with Foreign Sign Languages, *Sign Language Studies, 10,* 69-80

Jordan, I.K., Gustason, G. and Rosen, R. (1976) An Update on Communication Trends at Prograns for the Deaf, *American Annals for the Deaf, 121,* No. 6, 527-32

Kahn, J.V. (1975) Relationship of Piaget's Sensorimotor Period to Language Acquisition of Progoundly Retarded Children, *American Journal of Mental Deficiency, 79,* 640-43

Kari, J. (1979) Athabaskan Verb Theme Categories. *Alaska Native Language Centre Research Papers 2.*

Kegl, J. (1978) American Sign Language Agreement, paper presented at NSSLRT, Boston

Kegl, J. (1979) Further Breaking-down the A.S.L. Verb. Paper presented at NATO Symposium on Sign Language, Copenhagen.

Kegl, J. and Chinchor, N. (1975) A Frame Analysis for American Sign Language, in Diller, T. (ed.) *Proceedings of the 13th Annual Meeting,*

Association for Computational Linguistics

Kegl, J. and Wilbur, R.B. (1976) Where does structure stop and style begin? Paper presented at 12th Regional Meeting of the Chicago Linguistic Society, Chicago

Kelly-Jones, N. and Hamilton, H. (in press). *Signs Everywhere: A Collection of Signs for Towns, Cities, States, and Provinces in the United States, Canada, and Mexico.* Los Alamitos, California: Modern Signs Press

Key, M.R. (1975) *Male/Female Language.* Metuchen, N.J.: Scarecrow Press

Kintsch, W. (1977) On Comprehending Stories, in Just, M.A. and Carpenter, P.A. (eds.). *Cognitive Processes in Comprehension.* Hillsdale, N.J.: Lawrence Erlbaum

Kirk, R. (1968) *Experimental Design: Procedures for the Behavioral Sciences.* Belmont, Ca.: Brooks/Cole Publishing Co.

Klima, E.S. and Bellugi, U. (1972) The Signs of Language in Child and Chimpanzee. In Alloway, T. (ed.), *Communication and Affect,* New York: Academic Press

Klima, E.S. and Bellugi, U. (1975) Wit and Poetry in American Sign Language, *Sign Language Studies, 7,* 203-24

Klima, E.S. and Bellugi, U. (1979) *The Signs of Language.* Cambridge, Mass.: Harvard University Press

Klopping, H.W.E. (1972) Language Understanding of Deaf Students Under Three Audio-Visual Stimulus Conditions, *American Annals of the Deaf, 117,* 389-96

Kyle, J.G. (1980) Sign language and internal representation, in Ahlgren, I. and Bergman, B. (eds.)

Kyle, J.G., Woll, B. and Llewellyn-Jones, P. (1981) Learning and Using BSL, *Sign Language Studies, 31,* 155-78

Kozlowski, L.T. and Cutting, J.E. (1977) Recognising the sex of a walker from a dynamic point-light display. *Perception and Psychophysics, 21,* 575-80

Krauss, R.M. and Glucksberg, S. (1970) Socialisation of communication Skills, in Hoppe, R.A., Milton, G.A. and Simmer, E.C. (eds.). *Early Experience and the Process of Socialisation.* New York: Academic Press

Laberge, D. and Samuels, S.J. (1974) Towards a theory of automatic information processing and reading, *Cognitive Psychology, 6,* 293-323

Labov, W. (1966) *The Social Stratification of English in New York City.* Washington D.C.: Center for Applied Linguistics

Labov, W. (1972) *Sociolinguistic Patterns.* Philadelphia: University of Pennsylvania Press

Labov, W. (1976) *Language in the Inner City.* Philadelphia: University of Pennsylvania Press

Lackner, J. (1980) Speech production: Correction of semantic and grammatical errors during speech shadowing, in Fromkin, V.A. (ed.) *Errors in Linguistic Performance.* New York: Academic Press

Ladd, P. (1978a) TC or DCA? in Montgomery, G. (ed.), *Of Sound and Mind.* Edinburgh: Scottish Workshop with the Deaf

Ladd, P. (1978b) Communication or Dummification, in *Deafness, Personality and Mental Health.* Edinburgh: Scottish Workshop with the Deaf

Lane, H. (1980) A Chronology of the Oppression of Sign Language in France and the United States, in Lane, H. and Grosjean, F. (eds.), *Recent Perspectives on American Sign Language*. Hillsdale, New Jersey: Lawrence Earlbaum Associates

Lane, H., Boyes-Braem, P. and Bellugi, U. (1976) Preliminaries to a distinctive feature analysis of handshapes in American Sign Language. *Cognitive Psychology, 8,* 263-89

Lambert, W. (1972) A Social Psychology of Bilingualism, in MacNamara, J. (ed.), *Problems of Bilingualism*. Special issue of *The Journal of Social Issues, 23,* 2

Lang, J. (1918) *The Sign Language: A Manual of Signs*. Omaha, Nebraska: Dorothy Thompson Long

Lee, S. (1978) *Styles of Communication Interaction by Mothers of Deaf and Hearing Children*. Ph.D. dissertation, University of California, Berkeley

Lehmann, W.P. (1978) The Great Underlying Ground Plans, in Lehmann, W.P. (ed.), *Syntactic Typology*. Sussex: The Harvester Press

Lenneberg, E. (1967) *Biological Foundations of Language*. New York: Wiley and Sons

Levelt, W.J.M. (1980) On-Line Processing Constraints on the Properties of Signed and Spoken Language, in Bellugi, U. and Studdert-Kennedy, M. (eds.)

Lewis, M. and Freedle, R. (1973) Mother-Infant Dyad: The Cradle of Meaning, in Plimer, P. Krames, L. and Alloway, T. (eds.), *Communication and Affect: Language and Thought*. New York: Academic Press

Li, C.N. (1976) (ed.), *Subject and Topic*. New York: Academic Press

Li, C.N. and Thompson, S.A. (1976) Subject and Topic: A New Typology of Language, in Li, C.N. (ed.)

Liben, L.S. (1978) (ed.), *Deaf Children: Developmental Perspectives*. New York: Academic Press

Liddell, S. (1978) Nonmanual signals and relative clauses in American Sign Language. In Siple, P. (ed.)

Liddell, S. (1980) *American Sign Language Syntax*. The Hague: Mouton

Llewellyn-Jones, P., Kyle, J.G. and Woll, B. (1979) Sign Language Communication. Paper presented at International Conference on Social Psychology of Language, Bristol

Loach, I. (1978) *The Price of Deafness*. London: Disability Alliance

Lock, A. (1978) (ed.) *Action, Gesture and Symbol: the emergence of language*. London: Academic Press

Lock, A. (1980) *The Guilded Reinvention of Language*. New York: Academic Press

Loncke, F. (in press) *Ondersoek naar tekentaal van doven: de huidige stand van zaken. Bestaat een eigen Vlaamse Tekentaal?* Journal of the Free University of Brussels

Lowell, E.L. (1957, 1958) *John Tracy Clinic Research Papers II, V, VI, VII.* Los Angeles: John Tracy Clinic

Lyons, J. (1977) *Semantics*. Cambridge: Cambridge University Press

Mandler, J.M. and Johnson, N.S. (1977) Remembrance of things passed: Story, structure and recall. *Cognitive Psychology, 9,* 111-151

Markowicz, H. and Woodward, J.C. (1975) *Language and Maintenance of*

Ethnic Boundaries in the Deaf Community. Washington, D.C.: Linguistics Research Lab, Gallaudet College

Marmor, G. and Petito, L. (1979) Simultaneous Communication in the Classroom: How Well is English Being Represented? *Sign Language Studies, 23,* 99-136

Matthews, P.H. (1974) *Morphology.* Cambridge: Cambridge University Press

Mayberry, R. (1979) *Facial Expressions and Redundancy in American Sign Language.* Doctoral dissertation, McGill University

McDonald, B. (in preparation) *Aspects of the ASL Verbal System,* Ph.D. dissertation, State University of New York at Buffalo

McIntire, M.L. (1977) The Acquisition of American Sign Language Hand Configurations, *Sign Language Studies, 16,* 247-66

McIntire, M.L. (1980) *Locatives in American Sign Language,* unpublished Ph.D. dissertation, University of California, Los Angeles

Meadows, K. (1972) Sociolinguistics, Sign Language and the Deaf Subculture, in O'Rourke, T. (ed.)

Mehrabian, A. and Reed, H. (1968) Some Determinants of Communication Accuracy, *Psychological Bulletin, 70,* 365-81

Meyer, D.E. and Schvaneveldt, R.W. (1971) Facilitation in recognising pairs of words: evidence of a dependence between retrieval operations. *Journal of Experimental Psychology, 90,* (2), 227-34

Meyer, D.E., Schvaneveldt, R.W. and Ruddy, M.G. (1973) Loci of contextual effects of visual word-recognition, in Rabbitt, P. (ed.), *Attention and performance V.* New York: Academic Press

Meyer, D.E., Schvaneveldt, R.W. and Ruddy, M.G. (1974) Functions of graphemic and phonemic codes in visual word-recognition. *Memory and Cognition, 2,* (2), 309-21

McLaughlin, B. (1978) *Second-Language Acquisition in Childhood.* New York: Wiley and Sons

Miller, G.A., and Nicely, P.E. (1955) An analysis of perceptual confusions among some English consonants. *Journal of the Acoustical Society of America, 27,* 338-52

Miller, J.F., Chapman, R.S., Branston, M.B., and Reichle, J. (1980) Language Comprehension in Sensorimotor Stages V and VI. *Journal of Speech and Hearing Research, 23,* 284-311

Mindel, E.D. and Vernon, McC. (1971) *They Grow in Silence: The deaf child and his family.* Silver Springs: National Association of the Deaf

Minifie, F.D. and Lloyd, L.L. (1978) (eds.). *Communicative and Cognitive Abilities – Early Behaviour Assessment.* Baltimore: University Park Press

Montgomery, G. (1980) Effective Brains v. Defective Ears. *Supplement to the British Deaf News.* Carlisle: British Deaf Association

Montgomery, G. (1981) *The Integration and Disintergration of the Deaf in Society.* Edinburgh: Scottish Workshop with the Deaf

Montgomery, G. and Lines, A. (1976) A comparison of several single and combined methods of communication with deaf children. *Proceedings of the Newcastle Symposium*

Moore, M.K. and Meltzoff, A.N. (1978) Object Permanence, Imitation, and Language Development in Infancy: Toward a Neo-Piagetian

Perspective on Communicative and Cognitive Development, in Minifie, F.D. and Lloyd, L.L. (eds.)

Moores, D. (1972) Communication: Some Unanswered Questions and Some Unquestioned Answers, in O'Rourke, T. (ed.)

Moores, D. (1970-1974) *Research Reports 27, 39, 57, 81. Evaluation of Programs for Hearing Impaired Children, 1970-71, 1971-72, 1972-73, 1973-74*. Minneapolis, Minn: University of Minnesota Center in Education of Handicapped Children

Moulton, R.D. and Beasley, D.S. (1975) Verbal coding strategies used by hearing-impaired individuals. *Journal of Speech and Hearing Research, 18,* (3), 559-70

Namir, L. and Schlesinger, I.M. (1978) The Grammar of Sign Language, in Schlesinger I.M. and Namir, L. (eds.)

Nash, J.E. (1973) Cues or Signs: A Case Study in Language Acquisition. *Sign Language Studies, 3,* 79-92

Nelson, K. (1973) *Structure and Strategy in Learning to Talk.* Monograph 38, Society for Research in Child Development

Newport, E. and Supalla, T. (1980) The structuring of language by developmental processes, in Bellugi, U. and Studdert-Kennedy, M. (eds.)

Nicholich, L.M. (1975) A Longitudinal Study of Representational Play in Relation to Spontaneous Imitation and Development of Multi-word Utterances. ERIC Document – PS007 854

Nicholich, L.M. (1977) Beyond Sensorimotor Intelligence: Assessment of Symbolic Maturity Through Analysis of Pretend Play. *Merrill-Palmer Quarterly, 23,* 89-99

Ochs, E. (1979) Planned and Unplanned Discourse, in Givón, T. (ed.)

Odom, P.B., Blanton, R.L. and McIntyre, C.K. (1970) Coding medium and word recall by deaf and hearing subjects. *Journal of Speech and Hearing Research, 13,* (1), 54-58

Office of Demographic Studies. (1968-1972) *Annual Survey of Hearing Impaired Children and Youth.* Washington, D.C.: Gallaudet College

O'Rourke, T.J. (1972) (ed.) *Psycholinguistics and Total Communication: The State of the Art.* American Annals of the Deaf

Osterberg, O. (1916) *Teckenspraket.* Uppsala: Wretmans Boktrycker

Padden, C. (1980) The Deaf Community and the Culture of Deaf People, in Baker, C., and Battison, R. (eds.)

Padden, C. and Markowicz, H. (1975) Crossing Cultural Boundaries into the Deaf Community, paper presented at the Conference on Culture and Communication. Philadelphia: Temple University

Pedersen, C.C. (1977) Verb Modulations in American Sign Language, in *Proceedings of The National Symposium on Sign Language Research and Teaching.* Silver Springs: National Association of the Deaf

Piaget, J. (1962) *Play, Dreams, and Imitation in Childhood.* New York: Norton

Poizner, H., Bellugi, U. and Lutes-Driscoll, V. (1981) Perception of American Sign Language in dynamic point-light displays. *Journal of Experimental Psychology: Human Perception and Performance, 7,* 430-40

Poizner, H. and Lane, H. (1978) Discrimination of location in American Sign Language, in Siple, P. (ed.)

Prinz, P.M. and Prinz, E.A. (1979) Simultaneous Acquisition of ASL and Spoken English in a Hearing Child of a Deaf Mother and Hearing Father: Phase I – Early Lexical Development. *Sign Language Studies, 25,* 283-96

Putnam, V., Iscoe, I. and Young, R.K. (1962) Verbal learning in the deaf. *Journal of Comparative and Physiological Psychology, 55,* (5), 843-46

Quigley, S. (1978) *Test of Syntactic Abilities.* Beaverton, Ore: Dormac, Inc.

Rampton, A. (1981) *West Indian Children in our Schools: Interim Report of the Committee of Enquiry into the Education of children from ethnic minority groups.* London: HMSO

Reilly, J. and McIntire, M.L. (1980 American Sign Language and Pidgin Sign English: What's the Difference? *Sign Language Studies, 27,* 151-92

Ringeling, J. (1979) The shadowing task and familiarity with Dutch and English. *Progress Report,* 4, 1, Institute of Phonetics, University of Utrecht, The Netherlands

Rodda, M. (1970) *The Hearing Impaired School Leaver.* London: University of London Press

Rozanova, T.A. (1970) Memory of words in deaf children. *Defectologia, 3,* 8-15. (article written in Russian)

Rubenstein, H., Lewis, S.S. and Rubenstein, M.A. (1971) Evidence for phonemic recoding in visual word-recognition. *Journal of Verbal Learning and Verbal Behaviour, 10,* 645-7

Rumelhart, D.A. (1975) Notes on a scheme for stories, in Bobrow, D.G. and Collins, A. (eds.), *Representation and Understanding.* New York: Academic Press

Sapir, E. (1921) *Language: An introduction to the study of speech.* London: Rupert Hart-Davies

Sapir, E. (1929) The Status of Linguistics as a Science, *Language, 5,* 207-14

Sapir, E. and Hoijer, H. (1967) The Phonology and Morphology of the Navaho Language. *University of California Publications in Linguistics,* 50

Savage, R.D., Evans, L. and Savage, J.F. (1981) *Psychology and Communication in Deaf Children.* Sydney: Grune and Stratton

Schein, J. and Delk, M. (1974) *The Deaf Population of the United States.* Silver Springs, Md.: National Association of the Deaf

Schlesinger, H. (1972) Meaning and Enjoyment: Language Acquisition of Deaf Children, in O'Rourke, T. (ed.)

Schlesinger, H. (1978) The Acquisition of a Bimodal Language, in Schlesinger, I.M. and Namir, L. (eds.)

Schlesinger, H. (1978) The Acquisition of Signed and Spoken Language, in Liben, L.S. (ed.)

Schlesinger, H. and Meadow, K. (1972) *Sound and Sign: Childhood Deafness and Mental Health.* Berkeley, CA: University of California Press

Schlesinger, I.M. and Namir, L. (1978) (eds.) *Sign Language of the Deaf: Psychological, linguistic and sociological perspectives.* London: Academic Press

Schlesinger, I.M. and Presser, B. (1970) Compound Signs in Sign Language, in *Proceedings of the Stockholm Symposium. Volta Review Supplement*

Schumann, P. (1940) *Geschichte des Taubstummenwesens: Vom Deutschen Standpunkt aus dargestellt.* Frankfurt aM

Shirley, M.M. (1933a) The First Two Years: A Study of Twenty-five Babies: Vol. II. Intellectual Development. *Institute of Child Welfare Monograph Serial No. 8,* Minneapolis: University of Minnesota Press

Shirley, M.M. (1933b) The First Two Years: A Study of Twenty-five Babies: Vol. III. Personality Manifestations. *Institute of Child Welfare Monograph Serial No. 8,* Minneapolis: University of Minnesota Press

Shuy, R. (1973a) Language Variation and the Training of Teachers, in DeStefano, J. (ed.)

Shuy, R. (1973b) The Linguistic Problems of Teachers, in DeStefano, J. (ed.)

Sinclair, H. (1971) Sensorimotor Action Patterns as a Condition for the Acquisition of Syntax, in Huxley, R. and Ingram, E. (eds.), *Language Acquisition: Models and Methods.* New York: Academic Press

Siple, P. (1978a) Visual constraints for sign language communication. *Sign Language Studies, 19,* 97-112

Siple, P. (1978b) (ed.) *Understanding Language through Sign Language Research.* New York: Academic Press

Siple, P., Fischer, S.D. and Bellugi, U. (1977) Memory for non-semantic attributes of ASL signs and English words. *Journal of Verbal Behaviour, 16,* 561-74

Slobin, D.I. (1971) *Psycholinguistics.* Glenview, Illinois: Scott, Foresman

Slobin, D.I. (1973) Cognitive prerequisites for linguistic development, in Ferguson, C. and Slobin, D. (eds.), *Studies of Child Language Development.* New York: Holt, Rinehart and Winston

Smith, D. (1976) *The Facts of Racial Disadvantage.* London: Political and Economic Planning Office

Snyder, L.S. (1978) Communicative and Cognitive Abilities and Disabilities in the Sensorimotor Period. *Merrill-Palmer Quarterly, 24,* 161-80

Sperling, G. (1978) Future Prospects in Language and Communication for the Congenitally Deaf, in Liben, L.S. (ed.)

Sperling, G. (1980) Bandwidth requirements for video transmission of American Sign Language and fingerspelling. *Science, 210,* 797-99

Stelle, T.W. (1980) *A Primer for Parents with Deaf Children.* Edinburgh: Scottish Workshop with the Deaf

Stewart, W. (1973) Urban Negro Speech: Sociolinguistic Factors Affecting English Teaching, in DeStefano, J. (ed.)

Stevens, R. (1975) Children's Language Should Be Learned and Not Taught. *Sign Language Studies, 6,* 97-107

Stevens, R. (1980) Education in Schools for Deaf Children, in Baker, C. and Battison, R. (eds.)

Stokoe, W.C. (1960) *Sign language structure: An outline of the visual communication system of the American deaf.* Studies in Linguistics Occasional Paper 8, University of Buffalo

Stokoe, W.C. (1970) Sign language diglossia. *Studies in Linguistics, 21,* 27-41

Stokoe, W.C. (1970) *The Study of Sign Language.* Washington, D.C.: Center for Applied Linguistics

Stokoe, W.C. (1972) (ed.) *Semiotics and human sign language: approaches to semiotics*, 21. The Hague: Mouton

Stokoe, W.C. (1974) Classification and Description of Sign Languages, in Sebeok, T.A. (ed.), *Current Trends in Linguistics, Vol. 12*. The Hague: Mouton

Stokoe, W.C. (1978) *Sign language structure* (Revised Edition). Silver Springs: Linstok Press

Stokoe, W.C. (1980) The study and use of sign language, in Schiefelbusch, R.L. (ed.), *Non-speech Language and Communication*. Baltimore: University Park Press

Stokoe, W.C. (1980) *Sign and Culture*. Silver Springs: Linstok Press

Stokoe, W.C., Casterline, D., and Croneberg, C. (1965) *A Dictionary of American Sign Language on Linguistic Principles*. Washington, D.C.: Gallaudet College Press

Stoloff, L. and Matthew, D.Z. (1978) (Untitled) *American Annals of the Deaf*, 123, 452-54

Stone, L.J. and Church, J. (1975) *Childhood and Adolescence*. (3rd ed.). New York: Random House

Studdert-Kennedy, M. and Lane, H. (1980) Clues from the differences between signed and spoken languages, in Bellugi, U. and Studdert-Kennedy, M. (eds.)

Stungis, J. (1981) Identification and discrimination of handshape in American Sign Language. *Perception and Psychophysics, 29*, 261-76

Supalla, T. (1978) Morphology of Verbs of Motion and Location in American Sign Language, paper presented at the National Symposium on Sign Language Research and Teaching

Supalla, T. and Newport, E. (1978) How many seats in a chair? The derivation of nouns and verbs in American Sign Language, in Siple, P. (ed.)

Sutcliffe, D. (in press) *British Black English*. Oxford: Basil Blackwell

Sutton, V. (1977) *Quick Reading: The Sign Language Key,* Key 5. Newport Beach, California: The Movement Shorthand Society Press

Tartter, V.C. and Knowlton, K.C. (1981) Perception of sign language from an array of 27 moving spots. *Nature, 289*, 676-78

Taylor, D. (1951) *The Black Carib of British Hondouras*. New York: Wenner-Gren Foundation for Anthropological Research

Tervoort, B.T. (1961) Esoteric symbolism in the communication behaviour of young deaf children, *American Annals of the Deaf, 106*, 436-80

Tomkins, W. (1969) *Indian Sign Language*. New York: Dover Publications

Townsend, H.E.R. and Brittan, E.M. (1972) *Organisation in Multiracial Schools*. Windsor: National Foundation for Educational Research

Treisman, A. (1965) The effects of redundancy and familiarity on translating and repeating back a foreign and a native language. *British Journal of Psychology, 56*, 4, 369-79

Trevarthen, C. (1974) Intersubjectivity and initation in infants. *Proceedings of the British Psychological Society Annual Convention*. Bangor

Trevarthen, C. (1979) Communication and cooperation in early infancy: A description of primary intersubjectivity, in Bullowa, M. (ed.)

Tronick, E., Als, H. and Adamson, L. (1979) Structure of early face-to-face communicative interactions, in Bullowa, M. (ed.)

Trudgill, P. (1974) *The Social Differentiation of English in Norwich.* Cambridge: Cambridge University Press

Trudgill, P. (1975) *Accent, Dialect and the School.* London: Edward Arnold

Trudgill, P. (1978) *Sociolinguistic Patterns in British English.* London: Edward Arnold

Tweney, R. and Heiman, G.W. (1977) The effect of sign language grammatical structure on recall. *Bulletin of the Psychonomic Society, 10,* 331-34

Tweney, R.D., Heiman, G.W., and Hoemann, H.W. (1977) Psychological processing of sign language: Effects of visual disruption on sign intelligibility. *Journal of Experimental Psychology, 106,* 255-68

Ulfsparre, S. (1981) Panto Signs: A second attempt, paper presented at the second International Symposium on Sign Language Research, Bristol

Uzgiris, I.C. and Hunt, J. McV. (1975) *Assessment in Infancy: Ordinal Scales of Psychological Development.* Urbana: University of Illinois Press

Van Uden, P. (1970) *A World of Language for Deaf Children.* Rotterdam: Rotterdam University Press

Venezky, R. (1970) Nonstandard Language and Reading. *Elementary English, 47,* 342

Vernon, M. (1969) Sociological and Psychological Factors Associated with Hearing Loss, *Journal of Speech and Hearing Research, 12,* 3, 541-63

Vogt-Svendsen, M. (1981) *Undersøkelse av tegn språk. Tegn med fast nel komponent.* Unpublished Master's Thesis. Hosle, Norway: The Advanced Teacher Training College of Special Education

Volterra, V. (1980) Symbolic Development in Spoken and Gestural Modalities, in *The Sciences of Deaf Signing,* proceedings of the NATO Advanced Study Institute, Copenhagen

Volterra, V., Bates, E., Benigni, L., Bretherton, I. and Camaioni, L. (1979) First Words in Language and Action, in Bates et al

Wallwork, J., (1969) *Language and Linguistics.* London: Heinemann Educational Books

Weeks, T. (1971) Speech Registers in Young Children. *Child Development, 42,* 1119-31

Weinreich, U. (1953) *Languages in Contact.* New York: Linguistics Circle

Wilbur, R. (1979) *American Sign Language and Sign Systems.* Baltimore: University Park Press

Williams, F. (1970) *Language and Poverty: Perspectives on a Theme.* Chicago: Markham

Winer, B.J. (1971) *Statistical Principles in Experimental Design,* (2nd ed.). New York: McGraw-Hill

Wish, M., and Carroll, J.D. (1974) Applications of individual differences scaling to studies of human perception and judgement. *Handbook of Perception, 2,* 449-91

Wolfram, W. (1969) *A Sociolinguistic Description of Detroit Negro Speech.* Washington, DC: Centre for Applied Linguistics

Woll, B. (1981) Processes of Change in BSL. Paper presented at LAGB Autumn Meeting, York

Woll, B. and Lawson, L. (1981) British Sign Language, in Haugen, E.,

McClure, J.D., and Thomson, B.S. (eds.). *Minority Languages Today*. Edinburgh: Edinburgh University Press

Wood, D.J., Wood, H.A., Griffiths, A.J., Howarth, S.P. and Howarth, C.I. (1980) The Structure of Conversations with 6–10 year old Deaf Children Mimeo. Deafness Research Group, Department of Psychology, University of Nottingham

Woodward, J.C. (1972) A Transformational Approach to the Syntax of American Sign Language, in Stokoe, W.C. (ed.). *Semiotics and Human Sign Languages*, The Hague: Mouton

Woodward, J.C. (1973a) Some Observations on Sociolinguistic Variation and American Sign Language, *Kansas Journal of Sociology, 9,* 191-200

Woodward, J.C. (1973b) Manual English: A Problem in Language Standardization and Planning, in Gustason, G. and Woodward, J.C. (eds.). *Recent Developments in Manual English*. Washington, DC: Gallaudet College Press

Woodward, J.C. (1973c) Some Characteristics of Pidgin Sign English. *Sign Language Studies, 3,* 39-46

Woodward, J.C. (1973d) *Implicational Lects on the Deaf Diglossic Continuum*, unpublished Ph.D. Dissertation, Georgetown University

Woodward, J.C. (1978) Some Sociolinguistic Problems in the Implementation of Bilingual Education for Deaf Students, in Caccamise, F. and Hicks, D. (eds.)

Woodward, J.C. (1979) *Signs of Sexual Behaviour*. Silver Springs, Maryland: National Association of the Deaf

Woodward, J.C. (1980) Sociolinguistic Research on American Sign Language: An Historical Perspective, in Baker, C. and Battison, R. (eds.)

Young, R. and Morgan, W. (1980) *The Navaho Language*. Albuquerque: University of New Mexico Press

Zaitseva, G.L. (1969) Features of the Gestural Language of the Deaf with reference to expressions of spatial relations. *Defectology, 4*

Zaitseva, G.L. and Frumkina, R.M. (1981) Psycholinguistic aspects of the study of the gesture language of the deaf. *Defectology, 1*

Zeyskoy, E.A. (1973) (ed.) *Russian Speech*. Moscow: Ministry of Science